STEALING CINDERELLA

STEALING CINDERELLA

HOW I BECAME AN INTERNATIONAL FUGITIVE FOR LOVE

A TRUE STORY

Mark D. Diehl

FENCETREE PRESS

STEALING CINDERELLA
HOW I BECAME AN INTERNATIONAL FUGITIVE FOR LOVE
A TRUE STORY
Copyright © 2019 Mark D. Diehl

PUBLISHER'S CATALOGING-IN-PUBLICATION DATA
(Prepared by The Donohue Group, Inc.)

Diehl, Mark D., author.
Stealing Cinderella: how I became an international
fugitive for love: a true story / Mark D. Diehl.
[First edition.] | [Cape Elizabeth, Maine] :
[Fencetree Press], [2019]

ISBN 0781732819948 (hardcover) | ISBN 9781732819931 (paperback) |
ISBN 9781732819955 (Kindle) | ISBN 9781732819962 (ebook)

LCSH: Diehl, Mark D. | Intercountry marriage. | Fugitives from
justice--Korea (South)--Biography. | English teachers--Korea
(South)--Biography. | Interracial dating. | Chongqing da sha (Hong
Kong, China) | LCGFT: Autobiographies.

LCC HQ1032 .D54 2019 (print) | LCC HQ1032 (ebook) |
DDC 306.845092--dc23

For Jennifer

AUTHOR'S NOTE

This book is a factual retelling of some of the most significant experiences of my life. All events happened just as I have described them. However, every person's name (except Jennifer's and my own) has been changed, as have other details about their lives and careers. If you know a person with a name, job, hometown, or physical description that is similar to anyone here, it is purely coincidence.

Much of this story takes place in South Korea, in the cities of Taegu, Seoul and Pusan. Since the book is set in 1993, I used the spellings that were in use at that time, even though Taegu is now officially known as Daegu, and Pusan has become Busan.

Kimpo International Airport in Seoul, South Korea
Fall of 1994

We stood close together, hiding our faces and pretending to look out the window, resisting the temptation to look over each other's shoulders. There was no reason to make ourselves more conspicuous by raising our eyes. What could we do if we saw one of them, anyway?

They were not above ambushing us as we boarded a plane, or even above using violence in an airport. If they spotted us, we'd never escape. There were cameras and cops everywhere.

The garish yellow and red satin baseball jacket made a decent disguise for Jennifer, or maybe I just hoped it did. It was a dramatically different look from her usual designer suits, in any case. Even with the clashing pink cap and my black plastic wrap-around sunglasses, too much of her face could still be seen. Bruises were still visible on her cheeks and neck, though she'd tried to conceal them with makeup.

As for me, a white American, I would stand out no matter what.

We chatted quietly, without looking at each other. Talking seemed less likely to draw attention than standing in silence. It also kept the two of us connected, akin to holding hands, in a place where actually holding hands in public came with the threat of being beaten to death.

Jennifer turned her passport over in her hands, twice. I had never before seen her fidget. "Lucky I tried to change my major in college," she said.

"Yeah."

I tugged at my sleeve to make it billow out around the bandage Jennifer had affixed at my elbow, in case it had soaked through.

She looked exhausted. We had now been running and hiding for five days. If they found us, there would be more violence. If we missed the flight, we would soon be discovered and separated, and we probably would never see each other again after that.

"They're boarding," Jennifer said.

We kept our faces down, but everyone stared anyway.

This was where they'd cornered us before: at an airport gate, as we'd prepared to board a flight.

The trick we'd used, giving the ticket agent only a first initial instead of a full name, wouldn't be much help, at least not for me. My last name stood out as much as the rest of me did, and they would surely know my last name. Our former employer had only contempt for our privacy.

I slid my boarding pass out from my passport and examined it for the hundredth time, pinching it tightly between my fingers and white-knuckled thumb. It was smudged with ink from my new visa stamp. "If we have any chance of avoiding them, it's because we bought these after the counter was supposed to have closed," I said quietly.

"They could be checking right now," she said.

Ordinary Americans, lining up for ordinary flights, would probably look bored, so that was how we tried to appear as we shuffled toward the door. One passenger after another presented a ticket and made it onto the jet bridge. A gate agent motioned to Jennifer, took her ticket, and let her pass.

"Hello," a different one said to me, extending an open palm. "Boarding pass and passport, please."

I gave her the documents. The gate agent looked them over, and went to get someone else. Together they scrutinized the paperwork, especially the new stamp. Finally, they accepted the ticket and I proceeded into the tunnel.

I had almost caught up to Jennifer when someone pushed me against the wall.

I spun toward the offending hands. I would not go down easily.

It was an *ajuma* with a thinning perm, dyed coal black except for a quarter inch of gray roots, clad in thick black polyester. She shoved past me and continued down the walkway, using her elbows and shoulders to part the crowd. Two other *ajumas* followed in her wake, wearing the same hair and clothing. A Korean Air flight attendant stopped them at the front of the line, and passengers crowded behind them, waiting to board.

"She's asking for their tickets so she can show the *ajumas* where to go," Jennifer said. "They don't want to sit in their assigned seats."

The *ajumas* argued. The crowd at the end of the jet bridge swelled. It took four flight attendants to coax them from the door and into their correct seats.

We crossed the threshold. Jennifer was at the window and I was in the middle seat next to her. "It's a little cramped for a four-hour flight," I said. "And to think, just yesterday we were business class to Guam."

Together we watched as person after person stepped through the open door. What would we do if someone boarded the plane to get us? My mind ran through a possible scenario involving activating the emergency slide, running across the tarmac, and being gunned down.

Not easygoing people, Koreans.

It was the best plan I could come up with. If they got onto this plane, I would put an arm around Jennifer and dive for the emergency slide.

A man in a suit paused at our row. A fist in the gut would bend him over, and I could hit him in the jaw with the top of my head as I stood up to fight. I waited for a word or a grab, but none came. He placed his briefcase in an overhead bin and sat down next to me. A few minutes later, the plane door closed and a flight attendant stood up at the front to give her spiel about the exits and seat belts, first in Korean and then in English.

The plane taxied. I gestured out the window. "Want to take one last look?" I asked. "You may never see it again."

She gazed out at the concrete and glass, the tower, and the mountains in the distance. "I won't miss it," she said.

I didn't know it then, but more than two decades later, she still would not miss it.

The plane sped down the runway.

"The last time we thought we got away by airplane, it didn't work out so well," she said.

Our flight to Cheju-do had been just last week.

They would soon learn where we were.

"We may just be leaving one set of troubles for another," she said.

I took her hand as the plane accelerated, pushing us back into our seats, lifting off. Beneath us, the landing gear whirred and retracted, and I felt machinery clunking under the floor. Like taut rubber bands allowed to go slack, we collapsed against each other.

1

Above Kimpo International Airport
Eighteen months earlier

The plane's "nighttime" had ended maybe 90 minutes ago, and now it was starting to descend. I tried to wake myself up by playing a cassette tape. Most of my own stuff was pretty downbeat, but I had a B-52s tape that a college roommate had abandoned, and "Roam" was a peppy song about exploring the world.

The flight attendant recited the bit about the seat belts and tray tables over the PA. I craned my neck to look out the window but saw only clouds.

"Korea your final destination?" the guy in the window seat asked me.

"Yeah."

"Mine too. DOD?"

"Huh?"

"Oh. I thought you were a DOD contractor. Department of Defense."

"Ah," I said. "Nope. I'm coming to teach English."

"Ooh, don't get caught, man," he said. "If you're not with a Korean company, you're like an undocumented worker or whatever. This close to North Korea, people are always suspicious of foreigners. They take immigration pretty seriously. Come to think of it, they're pretty fuckin' hardcore about everything else, too. Not easygoing people, Koreans."

"I'll be with a Korean company," I said. "Got a visa and everything. And I know what you mean about Koreans being hardcore. This guy who's meeting me today at the airport once let me ride along as he and his friends, all Koreans, drove to a bar in a different town to watch two other Koreans play *Galaga* for a thousand-dollar bet."

"Yeah, see? They're intense."

"Oh, that's not even the story. I was in the back seat on the way there. A carload of black guys passed us, making chinky eyes at them and giving them the finger. My car of Koreans and another carload of Koreans coordinated with car phones and brought them to a full stop at the side of the highway. Then they got out and started kicking the car and spitting on the windows. When the black guys tried to get out of the car, the Koreans kicked the doors closed on their shins."

"Yep, that's what they're like," he said. "Whole country of that. One of those guys is meeting you here?"

"For a couple hours. I have to take a domestic flight to Taegu from here."

"I don't spend much time in Taegu," he said. "It's a big city but there aren't many foreigners there at all. Couple of bases. Camp Walker, and I think Camp Henry is there. I guess as a civilian you can't check 'em out, though."

"Not unless I want to get shot."

"Who knows what you'll feel like after some time teaching English in Taegu?"

He gestured out the window. "Mountains everywhere. Korea looks weird from the air at night. Bright lights, with big dark patches where the mountains are."

I leaned back in my seat so I could see more of the landscape. Obscured by smog, the mountains looked dark already.

"There's your new home, man!" the guy said.

The plane approached the runway and a mess of flat concrete roofs became visible, most edged with glossy brown ceramic tiles. "Those yellow plastic tanks are for water," he said. "Water pressure's unpredictable so everybody has one on the roof." Through the thick haze that stretched to the horizon I saw countless squarish little buildings and intermittent taller structures with backlit plastic signs. All had water tanks on top.

"Do you speak Korean?" the guy asked.

"No. I had Japanese friends and roommates in college, and I picked up Japanese okay. Not fluent, but I can get by. I'm hoping to do the same with Korean."

"Sounds like you had a lot of foreign friends in college."

"Yeah. Just curious about the world, I guess."

Curiosity had been part of it. A bigger part had been the fact that international students were clearly not cops.

The plane touched down and the guy disappeared. I had to look for my guide. Jae Won had been my first contact with Koreans, introduced to me by one of my Japanese roommates who had met him in English class. He was a perpetually calm graduate student in engineering, friendlier and more outgoing than most of his countrymen, which wasn't saying much. Even among the international crowd at school, the Koreans tended to stick to themselves.

Jae Won was waiting for me at the gate. He wore frameless oval glasses and business casual clothes with some logo on them to prove they cost a lot of money. If my parents had ever shown any interest in who my friends were, Jae Won was the type they'd have liked. My bag was checked through to Taegu, so I was free to leave the airport with him and find a nearby bar.

Jae Won drove, which I had never seen him do before. His car was a piece of shit that must have been several years old. As he was parallel parking, he scraped the side of another car that was trying to pass. Both drivers continued doing their thing without acknowledging that there had been an accident.

"You don't have to stop when you hit another car?" you asked.

Jae Won shook his head. "Korea traffic very bad," he said. "Korea is number one for traffic death in world."

We went into some restaurant and sat on the pale-yellow linoleum floor, in front of a low table.

Jae Won had a habit of restarting his English sentences. "I can't believe, I can't believe you are here in Korea," he said. He raised a hand toward the back of the restaurant and called out, "*Ajuma!*"

"What's that mean, *ajuma*?" I asked.

The waitress came over. She was about 50 years old, with permed but thinning hair dyed an unnaturally flat shade of black, and was dressed head to toe in black polyester. He said something to her in Korean and she went away again. "That is *ajuma*," he said. "Old, married woman."

We talked about my flight, and about how long Jae Won had been home in Korea. He would be heading back to Iowa City for the start of the new semester in about a week and a half. The *ajuma* brought successive liter bottles of beer, which we drank from little glasses like juice might have been served in back in the United States.

"Why did, why did you get job in Korea?" he asked.

"So I could see you!" I said. We both laughed as if the

joke had been funny. "Really, I'm here because it gets me out of Iowa City, and I think maybe I can be one of the first Americans with contacts here as Korea's economy really takes off. I've spent enough time with foreign people in school that I think I'll do okay at teaching English. Hopefully I'll be able to identify some opportunities."

"That is good plan," Jae Won said. "Korean economy growing very fast now."

"Yeah, I know. A lot of Americans are going to Japan these days, but I'm here so I can get in on the ground floor. Do you know what that means, get in on the ground floor?"

He waved his hand just over the surface of the table. "First level. Lobby."

"Yes, that's right. But when I say I want to *get in on the ground floor* in Korea, and we're talking about business, it's an idiom that means I'll be here at the beginning."

I held two palms to the tabletop and slowly raised them. "Korea is growing into a skyscraper. I'm here early, so I can ride with it as it grows. Businesspeople call it getting in on the ground floor. Usually they mean a business, though, not a country."

"Oh, okay. In on a ground floor."

"*The* ground floor," I said. "I'm getting in on *the* ground floor." I shrugged. "Besides, to get this kind of job in Japan, they require a teaching background and credentials in teaching English. I don't have those."

"But you must be good here," Jae Won said. "Not get in trouble."

He said this because of the way he saw me: Having provided him some weed so he could show off to his friends a few times, I was officially a serious American criminal. To the Koreans back in Iowa City, I was an authentic *Miami Vice*-style bad guy.

"Uh-huh," I said. "So, did you get to spend a lot of time with your girlfriend while you've been home?" I couldn't remember her name.

"No," he said. "I … I break her."

"Um," I said. "Oh! You broke *up* with her. I'm sorry about that, man."

"My older, my older brother, he getting married. His wife is younger, his wife is younger than my girlfriend. So I must … break up."

"Really? Is that a Korean thing, where you have to pay attention to everyone's age like that when you get married?"

"Of course. In Korea, in Korea we pay attention many things to get married. Age, school, job, father's job, brothers … Many, many things."

"Wow. That sounds complicated."

"Yes," he said. "Many rules."

My glass was empty so I grabbed the bottle to fill it again. Jae Won took it from my hands. "I pour you," he said.

"Oh, okay," I said. "Thanks."

"In Korea, do not pour yourself," he said. "I'm sitting … I'm sitting across you?"

"You're sitting across the table from me?" I asked. He nodded.

"I'm sitting across table," he said. "I must pour you. If you pour yourself, Koreans say it's bad for me." He smiled.

"Like, bad luck, you mean? It's bad luck if I pour for myself when you're sitting across from me?" I walked two fingers along the edge of the table. With the index finger of my other hand I traced a jagged line down through the air to the ambulating fingers. "Would you be struck by lightning?"

He laughed. "No. I will have a daughter. In Korea, always pour for older man, always pour for across table man. Never for you."

"Okay," I said. "Thanks, Jae Won."

"When older man pour you, it is honor. Drink is, drink is gift from man of higher status. You must drink. Must."

Jae Won's glass was empty so I filled it for him, Korean style. He took the bottle from me and filled mine. "Do you remember, do you remember Michiko?" he asked.

"Yeah." Michiko was a Japanese girl in English class with Jae Won. I had often seen Jae Won and Michiko taking study breaks or going to lunch together. She was tiny, sweet, and very quiet. Even her wardrobe—thin, fuzzy sweaters in neutral colors—seemed chosen so as not to draw attention. She was so shy that she had barely spoken to me at all.

"Michiko went, Michiko went to party with my friend."

"Oh, on a date? Michiko is dating your Korean friend? Like a girlfriend."

"No, no. We see Michiko at party. Michiko drank, Michiko drank too much and sleep."

"Oho! She passed out, huh?"

"Yes. She passed out." Jae Won nodded quickly a few times, smiling. "So my friend, my friend, he fucked her." He beamed proudly, as if he were telling me his friend was a Nobel Prize winner.

"I thought Michiko was your friend," I said. "You let some guy do that to her?"

He didn't understand the question.

"What time is it?" I asked. "I think I'd better check in for my flight."

"Yes, your flight. *Ajuma!*" He said something in Korean and the woman said something back.

"I got this one, man," I said. "How much is it?"

I opened my wallet and saw the single American twenty-dollar bill there. "Shit," I said. "I forgot to change this at the airport."

"That's all?" he asked, looking into the wallet. "You came to Korea with just twenty dollars?"

I shrugged. "It's what I have."

It was a little after 5:30 on my first morning in Korea, and I was already walking to work, dressed in a suit and tie. Leo, who was to be my roommate here as soon as the current occupants of the company housing unit moved out, walked with me. For now, we'd both been put up at a local *yogwan*, which my guidebook described as a traditional Korean hotel. Judging from its construction and décor, it was apparent that Korean tradition was big on poured concrete and yellow linoleum.

"Did Mr. Shin speak to you at all when he picked you up at the airport yesterday?" I asked.

"No," Leo said. "Korean Lurch didn't say a word."

"Heh. Korean Lurch. Perfect." Mr. Shin's appearance was dour and deadpan, and he had the personality to match. "Did he do the thing where he just held up the brochure?"

"Yes!" Leo said. "The same one they sent to us in the mail, where it's all in Korean with the logo and the English letters spelling SNM ACADEMY. I had to get right up in front of him to see what it was."

"And he knew what we looked like!" I said. "Remember, we had to send pictures? Why have us do that if they're not even going to wave to us at the airport?"

"To make sure we're white, maybe" Leo said. "They don't seem very interested in diversity, here. You're the only white guy I've seen in Korea, and there's nobody from any other race at all."

Together we followed the dark sidewalk toward the building Korean Lurch had pointed to the day before as he'd driven me to the *yogwan*. The only things that distinguished the school from the other boxes of concrete and glass were the two small red and yellow signs, in English, at its upper corner: *SNM Academy* and *SNM Junior*. It was about ten blocks from the *yogwan*, on the same side of the six-lane street.

"This is going to be challenging, starting to teach at six-thirty every morning," Leo said.

"And working until nine at night," I added.

"I think that's a pretty typical Korean schedule, he said. "At least we have time off in the middle of the day."

"Maybe enough time to sleep an hour," I said, "if we end up living close by."

The building was six stories tall, and occupied exclusively by our company, though the first two floors were empty. We rode a torturously slow elevator to the reception area on the fourth floor, where everything was a muted bluish-gray. The floor had been divided into small rooms by the installation of inch-thick panels that ran from floor to ceiling, which seemed to be made of the same stuff used in construction of office cubicles.

In the lobby was a black-and-white portrait of the founder, Moon Seung Nam, an expressionless and glassy-eyed old Korean man with age spots on his mostly bald head. "He looks embalmed," Leo whispered.

An American man came in. He was probably at the tail end of middle age, and he would have been a little over six feet tall, except for the fact that he seemed permanently hunched over. He had tangled, matted, graying hair around a mostly bald pate. The stubble on his face might have been two or three days of growth, and his lips were chapped and cracked. As required by company policy, he was wearing a jacket and tie. They were rumpled and didn't seem to fit quite right, but to Koreans he might have passed for the "exhausted business-man" type. To me, he seemed more like the "shopping cart full of empty cans" type.

He smiled and reached for my hand. "You guys are Mark and Leo, I'll bet," he said. He spoke too slowly and too softly, like Mister Rogers in an opium den.

"I'm Richard," he said.

"I'm Mark," I said, shaking his limp, leathery hand.

"So you're the boss, huh?" Leo asked.

"I'm *a* boss, I suppose," Richard said. "Just promoted when Jason left."

Jason had been the one who had offered me the job on the phone. Nobody had informed me that he'd be leaving before I arrived.

"Mr. Pock and I have the same rank," Richard said, "but I work with the expat teachers and he's in charge of the Korean staff. You'll meet him sometime, I'm sure."

"Have you been teaching long, Richard?" Leo asked.

"I worked in Taiwan before this," Richard said. "Before that I was tutoring foreign students back in the Baltimore area, where I'm from."

"How long have you been in Korea?" Leo asked.

"Four years." White and Korean teachers began passing by on their way to class. "This is James Lawson, from Atlanta," Richard said. "These are our two Canadians, Big Joe and Canada Katherine, and the ones coming in now are Roberta, Liz, David, Sue, Ryan, and Jennifer."

Jennifer was a beautiful, petite Asian woman in her early twenties, but mostly she looked like money. Everything was top of the line, from her pearl earrings and flawless makeup, to her imported (probably Italian) leather handbag and shoes. The brown silk designer suit she wore had to have set her back some serious cash, especially in a country with so many trade restrictions, and the suit had pants instead of a skirt, which I could already tell was unusual for dressed-up women in Korea. Her hairstyle, a straight perm with some shimmer coating stuff I'd seen a Japanese friend get once, was one of the priciest hairstyles I'd ever heard of. Even when compared to the obviously upper-class students I'd seen filing into the building, Jennifer seemed to be one of the elites. She was nice to look at, but the parading of wealth was off-putting. She was probably a rich Korean-American doctor's kid or something.

Richard mentioned a few people's credentials. David and Sue had certificates in teaching English as a second language, and James Lawson had taught in Japan. I wasn't listening all that closely, but I heard enough to realize that I was the least experienced teacher in the place.

"Our adult classrooms are up on floors five and six," Richard explained. "Offices and reception are here on four. The third floor, below our offices, has classrooms for SNM Junior, the kids' school, but you're both here to teach adult classes so you probably won't be down there much. There is a room at the back of the sixth floor that serves as a lab with cassette tape machines, and one at the front of the fifth floor that's more of a lounge where students and teachers can wait for classes, practice conversation, and watch AFKN."

"What's AFKN?" Leo asked.

"The military channel," Richard said. "Korea's still at war, you know. There are thirty thousand American troops here, but you won't see them because they never leave the bases. The American military has a TV station for its people, which they broadcast all over South Korea, with American shows like Good Morning America, Sesame Street, and news.

Watching it is good practice for our students, but the lounge usually is mostly populated with foreign teachers."

He opened the door to a room which could barely accommodate the three small desks it contained. "Mark, you'll be in here."

Canada Katherine was sitting at one of the desks. She was Asian, and a bit heavy, with glasses and unstyled hair that hung limply to her shoulders. She wore a frumpy polyester skirt suit in navy blue. Standing at the other desk was an older white woman in a long beige dress with embroidered flowers whose gray hair hung down to the middle of her back. She was wearing a lot of beads, and big, round eyeglasses halfway down her nose. "I'm Alice," she said. You're going to observe my class this morning. Are you ready?" She gestured at the clock. It was 6:25.

Richard continued down the hall with Leo.

"This class is a 101," Alice said as we climbed the stairs to the fifth floor. "It's our first adult level. We start at 101 and go all the way to 109, but there's only one class of 109 right now. I like the lower levels because they're easier to teach."

She opened the door to the room directly above the office I shared with her, revealing fifteen college-aged students in small desks squeezed in around three sides. Next to the door was a whiteboard and a larger, rectangular teacher's desk.

"Good morning, class!" Alice said.

"Good morning, Alice," they said back, flatly, in unison.

"This is Mark. He's going to be a new English teacher here. Mark, there's an empty seat there next to Petunia. Why don't you take that one?"

I sat down in the last available seat.

"Each of us teaches around a hundred students a day, in eight classes like this. Four classes in the morning, and four classes at night," Alice said. "The students have all chosen an

English nickname to use. That makes it easier for us to inter-act on a more personal level. In Korea there's such a strong hierarchy that everyone has to change how they address each other depending on age; it would make conversation practice a nightmare. Nicknames free everyone up a little, let them escape all the roles they play, all the rigid structure of Korean life. Anyway, this is the class."

One by one, she called on each of the students and had them introduce themselves by nickname. Some used real names like Kate, a few used professions like Musician, and some just chose random words, like the guy who called him-self Spoon. She followed each introduction by asking them, "How are you this morning?" Every student gave the same indifferent, mechanical response: "Fine-thank-you-and-you?" Alice responded to each, modeling other variations like "I'm doing well today, thanks for asking," or "I'm feeling good," but nobody gave anything but the canned answer on his or her turn.

"Okay, class, let's turn to page 54."

Page 54 had one large cartoon at the top, with a tall, smil-ing woman standing next to a short one. "Everyone together," Alice said. "Is Julie tall or short?"

"Julie is tall," they said, in unison, flatly.

"Is Sarah short or tall?"

"Sarah is short."

Smaller cartoons showed other opposites, like old and young, rich and poor, heavy and thin, pretty and ugly, expen-sive and cheap, quiet and noisy, and more. Alice went through each one the same way, and then broke them into pairs so they could practice on their own.

I got paired with Petunia, a short, serious young woman with thick glasses. When everyone had run through the whole series, Alice took over again and had them turn the page.

The next set of cartoons had one person assuming something, and the other person correcting them. "Tell me about your car. Is it new?" "No. It is old." "Tell me about your sister. Is she ugly?" "No. She is pretty."

When the class finished doing the exercises in unison, we all paired off again to practice. Then Alice pulled us all back together and started another page.

After an hour of this, there was a fifteen-minute break. I followed Alice back down to the office. "Some teachers stay in the room for break," she said, "but I need to get away."

"And that's the class? You just go through the book like that?"

"That's it."

Above Alice's desk was a poster, all in Korean. It had a black and white photo of a somber young woman. Alice saw me looking at it. "They push kids so hard in Korea," she said. "That was for a violin concert. You'll see music is a big thing here. It's another tool for teaching discipline, and the competition is brutal. She looks more like she's going to war than about to play the violin, don't you think?"

"If you hadn't told me, I might've thought it was a *Korea's Most Wanted* poster," I said. "I've learned from Koreans back at school that competition is fierce here, though."

Canada Katherine came in. "Did I hear you discussing music?" she asked. "Talking about *Revolution*?"

"Oh," Alice said. "We weren't, but that's a good example of life here." She turned to me. "The Beatles song *Revolution* was legalized last month. It'd been banned since it came out, twenty-five years ago."

"How did you even hear about that?" I asked. "Was that AFKN?"

"No," Katherine said. "AFKN is American. They just have news from the United States. There's a newspaper we get, here, called the Korea Herald. It's the only English newspaper in the country, so pretty much every foreigner here reads it. The school subscribes."

"I'm sure I'll check it out," I said.

Then we were back upstairs, slogging through the material again. The cartoons showed a sunny day and the students said "It is sunny." The cartoons showed a phone call where someone assumed the weather and got corrected. The class broke into groups. Petunia said nothing beyond what was in the book. I calculated that my contract obligated me to spend 2,496 hours doing this.

The next class I observed was Karen's. Karen looked to be about my age, a white girl from California with curly, blonde, shoulder-length hair.

This class was a 103. Karen had the students introduce themselves. There was another woman calling herself Musician, and a man who called himself Carmen. They were all college students except for a middle-aged guy who'd chosen to be called Old Man and an *ajuma* who called herself Polly.

This class also had the habit of answering "How are you?" with a robotic "fine-thank-you-and-you?" I started saying "It's nice to meet you," instead.

"Attention, everyone," Karen said. "I'm going to do a magic trick today. This is Mark. He's a new teacher here. You can ask him questions. Now, Mark, for this magic trick, I need you to hold this paper, but don't unfold it."

"Okay," I said.

Karen sat down in one of two empty desks. "Go ahead, class, ask Mark some questions."

"Where are you from?" a businessman who called himself Robot asked.

"I'm from Iowa City, Iowa," I said.

"How old are you?" Old Man asked.

"I'm twenty-three," I answered.

"Are you married?" Old Man asked.

"I am not married," I said.

"Do you have girlfriend?" Robot asked.

"Do you have *a* girlfriend," Karen corrected.

"Do you have a girlfriend?" Robot asked.

"No, I do not have a girlfriend," I said.

"What is your school?" a man named Charles asked.

At this, Karen interrupted. "He's not still a student, right Charles? He went to school in the past, so use past tense."

Charles tried again. "What was your school?"

"Better," Karen said. "Or we would probably say something like 'What school did you attend?'"

"What school … did you attend?"

"I went to the University of Iowa," I said.

"Why did you come to Korea?" asked Betty, a perky young woman with short hair. Her pronunciation was perfect.

"I want to learn about Korea," I said. "I want to make friends, and maybe someday I can do business here."

In this sea of somber, expressionless faces, Betty's warm and genuine smile was rather striking. "I like that you came here to make friends," she said.

"Okay," Karen said. "It's time for my magic trick. Mark, please open the paper and read what is there."

I opened the paper to find a numbered list. I read it out loud. "Number one: Where are you from? Number two: How old are you? Number three: Are you married? Number four: Do you have a girlfriend? Number five: What school did you attend? Number six: Why did you come to Korea?"

I clapped softly in Karen's direction with my fingertips, an approving audience for her trick. The class remained expressionless. Even Betty's face looked serious again.

"Now, yes, I do know this class very well," Karen said. "But it's more than that. Korean society is hierarchical, and most of these questions help people figure out where you fit. Where you're from is something everyone wants to know about foreigners, but the other questions are more important here than most Americans would realize."

"Okay," I said. "I understand. My Japanese friends and roommates were like that."

"Yes, okay," Karen said. "I've known some Japanese people, too. The cultures do share some characteristics, though Koreans will often tell you that they hate Japan. I would say that Koreans tend to be... let's just say they're blunter, here. Koreans are also... just... very intense about everything. You'll see what I mean, soon enough.

"Okay, class," she said. "Turn to page ninety-six."

It was lunchtime on my first day. Leo and I were sitting in the lounge.

"The bar at the *yogwan* has these same seats," Leo said.

Each seat was like a free-standing individual section of a couch, much narrower and a little taller than American sectional pieces, and upholstered in black vinyl. The current configuration had four of them lined up into something resembling a sofa, with two more crammed into the corners of the triangular room and a last one sitting next to the television, facing the others. The space was so small that the corner seats were inaccessible except by climbing over or sliding sections out of the main four.

AFKN was showing an episode of Jerry Springer, and it cut to commercial. Instead of the ads for laundry soap and maxi pads that would've come on back in the United States, it was a guy in a monkey costume being lectured by another in an army uniform on the importance of staying home when he was sick. "I don't want to work with a sick monkey like you!" he said into the camera.

Leo grimaced. "I guess the military makes its own commercials," he said.

"You are watching the Armed Forces Korea Network," an announcer said. Another commercial came on, this one showing two soldiers sitting in a restaurant, talking about their recent assignments. "Operations security is everyone's business," a voice said. Over the restaurant scene, the words OPERATIONS SECURITY appeared on the screen, then shortened and combined to form a single word: OPSEC. "Friendly communications can be used by the enemy to determine our capabilities, limitations, and activities. Always remember to practice good OPSEC."

David's red mop of hair appeared at the door. He and his wife Sue had come here from Seattle. "We're going to lunch," he said. "You guys want to come along?"

Leo and I walked with David, Sue, and James Lawson toward a Chinese restaurant near the school. People on the street stopped to watch as the little cluster of white people passed by.

"Looks like it might rain," Leo said.

"It always looks like it's going to rain here," David said. "Taegu is in a basin, between mountains like Los Angeles. They don't seem to have any pollution controls, so there's always this gray haze. You don't even notice it after a while, except that jackets and coats start to turn black a few days after you wash them."

"Maybe that's why I'm not feeling well," Leo said, placing a hand over his stomach as he walked."

"You didn't drink the tap water, did you?" Lawson asked. "That shit'll turn you inside-out."

"No. They gave us bottled water at the *yogwan*."

"Uh-oh," Sue said. "Was it frozen solid?"

"Yeah. Did you guys stay there when you first arrived, too?"

"Yep," Sue said. "And that frozen water they give you there is tap water, which you're probably already noticing."

What she said was true. My own guts were threatening to make me one sick monkey.

"Buy your own water while you're staying there," David said. Once you're in company housing, you'll get big bottles of purified water delivered regularly. They deduct the cost from your pay, of course."

"That's a solid idea," Leo said. "Does this place we're going have a bathroom?"

"I think so," Sue said. She and David were both very fair-skinned, but her short dark hair and porcelain complexion made a stark contrast to David's freckled Raggedy Andy look.

As we walked down the narrow street, we saw a collection of riot police on the opposite side. They were surrounding a charcoal gray building that was covered in brightly colored paint splatters. Most of the windows had been painted over with gray paint, and roughly a third of them had been cracked and broken, apparently by rocks or other thrown objects. About thirty officers stood in small clusters of four and five, leaning on their gray metal shields and smoking cigarettes. Above the entrance to the building was a black sign with steel letters reading "TAEGU AMERICAN CENTER."

"Most of the huge riots happen on the college campuses," Sue said. "But a lot of the anti-American stuff happens here. Sometimes when you walk by, there's tear gas wafting around."

"American Center?" I said. "What does this place do?"

"Officially it's called the American Cultural Center, and it's supposed to help people visit America," David said. "It offers college brochures, study guides for the SAT and the TOEFL, and probably some pamphlets for tourists, but I've never seen anyone go in or out. I think the United States maintains it so the protesters come here instead of demonstrating outside the military bases." He pointed a finger at the holes and craters. "If someone pulled that shit at Camp Walker, guys with machine guns would cut him in half. Much better to draw all the malcontents here. It's convenient for them, too." He nodded toward a grouping of round signs with Korean letters and times. "See the different bus routes?"

"Who are the protesters?" I asked. "What do they want?"

"They're college students," Lawson said. "They want us to get the fuck out of their country."

"Many of them are *our* students," Sue said. "They want all kinds of stuff, including more democracy. But they often protest American policies, too."

The Chinese restaurant had four tables, none of which was big enough for our group. We crowded around the only open one, our shoulders touching.

Suits were required for our jobs, and apparently for most other occupations, too. About half the restaurant's patrons were wearing business suits, all gray, with neckties in muted colors. The other half, non-management types like clerks and bus drivers, wore uniforms, which were basically suits as well, also in muted grayish shades. Most of the a*jumas* wore nearly identical black polyester outfits, and even the schoolkids I'd seen wore uniforms in blue and brown.

"Oh, another thing you probably wouldn't know if someone didn't tell you," Sue said. "If you're trying to save money to take it back home, start changing it to dollars right away.

Korea is super strict about controlling its currency. You can only change what you make from SNM Academy, and only with documentation and your passport."

"It's a pain in the ass," David said. "They actually stamp your passport every time you change won to dollars, and write in how much you change. They're paranoid about it and the bank tellers give you dirty looks if you bring in too much at once."

"Are you guys saving a lot here?" Leo asked.

"Not as much as we thought we would," Sue said. "But some. There's not a lot to spend it on here unless you're into Korean designer clothes. Transportation is the biggest expense—taxi fares."

A Korean man appeared at the table, just staring at us. "Oh," David said. "We should order."

"What's good?" Leo asked.

"Chinese food is different here than at home," Lawson said. Short and jowly with a buzz cut, Lawson gave the impression of being someone who liked to eat. "But you can get some things that are the same. *Chopchae* is an easy one to remember because it sounds like chop suey, which is pretty close to what it is, and there's another called *tangsooyook* that is basically sweet and sour pork."

"And everyone is proud of their regional differences in the way they eat, too," Sue said. "They'll show you what they do, like making a dipping sauce or mixing in this or that condiment, like vinegar or soy sauce or what have you, and say, 'In Taegu we do it this way.'"

I decided to go for the *chopchae*.

"Betty was trying to come along," Lawson said. "I told her the group was too big. She's super clingy."

"Well, she likes you," Sue said.

"Is this the same Betty I saw in Karen's class this morning?" I asked. "Perky, with short hair and wide eyes?"

"Yeah, that's her," Lawson said.

"You know if you have sex with her you have to marry her," David said. "That's the rule here."

"Yeah, okay," Lawson said. "Sure, I do."

"Mark?" Leo whispered. "I hope that's you standing there."

"Yeah, it's me," I whispered back. "I figured it'd be best to leave the light off. I don't want them coming up here."

"I had the same thought."

"Might as well have a beer," I said. "Doesn't seem like they're going to knock this shit off any time soon. Want one?"

"Sure."

Korean Lurch had moved Leo and me into our new apartment from the *yogwan* on Saturday afternoon. Now it was sometime around two-thirty Sunday morning, and the two of us were still awake, thanks to our battling landlords.

"There's only one liter left," I said. "I hope they wrap this thing up before we're out."

"There's always Sac-Sac," Leo said. Sac-Sac was a juice-like product that came in tiny cans sealed with pull-off aluminum-foil stickers. It had traces of what might have been tangerine pulp floating in a liquid that was sort of like Tang, or flat orange soda. Leo had been consuming multiple cans per day, in the belief that it was healthy.

There was enough light coming in from a nearby street-light that I was able to find the beer bottle in the mini fridge, pop the top, and pour it into two of the little juice glasses Koreans used for beer.

"Hit the heights," I whispered, handing him one of the glasses. This beer, called Hite, was allegedly made with spring water instead of whatever it was that gurgled from the tap.

There was no way to sleep, not when we were this close to the domestic death match going on downstairs between the husband and wife who owned the duplex. The battle had degenerated to sounds of breaking glass and heavy things tipping over an hour ago, and now they had spilled out into the garden, shouting and gesturing at each other. Leo and I stood at the bay window, watching.

"We need popcorn," I whispered.

"And subtitles," he said.

"Woman! Why you so damned gruesome!" I said. Switching to a higher-toned whisper, I answered myself: "Because I married a big pussy who can't even slug me in the face right!"

The houses in this part of the city were all small, two-story structures, each surrounded by a concrete wall that included enough space to park a single car. Our landlords parked in the street, leaving the space empty, perhaps so they'd have room to do this.

"I'm not even over jetlag, yet," I said. "How often do you think this happens?"

The woman's voice rose again into shouts. Illuminated by bright light coming through their windows, she raised her fist above her head and slammed it down into his face several times.

"Ooh! Shit!" Leo whispered.

The man reeled backward, waving his arms as if he were shaking out a bedsheet. He lurched forward and tried to kick her in the stomach, but missed. Her fist rose and beat him in the head and face again, with the same potato-mashing move. He raised his hands, shielding his head, and then seized a handful of her hair above her forehead and flung her to the ground. She landed face-first, but was up again in no time, clawing at his eyes.

"I wish we had more beer," I said.

Our contracts stipulated that the company would give us two hundred bucks spending money, in Korean won, just for showing up in Taegu. Richard had handed us each an envelope containing a short stack of *mon won* bills, denominated 10,000 won, which meant they were worth roughly twelve dollars each. This cash had turned out to be essential, because while the contract provided for housing, the apartment they gave us had no dishes, cooking utensils, or bedding. Leo, a granola-type from Colorado, had arrived with camping stuff, including a sleeping bag, but I had been sleeping on a bare mattress.

Leo had recruited a student who called himself New Clip to help us shop for things we'd need. New Clip's long, narrow face reminded me of an Easter Island head. He'd brought us to Taegu's crowded outdoor market, a jumble of tents, open-air tables, carts, and people sitting on blankets surrounded by their wares. Now we each carried big plastic bags full of sheets, pots and pans, towels, and other household items. Leo had found umbrellas, offered in varying plaids of muted blue, gray, green, and black. Like everything else we'd seen here so far—suits, uniforms, upholstery, buildings—the umbrellas only came in dusty, washed-out colors.

The chaos of the marketplace was nice. It felt like we

were no longer in the spotlight, though clearly still on stage.

"Think about it," I said. "When you go home to Colorado, are you going to stuff your suitcase with a giant soup pot? Not me. If anything, I might take some of those shitty little beer glasses we have that someone stole from the bars. You could almost call those legitimate souvenirs, but yet they're the only things the foreigners from our place decided to leave behind? No way. It's either Mr. Shin or the landlady, taking all that stuff when people move out."

"The landlady takes them, definitely," Leo said, "and uses them to clock her husband in the face."

"She does just fine beating the shit out of him without weapons."

"I see what you mean, though," he said. "A lot of people probably already have all that back home, anyway. I have my entire college apartment boxed up in my parents' basement."

"Yeah, see?" I said. "I actually don't own anything back in the States, but even to me, it seems weird to drag pots and pans back to the other side of the world."

"Nothing?"

"Everything I own is here with me in Korea. Contents of a suitcase and garment bag, and now this." I held up the plastic Santa Claus bag with all my new junk inside.

We approached a tent with handbags spread all over tables and hanging on poles. I managed to find a cheap vinyl brief-case with a zipper. Like everywhere else I'd shopped so far in Korea, there was no checkout line. People shoved and elbowed each other to get through the crowd. The *ajumas* were by far the worst because they would actually strike anyone who got in their way, sometimes punching with closed fists, instead of just pushing. One shoved me sideways by digging her fin-gernails into my shoulder and arm, leaving little red indenta-tions. When I finally reached the counter, New Clip helped me negotiate for the bag, and I ended up getting it for a single green *mon won* bill.

"Thanks for all your help today, New Clip," I said. "We really appreciate it."

"Is good for me," New Clip said. "For practice English."

"It's good for us, too, for sure," Leo said. "We'll buy you lunch."

"Thank you, Leo," New Clip said.

Three seats opened up at a little outdoor stand just as we were passing. "Hey," Leo said. "Sushi rolls! Want to stop?"

We snatched the seats before anyone could dig their fingernails into us. Stacked on a plate at one end of the counter were rolls of seaweed and rice. "In Korea, no sushi," New Clip said. "We say, *gimbop. Bop* is rice, and *gim* is, uh, green part."

"Ah!" I said. "The seaweed. *Gim bop*, seaweed rice. I got it. Thank you, New Clip."

"Got it?"

"It means I understand." I held my hands up like I was holding a football. "It's like, you have the information, whatever you're telling me—" I mimed throwing the ball and then catching it. "And then I tell you that now I have that information. *I got it*. Do you understand?"

"I got it," New Clip said.

"Ha! Yes. Just like that."

I showed Leo the shirts I'd gotten to send to friends back in Iowa. Cheap outdoor markets in Asia tended to sell unbranded merchandise with garbled English, and this place was no exception. I was sending two of the shirts to my friend Danny. One had a cartoon fish on it and read, "I am happy! Pants!" Another had small letters on the left breast that said "INTERCOURSE."

A grubby man came up and poked me on the shoulder. New Clip said something to him in Korean but he ignored it and poked me again. He held out his palm. The woman behind the counter shouted at him. He made a circle with is thumb and forefinger, a coin, and placed it in his other palm.

The woman from behind the counter picked up the stool next to Leo and came around behind me, still shouting. The man made another gesture at me. The woman jabbed him hard under the jaw with the stabilizing bar between the stool legs. He made a choking sound and fell to one knee. She ran at him and he scrabbled backward, disappearing into the crowd.

This *gimbop* was not raw fish. It had some cooked carrot, processed fish cake, and a yellow pickled radish.

The three of us finished eating and made our way toward the gates. On one table in front of a tent I saw six-inch-long dried centipedes, tied with twine into bundles that would've been too big to put my fingers around. "Are they for medicine?" I asked New Clip. "Yes," he said.

On our way out of the market area, we passed a table with various cuts of meat, including the skinless head of a dog about the size of a golden retriever, obvious because of its long canine teeth.

"I don't think we're in Kansas anymore, Toto," I said. Leo laughed. New Clip didn't understand.

"Do you know "The Wizard of Oz?" I asked him. His Easter Island face bobbed up and down but his expression did not change.

"Remember how in the movie, Dorothy had a little dog named Toto? When she got to Oz, things looked quite different, and she told him she didn't think they were in Kansas anymore."

He stared back at me, expressionless, as before.

"So, I said I don't think we're in Kansas anymore..." I gestured at the dog head. "...Because look at Toto! Do you get it, New Clip?"

"Ah, get it," he said. "It means understand. Yes. I get it. You talk to dead dog. Very funny."

Leo and I were the second and third people at the bus stop. Lately we'd been taking taxis to work, but on rainy days they became scarce. We'd both already been passed many times by taxis that picked up Koreans instead of us.

"Aren't you glad I thought to buy umbrellas?" he asked.

"Yes, yes," I said. "Very forward-thinking of you." We stood back from the other person there, an *ajuma* holding an umbrella with a navy and gray spotted pattern that clashed with the two plaids of the ones we'd bought at the open market, even though they all shared the same flat colors.

"It doesn't stink as much when it rains," Leo said. "You know that smell that's always around? A class told me it's because the economy grew so fast, there was no time to improve the sewer system to match development. They got modern buildings but the streets smell like shit all the time."

A man approached from one side, and another came from around the corner, both in suits. A younger woman walked up next, wearing some uniform from a bank or convenience store. Soon there were more than twenty Koreans waiting for the bus.

One man began shouting at me as he approached, pushing his way through the crowd and tilting his umbrella behind his back in order to lean under mine. He was middle-aged, wearing what might have been a shop foreman uniform, consisting of a brown shirt and brown pants. He continued shouting, now inches from my face. He smelled like garlic.

"Leo?" I said. "Do you have any idea what this is about?"

"Nope. Glad it's you and not me, though."

The man pushed me out of the way and began to yell at Leo. Someone next to me spoke English.

"He say America NAFTA plan bad for Korea. NAFTA cheat Korea!" This translator had glasses and was wearing a suit. He, too, was shouting.

The green and white bus arrived, and the crowd got on. Leo and I waited for the next one.

The new crowd that formed around us didn't say anything, though they all stared. None of them ventured too close. They left a wide gap around us, as if they feared we might infect them with something.

When we boarded the next bus, there were no seats. Leo and I rode standing up, halfway down the aisle. We were once again the center of attention. "It's like theater in the round," Leo said.

It would be the last time either of us took a city bus in Taegu.

Korea had a lot of taxis, so I was usually able to find adequate transportation in spite of the ones who refused to pick me up. Near our apartment was *Mu Goong Hwa Juyuso*, which translated as "Rose of Sharon Gas Station," and was known by all taxi drivers. I could get back there in a taxi by saying the name and adding *kapsida* ("let's go"). Work was near the Grand Hotel, which they all knew, and most downtown attractions were near a famous movie theater called *Han Il Geukchang*. Taxis were my biggest weekly expense, but when possible Leo and I rode together to save money.

One day he and I returned to work with plenty of time to prepare for our afternoon classes. My office was closer to the front door than Leo's was, and he stopped there with me to finish the conversation we'd been having on the ride in.

"I agree, it's pretty weird," I said.

"What is?" Alice asked.

"That place in the basement next door," Leo said. The sign that's all in Korean and except for the words *room salon* in English. Why are they only open at night? It's always closed when we get here in the afternoon, and open when we're leaving. Who needs a haircut at nine at night?"

"Ha. Haircut," Alice said. "*Room salon* is what they call a prostitute bar. Businessmen go there after work. Pretty girls hold their hands, drink with them, and laugh at their jokes. Then if they want, they can pay an extra fee to take the girls home. Or, much more likely, to that *yogwan* you stayed at."

"Really?" Leo asked. "So, all these parents are taking their kids to the academy downstairs, and we're next door to a whorehouse?"

"There are probably a hundred of them in Taegu," Alice said. "Maybe several hundred. They're easy to spot because they always have the English words *room salon* on the signs. Ask your classes. They'll tell you."

"Wow," Leo said. He continued on to his office, which he shared with Gerri and Sue.

New Clip appeared in the doorway. "Hey, Mark," he said. "I talked to English professor at my school, like you wanted."

"You did?" I said. "Thanks, New Clip! That's really nice of you to do that for us."

New Clip had been hired as the academy's errand boy. One day he'd heard Leo and me discussing how we wished there was a program here to teach foreigners the Korean language the way SNM Academy did for English. He'd volunteered to contact the English department at his university and try to set something up. The assumption was that an English professor would be better able to communicate with us than someone who regularly taught Korean.

"Tuesdays at one-thirty," New Clip said. He had a piece of paper saying as much, with a room number. "I will help you get there first time."

"*The* first time," I said. "You'll help us get there *the* first time."

"*The* first time," New Clip said. "I will help you get there *the* first time."

This was easily my favorite class of the day, the school's only level 109. Alice had told me that nobody wanted to teach this class, because they were bored with the book and, as graduates of Korean high schools, they already knew English grammar better than most Americans. I jumped at the opportunity to teach it because I saw that these students wanted to practice, to be engaged in actual, meaningful discourse, and to learn about more than just pronunciation and the assembly of sentences. After nearly a month here, this two-hour block was the one time of the day when my brain felt alive.

This class was the event horizon for the three men and three women comprising it, halfway between the colleges they had just graduated from and the uncompromising world of full-fledged Korean adulthood. They clung to it. I had come to think of the group as the Deadbeat Club, like the name of a song on my former roommate's B-52s tape.

On the board, I'd written each of their nicknames and asked them what their major had been.

"Okay," I said. "Now, why did you choose these majors?"

"Nobody chose," Paul said. "The Korean college system is different than the U.S. system."

"Oh, really? How so?"

"In America, you apply to many different colleges and choose one that admits you," Sarah said. "In Korea, you may only apply to one college."

"Not just college," Groundhog said. A former SNM Academy class had so named him because he had the same face and vacant puppy-dog expression as comedian Bill Murray. "Major. One major at one college."

"So, Koreans apply just to one major at one college, and that's it?" I asked. "What if you're not accepted?"

"If you're not accepted, you don't go to college," Sarah said.

"You can study and take the test again the next year," Paul said.

"Wow. So, you apply to one major at one college, out of all the majors and colleges in Korea. How do you know where to apply?

"Practice tests," Groundhog said. "And parents."

"We take a lot of practice tests, and we know around what our official score will be," Sarah said. "Then in that range there are different majors and schools that accept students with scores like that. Past scores that were accepted for each major at each school show what it will probably be again this year. Every major is a separate competition."

"It's on the news," Groundhog said. "Not every school, but when there is a big change. Like the stock market. They say,

'The chemistry major at Seoul National University is seeing more competition this year. They will accept this many and already have one-third.'" he shrugged. "I don't know how many. Whatever number."

"Wow," I said. "So, do any of you know what you'll do, what your jobs will be, with those majors?"

"Housewife," Strawberry and Sarah said, almost simultaneously. Strawberry had majored in home economics and Sarah in English.

"You know this already?" I asked.

"There's nothing else," Sarah said.

"I'd be doomed," I said. "I can cook a few things, I guess, but I'm not good at cleaning. What about the rest of you?"

"Banker," Groundhog said.

I gestured to the board, where it showed he'd been a business major. "That makes sense. You are trained in business, and you choose to apply that education to a career in banking."

"I didn't choose it," Groundhog said. "I don't want to be a banker. It will be very boring. I want to work for a small company, have more control. My father says I should be a banker because it is more secure."

"And so, you have to be a banker, because your father says so?" I asked. "Is that common in Korea, that your parents choose your career?"

"Very common," Paul said. Everyone agreed.

"Maybe everybody," Strawberry said.

"I'm sorry you have to be a banker, Groundhog," I said.

Major Byun was a married, middle-aged 103 who told me he attended SNM Academy in order to meet young women. He and I had agreed to get together downtown. I had come to Korea to network and look for opportunities, and pretty much anything beat sitting on the vinyl sectional watching AFKN, so I tended to accept every invitation I got.

It was Saturday so I wore jeans and a tee shirt. He was a major in the Korean Air Force, and he dressed like Major Nelson from *I Dream of Jeannie*. We went to see the movie *Cliffhanger*, in what must have been some sort of unlicensed or pirated showing. The "theater" was an old store filled with rows of folding chairs. Two-thirds of the seats were empty, but Major Byun chose to sit down next to a woman who seemed to be there alone. He offered her his popcorn and she refused. For the first ten minutes of the movie, he continued to push the popcorn at her, and she continued to refuse. Then she got up and moved away.

After the show, I drank soju with him in a tent made from rubbery orange material like the stuff used for carnival bouncy-houses. He was older than me, so by Korean custom I had to down shot after shot as he poured for me and I recip-rocated, pouring for him as he reminded me to show respect by holding the bottle with both hands.

"Soju is maybe too strong for Americans," he said once when I shuddered. Soju was only half the strength of vodka, which I drank like water back in the States. The shudder had come from the realization, as I had tilted back the glass, that the stuff smelled like urinal cakes.

Korean Lurch had shoved a scrap of paper at me. It was a note: "SEE ME. RICHARD."

The landlords downstairs had been at it again the night before, though they'd finished early, around one o'clock in the morning. On the taxi ride in at 5:30, Leo and I deduced that the wife must have knocked the husband out cold.

I finished another can of a chemical-tasting Korean energy drink called Bacchus F, which made me feel as if my eyes were being pulled from their sockets with suction cups, and knocked on the flimsy metal frame of Richard's open door.

It had been several days since I'd been out with Major Byun and endured the subsequent hangover from hell. In the interim, two different classes had confirmed that soju was made from petroleum.

In the two chairs across from Richard sat David and Karen. Both looked flushed and upset. Richard, as always, looked like he'd just been awakened from behind a Dumpster.

Richard turned to me. "Just wait in the lobby a minute, Mark. You can come in when these two are finished."

"No, stay here, Mark," David said. "You can be a witness."

"Richard," Karen said. "This is serious. We used to think it was funny that Gerri talked about how all three of her husbands died in freak accidents, but now she's accusing me of really weird things, like going through her stuff. When she said it, I asked if anything was missing, and she said, 'No, you're too crafty for that.' It's getting scary. I can't keep living with her."

Richard ran a hand along the side of his face and into his hair. It was too tangled to continue that direction, so he pulled it back down in front of him again and wiped his fingers on his shirt. "Her contract is up in a month," he said.

David turned to me. "Gerri is Karen's roommate," he said. "You may have noticed that Gerri is insane."

I shrugged. "She hasn't crossed my path much."

"Today, she was talking to me at the copy machine," David said. "Her eyes got this glassy look. 'Karen's making me nervous,' she told me, just like that, in this really distant, flat voice. Then she leaned close and whispered, 'I suspect that she's plotting to kill me.' The hair on the back of my neck stood up. Gerri went off to her class, and I went through the offices and hid all the scissors. It was all I could think to do."

"Well, I can't think of anything else to do, either," Richard said. "If she were to leave early, I'd have eight classes to fill for a month. I'm not going to do that just because she's creepy."

"I'm not asking you to send her home early," Karen said. "I'm just afraid to live with her. Just let me go to a *yogwan* or something until she's gone."

"I don't have the budget for that."

"Karen, I don't think you'll get anything this way," David said. "Why don't you just come stay with us? There's an extra bedroom because Sue and I share the big one."

"There you go," Richard said. "Problem solved. Karen will live with David and Sue. Now, go prepare for your classes. Mark, come in."

David and Karen squeezed past me in the narrow hallway. I entered and sat down.

"So, what's up?" I asked.

"One of your students told me you like to discuss cultural issues in your class," he said.

"Yeah, I do," I said. "It's more engaging, and the ones who tend to be the least motivated in learning English become the most eager participants, trying to show me what's so great here."

"Well, they don't like it, and that's not your job."

"I don't know who it is you spoke with, but they truly don't seem to mind my teaching style. Some have told me they enjoy it because it's more interesting."

"Koreans don't think of what you're doing as education," he said. "Korean education is ordered and structured, like the rest of the society here, always peaceful and efficient. Nobody has to listen to subordinates or students. What's important to Koreans is the knowledge you possess, not your opinion about that knowledge. You make them lose respect for you when you make them explain their society."

"I'm teaching in a way that's not just empty memorization," I said. "They talk in my class because they *want* to talk. The students help each other put together vocabulary and grammar to say what they want me to know. And by the way, it's a lot harder to come up with challenging topics of conversation than just reading the book all day."

"They think you're wasting their time," Richard said. "Education in Korea is when you open the book and teach them what's there. You present it, and they accept it. There's no squabbling, no back and forth. It's all methodical and serene. That's what we do here, and it's what makes this country so incredibly productive. Don't come here and try to fuck it all up. Got it?"

"Whatever."

My 102 ended at noon. Most of its members were free to stick around, and they offered to take me to lunch. I dropped my class materials at my desk and came out to join them in the lobby.

One of my students, Sally, was standing there talking to my coworker Jennifer, in Korean. Sally said something to the rest of the class and they all agreed with her. Especially the men seemed particularly enthusiastic in their support of whatever she'd asked.

"She will come to lunch, okay?" Sally asked.

"Sure," I said to Sally. "Hi," I said to Jennifer. I decided against telling her I hadn't known she could speak Korean.

"Hi," Jennifer said. "So, where are we going?"

A discussion ensued, in Korean, as everyone headed for the elevator. They came to a conclusion about where to go, and all eight of us walked down the street together. A few passersby still watched me, but this time it was probably clear that I was an English teacher with a class. The scrutiny felt more forgiving than usual.

Taegu Mondu was a typical Korean restaurant, with glaring white walls, overly bright fluorescent lights, and gray laminate tables. Our group arrived at the start of the lunch rush, but the tables were long enough that we were able to sit together comfortably. A mother sat at the next table over, with a little girl about four years old and a little boy who might have been five. Sally sat next to Jennifer, across from me in the middle of the group. "Mondu" is the Korean word for "dumpling," and dumplings were all that were on the menu, in at least a dozen forms, including steamed, fried and soup varieties.

A woman next to me who called herself Silver pointed to a photo on a laminated menu. "This one Taegu style. Only we have in Taegu."

The one she'd pointed out was called *bi bim mondu*, which was fried dumplings covered with a mound of shredded raw cabbage and sticky hot red pepper paste. The dish vaguely reminded me of Mexican food, which I was already starting to miss.

"Thank you for telling me, Silver," I said. "I always like to try foods the local Taegu way. I'm going to get that one today."

We all ordered and waited for the food to come. The little boy at the next table climbed up on top of it and leapt onto the end of ours. He jumped up and down, causing the legs to bang loudly against the linoleum, and then leapt to another table. His sister tried to get out of her seat, but the mother grabbed her shoulders and slammed her back down, hard, chastising her.

"Why does she let the older one do whatever he wants, but yet act so strict with the little one?" I asked, knowing the answer. At least they'd practice English.

Jennifer spoke. "Because one is a boy. Korea treats boys and girls differently."

"We Koreans say women must be calm," a student called Kevin said.

The food came. Mine had crispy brown dumplings that gave a slightly spicy smell. Everyone took metal chopsticks from a can at the center of the table. I snatched up a dumpling and a little cabbage with chopsticks and dipped it in sauce. I bent to take a bite when Jennifer raised a couple of fingers at me. It had the effect of raising a palm, like a policeman stopping traffic, and I got the hint. This class, too, had an Old Man, who might have been forty-five. Everyone sat frozen, waiting for him to take a bite of his dish, which was coincidentally the same one I had ordered. He did, and time started again.

"But what if a girl is just naturally active?" I asked. "Like a female athlete?"

"No," Old Man said. "Korean woman not active. Always calm."

"Nobody like women athlete," Kevin said. "They are like men."

"What do the rest of you think?" I asked. "Do you feel boys are born to be more active than girls?"

Most did.

"It doesn't matter," Jennifer said. "Boys get to run around when they're little. Then in high school they're just as controlled as girls, and then they all have to go into the army. Girls are kept still even when we're really young, but boys get beaten into compliance later." She smiled slightly. "Everybody ends up calm here. Nobody escapes."

So, the princess was smart. It was an astute observation.

"I am sorry," Sally said, putting her arm around Jennifer's shoulders. "I am sorry for my friend," she said. "We go high school together. She always like this."

I looked back at Jennifer. "You two went to high school together? Where was that?"

"Here," Jennifer said. "Taegu."

"You're ... *from* Taegu?"

"Of course I'm from Taegu."

"Korean women are more independent than American women," a guy with big eyeglasses called William said. "When Korean women get married, they keep their same name. American women get married and get husband's name."

"That's an interesting point," I said. "In fact, many American women now say it's a sign of independence to keep their maiden names—their names from before they were married."

"But that's not very accurate, about Korean women keeping their names," Jennifer said. "Nobody calls them that name anymore after they're married, except maybe official papers. Married women are always just called *so-and-so's wife*, or *so-and-so's mom*."

"Korean woman like that," a female student calling herself Maria said. "For Korean woman, pleasure is take care of baby, husband, house. When Korean woman hear 'hey, you, somebody's mom,' it make her very proud."

"If it's such a wonderful pleasure to take care of babies and do housework, shouldn't we let men enjoy it, too?" Jennifer asked.

"No," Maria said, scrubbing her hand through the air in front of her as if erasing a white board. "Men are different. To men, most important is respect. Way to get respect is to be a manager. When every man is manager and every woman is mother, then everyone is happy."

Some of the class began talking in Korean.

"So where did you learn English?" I asked Jennifer. "Did you live in the States?"

"Right here," she said. "SNM Academy. I started taking classes here about three years ago."

"So … You didn't speak English at all until you were, like twenty years old?"

"Right. I'm the success story. If other young ladies come here to study, and they practice hard, maybe they can get a job making less than half of the money you do, too."

2

Korean Lurch caught me in the hallway on the way to my new 103, for which I was already late. He was clutching another scrap of paper from Richard. He shoved it at my hands and I jumped back as if he were trying to stab me. He took two steps forward and extended his arm at me again. I flattened myself against the wall, but he stuffed the note in among the books and papers I was holding against my chest as I shuffled past him.

"Hello, class," I said, entering the little room. "Sorry I'm late. I couldn't get a taxi. Since this is our first day together, let's get to know each other before we work with the book. Please ask me questions now, and then we'll go around the room and ask each other some questions, later."

I answered all the standard questions, telling them about my hometown, age, marital status and the like. Then a young man in rimless rectangular glasses asked, "What famous buildings did you see?"

"That's an interesting question," I said. "Nobody has ever asked me that before. Do you have a nickname?"

"Uh, yes. Pei."

"Do you mean famous buildings here in Korea, or in other countries?" I asked.

"In other countries," Pei said.

"Let's see," I said. "I've been in the Sears Tower, the Hancock Building, the Empire State, the Twin Towers... Would you count the Saint Louis Arch?" Pei nodded. "Tokyo Tower, and one other one in Japan I can't remember the name of. Are you an architect, Pei?"

"No," he said. "I am student of architecture."

"Ah, and what famous buildings have you seen?"

"All Korean," he said. "The Sixty-Three Building, Trade Tower... I want to go Europe. Korean architecture is boring. European architecture is more interesting."

"How can you say this?" a different young man asked angrily. "Are you Korean? How can you say such a terrible thing about our country?"

"Wow, that's a fascinating idea to explore," I said. "Do you have a nickname?" I asked, gesturing to him.

"Mr. Big," he said.

"Okay. It's nice to meet you, Mr. Big, and you, too, Pei. Let's think about this issue a moment. Now, Mr. Big, I can see that you love Korea. Is that true?"

"Of course!" Mr. Big said.

"And Pei, do you love Korea, too?"

"Yes. I love Korea very much."

"Now, I think Mr. Big feels that someone who loves Korea should love everything about Korea. Like architecture. He feels that if Pei is Korean, Pei should love Korean architecture most. Is that right, Mr. Big?"

"Yes."

"Now, we all love Korea, don't we?" I asked. "But Pei feels that he can be Korean and love Korea, but also see something from another part of the world that he likes best. Is that right,

Pei, that you're Korean and love Korea but you appreciate European architecture more?"

"Yes," Pei said.

"What do the rest of you think?" I asked. "How many of you agree with Pei, that Koreans can have favorite things that are not Korean? Raise your hands." I raised my hand. Pei raised his hand, but nobody else did.

"How many think that if you're Korean, you have to love everything Korean most?"

The other fourteen students raised their hands.

Alice stood next to her desk, shaking her head. This was her last month, and some students had given her a gift. "Do I want to take this all the way home?" she asked. On the desk was a painted woodcarving depicting two girls in traditional Korean dress jumping on a seesaw, where one had just landed and launched the other into the air.

"Ask yourself how often you play with it now," I said, smirking.

"Har har. It's not a toy, it's a conversation piece. *Neolttwigi*, they call this game. You know why this is a traditional thing, right? Girls played this because they were always locked behind their garden walls. Leaping into the air like that let them see the outside world."

"Charming. I wish I could see the outside world. Instead, I have to see Richard. Again."

"Ah. You know his daughter is coming to visit him soon. Maybe that will distract him."

"From his vendetta against me?"

"Your word, but yes."

"I might as well get it over with." I went out past the reception area and down the narrow hall to Richard's open door.

Richard was sitting behind his desk. "Ah, there you are," he said. "Look, sorry I had to call you in like this. It's not even a big deal, so I'll make it quick."

An air raid siren sounded then, like the tornado sirens I'd heard growing up, but deeper and haunting, more suitable to a country that was still at war after 40 years and anticipating chemical weapons attacks. There was no point in talking while it droned, so we both waited.

"Your landlady called yesterday," he said as the siren wound down. "You left dirty dishes in your sink, and it's not the first time. I know you and Leo are two young bachelors living alone, but this is Korea, and here people show respect. If you don't want to wash your dishes, get a maid."

"Wait," I said.

It was impossible to see the sink from the windows.

"My landlady came into my apartment?"

"Yeah. It's what they do, here. You don't have an apartment. *She* has an apartment, and you live in it."

"But I assume the company pays rent. That means it isn't her apartment, during the time I'm there, because the rent makes it temporarily mine. I have a right to privacy in my own apartment."

"No, you don't. She owns the place, and she has the power. She is right, and you are wrong. See? Harmony. Peace. We can all get back to work."

"But that's—"

"Look," Richard said. "You know you ought to wash your dishes, anyway. If I let you stay here, you are going to behave properly." He leaned a little closer and lowered his voice. "It doesn't seem like this job is going to work out for you, Mark. You might want to start getting some money together for a plane ticket home."

"You missed it," Karen said as I stumbled in, drunk from going out with my last class of the day. "Your landlords were at it early tonight. She was on him the second he came through the gate, screaming and swinging. He brought his briefcase up in front of him and then shoved it forward like passing a basketball, right into her face. She dropped down to her knees, and he walked around her and went inside. After a while she picked herself up and followed him, but she was really slow."

"Huh," I said. "Maybe they'll both just die. Wouldn't that be nice?"

"Hey, Mark," Leo said. "We met Richard's daughter today."

"You're still trying to be friends with that freak?" I said. "You'll never get back the minutes of your life you waste on him."

"You should be grateful," Leo said. "Otherwise, I might not have been able to talk him out of firing you. It helps to try and get along with people."

"Right. So, is Richard's daughter hygienically challenged like he is?" I asked.

"No," Leo said. "She's normal."

"She is *not* normal," Karen corrected. "She's … relatively ordinary in appearance."

"Well, except that she looks just like Richard. Like, a younger, cleaner, female Richard," Leo said. "She looks like a college student. Which she is."

"Until she snuggles up with Daddy," Karen said.

"Huh?"

"They are *weird* together," Karen said.

"Remember I said he'd told me he'd left the States because he didn't like how the U.S. dealt with 'family matters?'" Leo asked.

"Yeah," I said. "He even went on about that with me once in the elevator. I think he was trying to make me see the beauty of Asian society. He said something like, 'Families here are autonomous and not being harassed by the government, so nobody disputes the father's authority and there's peace and harmony."

"Ha!" Leo said. "Peace and harmony. Whatever the issue, that's his answer to it."

"Yeah," I said. "Especially when he's threatening to fire me for offending Korean values or pissing off our oh-so-peaceful-and-harmonious landlady."

"Richard's daughter calls him by his first name," Karen said. "But lots of hippie parents have their kids call them by their first names, so I didn't think anything of that. Then we went to the *kal gook soo* restaurant he likes—have you had *kal gook soo* yet? It's this noodle soup where you mix in your own stuff."

"It keeps your hands busy, mixing in sauce and peppers and seaweed flakes or whatever," Leo said. "Before the soup came, Richard was resting his hand on her thigh. Then we were all holding spoons and picking up noodles with chopsticks. When they took the bowls away, he put his hand *back* on her thigh," Leo said. "And this is a traditional Korean restaurant; everybody sits on the floor."

"Then we all walked back to Richard's place, so he could get his stuff before we went back to work," Karen said. "There was extra time, so Richard wanted to make tea with his

Korean tea set. They sat together on the couch and cuddled, and then he whispered in her ear and she melted. Just went limp against him."

"Since Richard's the director, he has an apartment to himself," Leo said. "Just like this one, the upper floor of a duplex. Two furnished bedrooms, kitchen, bath, living room, just the same. So in the guest room, she'd emptied her suitcase and laid all her stuff out on the bed. She saw me looking at it through the door and said, 'I should probably put it all away, but I won't be here very long. It's easier like this, and Richard and I don't mess up a second set of sheets.'"

"Wow."

There was nothing I could add to the conversation, so I went to change out of my suit. When I came back, Leo and Karen were settling onto the couch with dumplings and beer.

"Check it out," Leo said, nodding at the screen. He had brought a VCR from work, and there were a few movies on top of it. "Rented it at the little store down the street: M*A*S*H, subtitled in Korean!"

"We got it for the irony of watching it in Korea," Karen said.

I decided to leave them to their date.

The taxi let me out on a street lined with little carts. Each was tended by an *ajuma* in black polyester selling some kind of Korean street food: deep-fried fish cakes on sticks, rolls of *gimbap*, and paper cones of wok-fried silkworms called *bundaegi*. Major Byun had given me the address of a restaurant, which at eleven at night still had a decent crowd.

I had pleaded on grounds of genetic weakness to forgo soju and drink beer instead. He had promised that he would do so if I showed up.

I scanned the room for him but saw no Korean Air Force uniform. Major Byun, now dressed in civilian clothes, found me instead. "Mark! Mark!" he called.

Three other men sat with him in short black vinyl lounge chairs, all dressed in business casual clothes in patterns of black and brown, all middle-aged. There were beer bottles on the table. Hopefully they'd stick to beer all night. They waved at the waiter and got him to bring me a glass.

Since they were all clearly older than I was, I could immediately tell that my assigned place was at the bottom of the hierarchy. I shook hands with each as he introduced them, always taking a single hand with both of mine. He slurred their Korean names and I didn't catch any of them, but it didn't matter much when I could only speak through Major Byun, anyway.

"He is owner of this restaurant," Major Byun said of the first one. "He have one wife and one girlfriend." He introduced the next one, who he said had a delivery company, and added, "He have one wife and two girlfriend, like me." His voice changed in tone as he introduced the third friend, which seemed to indicate particular admiration or awe on Major Byun's part. Perhaps this guy was merely the eldest of the group, but the major showed more deference around this last one than he had with the others. "He own grocery store—no! Supermarket. He own supermarket."

"Does he have a girlfriend, too?" I asked. Since to these guys it was so prestigious, asking seemed the polite thing to do.

"For him is different," Major Byun said. "He find old women." The major's face contorted into hideous disgust and he raised his fingers up by his face as if they were claws. "Ugly. Nobody want them. But he say, 'Oh, you are so beautiful, you are so sexy.' Oh!"

Noticing that his friend's glass was empty, he filled it, and mine. I quickly put both hands around my glass, showing respect as he poured. Then I took the bottle and poured for him.

"It take a long time, weeks, or maybe months, but then they go to bed. He fuck them, the ugly ones. Then he say them they are bad women and he will tell their husbands. He keep fucking, every week, and make them give him money. Then he find new woman, and keep doing again. Now he is rich and have big supermarket. He is very respected in Taegu."

"Ah," I said. "I see."

Major Byun translated a few questions from the friends, the same ones I always got, and then they talked to each other in Korean. From time to time, one or another of them would exchange bows with someone passing by the table. Eventually, Major Byun said, "These guys know everybody. We look important with an American here!"

I drank quietly, watching them, picking up a word here and there. Major Byun, as my elder and superior, leaned in from time to time to give me advice about issues like using two hands to accept anything from anyone older, not smoking in front of older men, and proper procedure for pouring drinks.

He looked around the restaurant and I followed his gaze. He pointed out the few women in the place, one by one. "They are bad girls," he said. He said something to his friends, and they all looked at the women too. Each one sat at a different table, fawning over some man next to her. "If a woman is out after 10:00 p.m., she is bad girl. Dirty girl. They like everything. If you see woman out at night like this time, you can do anything you want to her, it's okay." He explained to his friends what he was telling me. The delivery guy said something and Major Byun translated. "Or smoking. Smoking woman very bad, very dirty." The restaurant owner contributed something else. "He say chewing gum. This kind of girl is very low. Man don't have to worry about her family. Anything is okay."

The blackmailer spoke up and they all nodded deeply in acknowledgement of his wisdom. "He say worst is when you see girl with American. That mean she is garbage, have no family at all. Girl like that, she want to be fucked, any time. Anybody can do whatever he want to her and she gonna like it, because she know she is garbage shit. Shit girls, they want be punished."

They drank more and smoked more. Major Byun got drunker. After a long while, everyone drained their last glasses, and Major Byun stood to escort me out. He took me through some back streets and eventually to a place that looked a lot like the restaurant we'd just come from. "It's room salon!" he said, marching me up to the door.

"Wait!" I said. "Major Byun, I don't—"

A neckless Korean bouncer in a black suit stopped us. He and Major Byun exchanged words, and then Major Byun turned away. "You can't go there," he said. "I take you your apartment. My car is near here."

"Can you drive, Major Byun?" I asked. "I think maybe you had too much."

"Don't worry. Don't worry, Mark. I'm Major in Korean Air Force. Police won't arrest me. They treat me same as executive of big Korean companies. It's okay."

"Korean children only study," a usually quiet young business-man called Spring said. "There is no time for a part-time job."

"Yes," Lucy said. "Really, no time. In Korea, we say students who sleep five hours cannot go to college, but students who sleep four hours can attend."

The class concurred.

"Wow," I said. "So, the average high school student in Korea only sleeps four hours a night?"

"Yes," Spring said. "School begins at eight in the morning and stops at midnight."

"That is for boys," Lucy said. "Girls high school is until ten."

"Yes," Spring said.

"That sounds like torture to me," I said, smiling. "You Koreans are tough! You know, it really is used as torture, like with war prisoners, not letting them sleep, and then brain-washing them. Have you heard of brainwashing?"

"Yes," Spring said. "China did brainwashing during the Korean War."

"Yes," I said. Switching to what I hoped was a comically spooky voice and peering at them sideways like a conspiracy theorist caricature, I added, "Maybe someone is trying to brainwash Korean kids, trying to make them all the same!"

"Of course," Pen said. "Schools make kids all the same."

"Is that a good thing?" I asked. "To be the same?"

"Yes," said a cute girl with bangs, who called herself Cookie. "In America, you say something is different, or you say something is wrong. In Korea, we have only one word. Different and wrong are the same word."

"I was late to my first class again this morning," I said to the Deadbeat Club. "So, I got to talk to Richard again, today. Apparently, classes are still complaining because I talk to them about real issues instead of relying on the book. He told me that he'd rather have me quit on my own schedule than fire me, because he's such a kind and understanding guy. I don't think I'll be here very long."

"Oh, no," Strawberry said. "That's sad. We will miss you, Mark."

"You should do like Koreans when there's a difficult problem," Groundhog said.

"What's that?" I asked. "I hope it involves beer rather than soju."

He said something to his classmates in Korean. The rest of the Deadbeat Club responded enthusiastically.

"We want to take the class out," Sarah said.

"Oh?" I asked. "And where will we go?"

"Do you know about Korean fortune-tellers?" Paul asked.

"I don't know anything about Korean fortune-tellers," I said.

"I heard about a fortune-teller near here, just behind the Grand Hotel," Groundhog said. "We can go now."

"If you are all fine with taking our class out of the building, I am, too," I said. They were already packing up their things.

We passed the American Center on the way. Dozens of student protesters were gathering in the street, all dressed in dark colors with handkerchiefs over their faces. Around sixty riot police had lined up in front of the building. Half of the students were holding broom handles and other weapons. "Many college students do this," Groundhog said. "Maybe most college students. If they get arrested, then they must become the riot police when it is their time for military service. All the riot police begin as protesters."

"Wow, look at that!" I said. "At least four big signs that say 'Yankee Go Home.' I didn't know people actually made those."

We turned a corner, then another. More students passed us on their way to the confrontation. Unlike the usual expressionless, staring crowds on the street, these faces were tinged with worry and excitement, which turned universally to anger when they looked at me. "In Korean history," Groundhog said, "Korea was invaded over nine hundred times. Japan invaded us to get to China, China invaded to get to Japan. Before that, Mongolians. Always the buildings were burned, always the men were killed, always the women were raped. Now, North Korea is invaded by China, and South Korea is invaded by the U.S. Now your government in Washington, D.C. manipulates our government and our economy. Our women are prostitutes outside military bases, and American soldiers sometimes rape and kill them. Koreans want to just be Korean."

"But wouldn't that mean everyone would be North Korean?" I asked. "They're very powerful, militarily. If the United States were to leave the peninsula, North Korea would be a huge threat."

"Because of China," he said. "This time, two invaders agree with each other to each only take half of Korea. These protest guys want our own land, our own women, our own language."

We turned down another street and could now see the Grand Hotel. "We're going behind it," Groundhog said. "There are two kinds of fortune-teller in Korea. One kind looks up dates in books, like birthdays. The other kind is like this one, with a ghost."

Gerald said something in Korean, and Ivy replied. The group chatted briefly among itself.

"Hey, folks," I said. "This is still our class time. I feel I'm not being responsible if you're all speaking Korean. Let's practice English, please."

"I don't like when the people stare," Gerald said. "The group of old ladies back there all watched us. The students are looking angry at us."

"I said Gerald should know this," Ivy said. "He has been at SNM Academy long enough. He should expect what happens when you walk with foreigners."

The alley behind the hotel was unpaved and muddy. The towering, gleaming white walls on one side mocked the little corrugated tin shacks on the other. The fortune-teller's shanty was near the far end of the hotel. Inside sat an *ajuma* in a traditional Korean dress, but not the fancy silk *hanbok* I'd seen in pictures of weddings and other special events. This *hanbok* was made of some tough, heavy dark green fabric of the type that might be used for work coveralls. The rest of the room, however, was cluttered with traditional silk outfits for children, as well as toys, books, and games.

"She looks too old for kids," I said quietly to the closest person, who was Sarah.

"These people never have kids," she said. "Their lives are sad. They never get married, never make any money. It's like a curse. Every fortune-teller lives like this."

"So why does she have all this kid stuff?" I asked.

"It's not for her," Paul said. "Customers bring these things for the ghost."

"This one has a ghost of a little boy, so all the gifts are for the little boy," Groundhog said.

"Oh," I said. "Have you been here before?"

"No. I heard about this from a different English class at SNM, last year."

"Should we have brought some gift like that?"

"We can just pay money," Groundhog said.

"Oh, well, since this field trip is for me," I said, reaching for my wallet.

"We already paid for you," Paul said.

"Oh, thank you."

The fortune-teller was seated on the floor in the corner of the room. We all approached and sat down around her. Her gaze panned slowly across the group until it settled onto Groundhog. Her soft smile hid her teeth but did not touch her eyes. She spoke to Groundhog and his face went slack. Strawberry asked him something in Korean and he responded, his voice flat.

"What's happening?" I whispered to Groundhog.

"She said to me, 'you have three grandmothers.' I do."

The woman asked the group a few questions, and the group gestured to me, explaining. She nodded and bowed her head. Her voice deepened and her body rocked, but I had no idea whether she was speaking, chanting, or merely moaning.

When she looked up—

How had she done this? I didn't speak the same language, so it was unlikely that I would have been hypnotized. From their expressions, it was clear that the class saw the difference, too.

It was as if I'd been watching a movie and someone had stood up between the projector and the screen, so that my attention was drawn more to the person standing than to the film that continued to play. When the woman raised her eyes, there was a little kid there, with what seemed like a movie of the old woman playing over him. The boy stared at me, apparently amused by my uniqueness. Groundhog translated as he spoke.

"You have nowhere to go. Your boss will go away and you will finish your contract. You cannot, you must not leave Korea yet. There is something very important you must do here first."

I was already smoking in the living room by the time Leo and Karen came back for lunch. An AFKN commercial was teaching me about the benefits of using underarm deodorant.

"I didn't know you smoked, Mark," Karen said, taking off her shoes. Karen had started sharing Leo's room full-time. I'd thought for sure the landlady would pitch a fit about having three people staying in the place instead of two, but though she had frequently seen Karen in the early mornings and late nights when we'd all come in and out, she had said nothing. Leo's room was now crowded with her clothes and other belongings, which the landlady had no doubt also seen.

"I don't smoke, usually," I said. "My 105 is taking me to lunch tomorrow. Some soup they say I've got to try."

"Oh, yeah?" Leo said. "I love when classes take me out. Good group?"

"Not really. And it looks like I'll be paying, which is fine. Whatever. But this class is super nationalist and generally uncomfortable. One guy last week said he hopes North Korea develops a nuclear weapon so that Koreans will have power over the United States after they unify. The class always seems to have that *fuck-you* vibe, you know?"

"Ooh," Karen said. "I hate the *fuck-you* vibe classes. And you're going to lunch, huh?"

"Yeah. I have a few tricks up my sleeve to help me cope, though. For one, I asked Jennifer to come along."

"Jennifer, the teacher who works with us?" Karen asked.

"Yeah. She came to lunch with another class of mine once. I was shocked to learn she's actually from here."

"She certainly is unusual for a Korean woman," Karen said. "She's brilliant and she's tough. Having her there will definitely make a more interesting lunch for you. She's probably just the ticket for a *fuck-you* vibe."

Leo sniffed the air. "What is that you're smoking?"

I smiled at him. "Smells vaguely tropical, wouldn't you say? I made it from banana peels."

"Oh, I knew someone who tried that," Leo said. "It didn't work."

"You're supposed to get high from it or something?" Karen asked.

"Yeah," I said. "But the recipe everyone uses is from this book *called The Anarchist Cookbook*, and I figured out that the recipe is wrong. Or, not wrong. Just incomplete."

"Are you saying you did it?" Leo asked. "It works? You can get high off of it?"

"Yeah. It's ... You know, don't expect miracles. It works, to the extent that smoking a shitload of it gives you the sensation of spray-painting in a poorly ventilated Tilt-A-Whirl."

"Sounds lovely," Leo said, reaching for it.

I gestured broadly at our surroundings, meaning to implicate all of Korea. "Beats sobriety."

"So this is why you were keeping kimchee jars full of rotten bananas?" he asked, puffing.

"Yep," I said. "Fermentation. Fruits aren't known to be psychotropic, but fungi are. I reasoned that there must be a fungus growing inside the banana peels, so I let them turn black before harvesting the peels."

The apartment filled with thick, sickeningly sweet smoke. "It's like having our own chemical weapon," Leo said.

Jennifer and I were standing in the lobby with Kate, one of the 105s who were going to lunch. Kate liked my suggestion of bringing Jennifer along so that there would be more English conversation. Hopefully the others would, too. My offer to buy lunch for the whole class rendered moot their feelings about it, though, at least from my perspective, which was why I'd offered.

The lobby was crowded since classes had just let out for the afternoon break. We weren't far from the spot by the reception desk that Korean Lurch preferred, directly under the photo of Moon Seung Nam. He stood there now, at the Lurch perch, with his hands behind his back, watching the students flowing in and out. He even tried to speak English at these times. All I could figure was that he was trying to impress the receptionists, who spoke even less English than he did.

Korean Lurch was staring at Kate's sandals. When he saw the three of us looking back at him, he spoke, in halting English at maybe the 102 level: "My friend saw girl wear this kind of shoe, with red polish on toes. He put his foot down hard on her toes to correct her."

Jennifer didn't miss a beat. "Is he your hero?" she asked.

"Yes," Korean Lurch said. "My superior."

"And you want to be just like him, so you threaten our school's students?"

He scowled at her and returned to surveilling the crowd. "This student does not have red polish so it is okay."

"Hey, Mr. Shin," I said. "Is that an SNM Academy pin on your lapel?"

"Of course."

"Because you work for SNM."

"Of course because I work for SNM."

"I work for SNM, too," I said. "Why don't I get a pin? I bet

people would treat me better at bus stops if I had a pin showing I work for a Korean company."

"I work for SNM," Korean Lurch said. "I am employee.
You are … product." He gave up the Lurch Perch and headed
down to his office.

Jennifer and Kate were talking in Korean. "We think
everyone who's coming is here, now," Jennifer said.

The group headed out. It took some maneuvering on the
street before I was walking next to Jennifer. "Nice job handling Mr. Shin back there," I said.

"Thanks. You, too."

At the restaurant, we all settled on woven mats around
a long, low table. There was a brief discussion, then a male
student called Cassette ordered for everyone. Cassette had
been the one who'd said he wanted North Korea to have
nukes, and also the one who had suggested coming here.
He was sitting directly across from me at the center, next
to Kate, who was next to Jennifer. "Mark," he said. "We
ordered special soup, because this place has the best, like
we told you."

"And this soup is only available in Taegu?" I asked.

"No, it's Korean soup. You can get it everywhere," Cassette
said. "In other cities, they put the rice into the soup. In Taegu,
we keep rice alone. We call this *ttarogukbap*. It means *separate,
soup, rice*. People from Taegu have soup this way."

"Ah!" I said. "I had Japanese roommates and spent some
time in Japan. They keep rice separate there, too. Taegu has
that in common with Japan."

Cassette and two of the other male students reacted
with grimaces and low, growling comments in Korean. "We
Koreans don't like Japan," Cassette said.

"I've heard that before," I said. "Please tell me more about
that, class. Why do Koreans dislike Japan?"

Pharaoh, one of the other two young men who had expressed disdain, spoke up. "They...invade? Invaded?"

"Hm," I said. "It depends on how you mean it. Do you mean it is their habit to invade Korea, and they still do it now? If you mean it's a habit that continues now, you should say 'they invade.' If it's something they did in the past, but they don't do it now, say 'they invaded.'"

There was a brief discussion in Korean, and then Pharaoh continued. "Korea is too strong now to invade. In the second world war, Japan invaded Korea. Look at our mountains. Right now, Korean mountains have little trees. For a long time, there were no trees. Japanese cut them all down and took wood to Japan. And do you know about *comfort women*?"

"Comfort women?" I asked. "What are comfort women?"

"Japanese soldiers caught Korean women and kept them for sex." Pharaoh said. "They were slaves of the Japanese army. It took them to follow the soldiers. Even when the war ended, the women's lives were still ruined."

"We Koreans never forgive Japan for this," Cassette said.

Jennifer had been listening to the conversation. I was tempted to single her out, to call on her to share her perspective, but it wasn't my place to do so. This was a lunch, not a classroom, and she was not my student.

"I had not heard of the comfort women," I said, mostly to Jennifer. I didn't have to call on her to show her I was interested in what she thought about the issue. "That is truly a horrible thing to have happened."

"It is," Jennifer said. "What Japan did ruined their lives during the war. But Japan didn't decide that those women's families wouldn't take them back after the war ended. Japan didn't say they could never have normal jobs and support themselves, so that they just had to keep on being prostitutes or starve. Even now in Korea, young girls are kidnapped on the street, raped, and sold as prostitutes. I was almost kidnapped once because I came out of my high school a little later than everyone else. Someone held a knife at my neck and tried to pull me into a van, and a teacher saw them and shouted. The kidnapper froze for a little bit and I struggled, and he let go. If they had taken me, even if I'd been kept right next door to my parents' house, I couldn't ever go to them because my parents would have rejected me. I would've brought shame and been a lifetime burden. Japan did an awful thing to those comfort women, but it was Koreans who treated them terribly for 40 more years, and Koreans still behave the same way."

The soup came, with beef and radish, spicy with red pepper and laden with garlic, enveloping the whole table in steam and warmth. I kept the rice separate, as Taegu people did. Everybody talked, mostly in Korean, as they ate.

The third time Jennifer caught me staring at her, she stared back. "What?" she said.

"I want to know you better."

"A class told me about kidnapping here in Korea," I said. This class was a 103, so the students were less able to express themselves on such topics. That was okay. My main objective in raising the subject was to break the monotony of book-slogging for a few minutes, in hopes of saving my own sanity.

"They said young women are kidnapped and made into prostitutes, and they can't go home again," I said.

The class concurred.

"The ugly ones peel garlic," a young man called Rudy said.

The class laughed.

"Mark, do you know eunjangdo?" a young woman calling herself Sue asked. "Korea woman knife? Traditional Korean woman wear knife on ribbon around her neck."

"Oh, really?" I asked. "Women carried knives to protect themselves, to fight back? Maybe they should still carry them today."

"No," Sue said. "Not fight." She mimed stabbing herself in the chest. "She kill herself so man cannot rape."

"Really?" I asked. "So every woman carried a knife all the time, just so she could kill herself?"

"Not every woman," Rudy said. "Good women from good families. To protect family name."

"He say engine is air-cooled," New Clip said.

"He says," I corrected.

The fact it was air-cooled was obvious to anyone who knew anything about engines. It was a 125cc dirt bike, and the fin-covered engine was the same type, and roughly the same size, as the old Lawn Boy mower I'd pushed as a kid. The shop guy kick-started it, producing the classic dirt bike sound: *REE-dee-dee-dee-de*.

This three-block stretch of a two-lane city street was crowded with stores selling and fixing motorcycles. I'd brought New Clip along to help. He didn't know anything about bikes, but his translating was handy, and he got English practice and a free lunch out of the deal. New Clip was a rich college student, though, and he was clearly out of his element among these tough guys with grease under their fingernails. He fidgeted and his eyes darted around a lot.

"He say bike is one year old."

"Says," I said. "He *says* the bike is a year old."

"He says."

"But how do I know whether that's true?" I asked. "Some Korean company must've bought the rights to produce this one model, because every dirt bike on this street is exactly like it. I think they make the identical bike here, year after year. It looks like maybe a late 1970s model."

I knew they bought foreign rights to manufacture international products here because a class had told me about the Mercury Sable, a lower-end American car some company had rights to assemble in Korea. Import restrictions and tariffs made the Sable Korea's most expensive production car, even though it was essentially brought in as a kit.

New Clip talked to the bike guy in Korean. "He says that is true. Same bike every year, but he says colors different. This last year color. Blue was year before, and yellow before."

"*Last year's color*," I said. "The color of last year. We add an 's' at the end. 'Mark's bike.' This is last year's color."

I decided to go with the orange. It looked solid and was only a year old, so the bike would probably be reliable. It would also hold more of its value than a brand-new one, which would be important when it was time to cash it out and leave the country.

I negotiated a price and bought it. The guy didn't stare, or ask me a lot of stupid questions, or condescend to me. In spite of the fact that I was spending nearly all of the money I'd saved so far, this investment was quite comfortable for a business transaction in Korea.

I was getting better at teaching. Classes told me about issues in Korea, and I drew more details out of them with questions, correcting grammar and pronunciation as I went.

The discussions were always predictable. Most of the volunteers were traditionalist, and when I called on people to find out what they thought, almost everyone fell in line. If any of them expressed a dissenting opinion, the others ganged up. As every topic ran its course, I found myself wondering what Jennifer's take on it would have been.

I made my way across the campus to the Korean language class New Clip had helped me arrange. Since parking regulations were unclear, I had parked the motorcycle outside campus and walked in. Someone had painted a giant American flag, on fire, in the street, and all around the gate were impact marks from projectiles like rocks and burns from Molotov cocktails.

The professor took himself very seriously and was clearly uncomfortable with the casual demeanor of his American and Canadian students. He taught us the Korean alphabet, and showed us how the characters, each representing one syllable, stacked and combined on paper. The stacking made

Korean the world's most efficient written language, so that the same book in Korean would use only one-third as much paper as in English. He taught us all the letters and all the sounds, and made it clear that he expected them to be memorized by the next week.

"Hello to my favorite class in entire country of Korea!" I said. "No! You're my favorite class in the whole world! I'm so glad we get to spend another month together."

"You seem happy, Mark," Groundhog said.

"I'm having a pretty good day, Groundhog," I said. "I told you last week that I bought a motorcycle, right? Now I can go straight back to my apartment for lunch, with no waiting for a bus or taxi. I haven't had any complaints from my landlady or any of my classes in two weeks, and now I'm back with you folks. Even Richard seems to be leaving me alone."

Groundhog and Strawberry and Sarah exchanged sly looks. "Okay," I said. "You seem to know something I don't. What's up, friends?"

"Maybe we helped you, a little bit," Strawberry said.

"Oh, really? How did you help me?"

"We went to the front desk, and requested only you for this class," Groundhog said. "Nobody else, just you, we said. We had to write on a form."

"Wow," I said. "That's really nice of you. I think it got Richard off my back. It's a cool thing you did for me. Thank you."

"Sarah had a friend in one of Richard's classes," Strawberry said, "and I had a friend in a different class Richard teaches. We asked them to complain that Richard's class is too boring."

I laughed. "That's amazing! I'm so proud of you, class. Thank you, thank you. My birthday is next week, and I want to take you all out. Can you make it, say, Saturday afternoon?"

With women in the class, I knew better than to try and schedule things at night.

"You should bring your friends who complained about Richard, too," I said. "I'll pay. We say in America, 'My treat.'"

"Should we bring Jennifer, too?" Sarah asked.

"My friend in your class said you took her out with them and you stared at Jennifer," Strawberry said.

"How do you know Jennifer?" I asked.

"She used to be in this class," Ivy said. "She's our friend."

"Oh," I said. "Well, then, yes. By all means, bring Jennifer."

3

I t was Saturday afternoon, and the Deadbeat Club was coming to meet me at four-thirty. The fact that I had Saturdays off was one reason, among many others, that Koreans felt I had an easy schedule. Fortunately, the school gave Korean teachers the same schedule. Jennifer was the first one to arrive. She waited with me for the others to show up, looking like she just stepped off a fashion show runway in a designer olive-green silk suit. I had noticed her suits always seemed to have pants, never a skirt.

"Happy birthday!" she said.

"Thanks," I said. "My twenty-fourth! And thanks for coming. I promise I didn't bring you to argue with anybody today."

"Oh, but you did before?"

"Of course I did before. I was a little tired of being the one they all gang up on."

"Tell me how tired you are in another twenty years," she said.

We'd all decided to start at Cujully coffee shop, just a few streets over from the school. I looked down the street in each direction but didn't see any of the Deadbeats approaching.

"Maybe they're already in there," she said.

I had been to Cujully before. It was a windowless concrete shoebox, painted a semi-gloss brown inside, and crowded with little laminate tables. The place was full, but I didn't recognize anyone. I had thought I'd gotten used to the scowls and prickly stares in Korea, but today they were significantly, shockingly worse.

We ordered coffee and found a table. If I kept my eyes on Jennifer, I wouldn't meet the challenging stares. She seemed to have a similar idea, which left us both looking mostly into each other's eyes.

I wanted to ask Jennifer how she had come to be so different from the other few hundred people our age I'd gotten to know in South Korea. How had she remained so independent in a country where the word for "different" was also the word for "wrong?" That was also the reason I held back. In Korea, the question itself was an insult: Why *are you so wrong?*

"So how long were you in this class before you became a teacher?" I asked. "How long have you known these guys?"

"Different ones were in my classes at different levels," she said. "One here, one there. Then in the upper levels, it was always the same people in every class. I stayed in that one for about four months, I think, before I interviewed for the job. I started the month before you got here."

"Were you an English major in college?"

"No. Library and Information Science. I was supposed to go to a teacher training program in Seoul when I got hired, but they needed a new teacher right away. I have no credentials for this job."

"That's good to know. I also have no credentials for this job."

"I hear you're getting popular, though."

"Yeah, right. If you heard that, you also probably know it's because of tampering by this class."

"I think maybe there are some others who like you, too. You probably have a natural talent for teaching."

"I'm a circus elephant. I'm exotic, so people pay to look at me and hear me trumpet."

We chatted for half an hour. None of the Deadbeats showed up. Several people in the place stared directly at the two of us while talking to their tablemates.

"Where are they?" I asked.

"Koreans are often late. Foreigners call it *Korean time,* and I know it drives Americans crazy."

"I've heard of Korean time," I said. "But isn't it strange that *all* of them are more than thirty minutes late?"

"Maybe they went to the restaurant instead," she said. "I don't want to stay here, in any case."

"I don't, either."

When I was alone, it almost always took me more time than the average Korean to hail a taxi, perhaps on the order of five or ten minutes longer. Having Jennifer standing next to me made it worse. Neither of us could get one to stop at all.

"What do they think we're going to do, rob them?" I asked.

We decided to try standing at different spots along the street. Finally, a taxi stopped for Jennifer and I ran to join her. She told the driver where to go. "This birthday is already quite an adventure," I said.

"I've been out with Americans as part of a class," Jennifer said, "but never alone like this. Is this the way it is for you all the time?"

"There's always staring," I said. "Like I'm in my own personal spotlight wherever I go. But it doesn't usually feel quite so hostile. They're saying things about us, aren't they?"

"I was hoping you didn't realize that, but yeah. I don't hear everything because a lot of it is under their breath or spoken to someone with them, but once in a while they say it directly to me."

"What do they say?"

"I don't want to translate it. Crude things."

The taxi stopped. "I'll pay for it," she said. "It's your birthday."

"Thank you," I said. "That's nice." I sat in the car with her while she paid. The taxi driver talked to her gently, almost cordially—not for a long time, but a few sentences more than I'd have expected. Jennifer said something back that was not gentle. He gave her change, and together we exited the taxi. "What was that conversation about?" I asked.

"He told me I was pretty and asked how much I charge for sex. I told him that you and I are both English teachers. He had nothing to say after that."

We went into the restaurant. It was still early enough that there were a few available tables, but no sign of the Deadbeat Club. Jennifer spoke to the host, who stared at her without speaking.

"I told him we're waiting for the rest of our English class," she said.

"He doesn't seem particularly impressed," I said.

Jennifer and I stood at the front of the restaurant while the seated patrons took long looks, sizing us up. The activity in the room hadn't stopped, but the menace was slowly intensifying, like sharks circling closer to prey.

Neither of us spoke for a while. "Have you tried *samgyetang*?" she asked. "It's the only thing on the menu here."

"No. It's chicken soup, right?"

"Each pot is a small whole chicken. Inside it's stuffed with rice, ginseng, garlic, and do you know jujube? Americans never know what that is. I think it's a date, or fig? Some fruit like that."

"It smells good," I said.

It was getting harder to keep my head up as we waited.

With so many eyes on us, there was a palpable compulsion to curl downward, to shrink, to hide.

"I don't think they're coming," she said.

"That's not a very nice thing to do to me on my birthday," I said.

"They probably think they're being cute," she said. "They don't show up, so it's like a date for us."

"If we were both Korean, that would be sweet," I said. "As it is, I don't think we should stay here."

"I understand. Let's go."

We left the restaurant. "There's an intersection up this way that should have a lot of taxis going by," she said. We walked that way together. The crowd on the street was mostly young people about our age, out on dates or, much more commonly, in big groups.

"I'm sorry your birthday wasn't much fun," she said.

"I was really looking forward to spending time with you today," I said.

"Me, too."

We reached the intersection. People were hailing taxis and getting into them. It looked so easy.

"Should we get separate cars?" I asked.

She hesitated before answering. "I guess so."

"I wish there was someplace we could go," I said. "I wish it could be like a date for us."

"I do, too."

We stood there in the milling crowd. The circling shark feel was overwhelming.

"Well," I said. "Thanks for coming out with me. I know today was harder for you than it was for me."

Was it even safe for us to separate here? Major Byun and friends had said that seeing a woman with an American man meant she was dirty and wanted to be hurt. An entire crowded intersection had seen her alone with me.

But how would I protect her? What could I do if the crowd decided to turn on her?

"A class told me there are bars by the American bases," I said. "We might not stand out there so much."

"Let's try it," she said.

It took some time to get a taxi but eventually we managed. "Have you been there before?" she asked once it was rolling.

"No. You?"

"No. The area has a bad reputation," she said.

"Oh. I guess that makes sense. I appreciate you checking it out with me."

The driver didn't say anything at all. I paid for this one.

Taegu had two American army bases, both relatively small, and the entertainment area was just a few bars and night clubs across from the gates. There were a few Americans milling around there, the majority of whom were teenagers with shaved heads, but the place was mostly empty. "I suppose it's pretty early for the club crowd," I said. "I hope there's a place with food, though."

We looked in one doorway and then another, but both places were loud nightclubs with flashing lights and mostly empty tables. A sign above a doorless flight of rickety stairs said "Texas Saloon & BBQ."

"How about this place? It says barbecue."

"It does?"

"Yeah. BBQ is what they write on signs."

"That sounds good," she said. We climbed the stairs. The place was a narrow room with a bar along one wall and three booths filling the other. Country music was playing, but softly enough that we could still talk over it. Three American guys sat at one of the booths, and two others at the bar. We took a booth.

A mirror behind the bar reflected the attempt at American décor, with pictures of cowboys and classic cars. Near the register was a menu offering chicken and burgers, in addition to a few Korean beers. An *ajuma* came out to take our order, and we decided on chicken and Hite.

The table was etched and marked with bits of graffiti, mostly hometowns and states. We looked together at the various locations: *NYC; Chisholm, AR; Salt Lake Baby Yeah!*

Jennifer put her finger on an especially large one in black marker: *TEXAS ENVENTID BBQ!* She circled the middle word. "Is that some restaurant name?"

"It's supposed to say 'invented.'"

"Ah!" Jennifer said. "I remember that story. Some Koreans were having barbecue a thousand years ago, and one of them said, 'Someday this will be invented in Texas.'"

My birthday had turned pleasant, after all, there at the Texas Saloon. I poured her drinks and she poured mine, just for the hell of it.

"About half my students tell me they think it's terrible for women to have jobs," I said. "Is that true for Koreans in general, that half think it's bad?"

"Yeah," she said. "In general. My mom works. She owns an academy that teaches little kids to use an abacus."

"So why did you study to be a librarian?"

"Do you know how it works in Korea? We can only apply to one major, and we predict where we can get accepted, based on our practice tests. I wanted to go to medical school, but my parents said it was foolish. No man from a good family would want to marry a woman whose job would be publicly

showing off how smart she was. And my father is a professor at a medical school, so I guess that's pretty sad for his
female students."

"So they decided you were going to study library science."

"Yes. But I told myself that if all I could ever be was a wife
and mother, or maybe a tutor, I could at least paint and draw.
There's a test for people who want to change their majors, so
I signed up to take it so I could change my major to art."

"Why couldn't you be a librarian? It seems like a job your
parents could be okay about."

"They don't hire women. One of my professors announced
to the class that women shouldn't ask him for job recommen-
dations, because he only recommends men for work."

"I should have known. Do you draw and paint a lot?"

"I enjoy it, but I don't do it much. Do you draw or paint?"

"No, I'm terrible at that stuff. I was never allowed to do it
growing up, so I never developed any skill."

"Your parents wanted you studying all the time?" she asked.

"My parents?" I said, laughing. In Korea, where everyone is so expressionless all the time, even small shows of
emotion seemed exaggerated. I had to be careful not to
make her think I was laughing at her, so I made an effort
to avoid being overly expressive. "No. Growing up, I was
never even asked whether I had homework. Nobody paid
attention to what I did or didn't do, but I couldn't make
art at my house because I wasn't allowed to have crayons
and markers."

"Ah!" she said. "Because kids sometimes draw on the walls
and furniture."

"No. It was because I might not have put them away. My
mother talks of how she had this great idea for keeping the
house clean: I was never allowed to have toys smaller than a
breadbox. Do you know what a breadbox is? A box to hold

bread. It's a little bigger than a loaf of bread, like this." I held up my hands. "So, I could have toy trucks, stuffed animals, big things like that. I never got to develop fine motor skills; my handwriting still looks like I'm five years old."

"Could you have toy guns?" she asked.

"As long as they were big," I said.

"That was one of two toys I had," she said. "A toy gun that was also a whistle. I had that, and a plaid bear. That was it, for most of my childhood, because it was important that I look like a boy. It made the family seem more successful. But even *I* had crayons and markers." She gave me one of her mini smiles.

"A toy gun and whistle, together," I said. "I don't think I've seen one of those."

"It looked like a gun, but then it was a whistle when you blew in the—" She gestured, a closed fist with a trigger finger, and waved her hand out in front of it. "What do you call it? The tube."

"The barrel? Where the bullet comes out?"

"Yeah. The barrel."

The food came. The chicken had a tasty sauce that seemed almost like something one might find in the States. I suspected it was made mostly of ketchup and Sac-Sac.

"So, what happened with the test to change your major?" I asked, pouring more beer for her.

"My parents found out I was signed up for it. I think they read my mail. They told me I was not to take the test, but they didn't trust me to stay away, so they sent me to Japan for some student tour during the week of the exam."

"Oh? When were you in Japan?"

"The … winter before last winter."

"Really? I was there then, too, over the school break. It was my one paid English teaching experience, tutoring to pay for my ticket back to the United States."

There was a pause as we both drank.

"Why were your parents so insistent that you be a librarian, when they must have known you weren't even going to work in the field?" I asked.

"They didn't want me to be an artist. It's a messy, disorganized life, they said, and they thought it would look like I was too dumb to get into school for anything else. A husband, and his mother, who will live with him forever, want the organized home of a librarian. They also want the children to be read all the best books."

"Again with that. They really, really want you to get married, huh?"

"They want me to marry someone they choose. They think that if I do all these things, they get to choose me a spouse from another top family, so both families benefit."

"They choose?"

"It's like a business deal. They chose for my sister. She's getting married in a few weeks."

"Wow. They just brought home some guy and told her 'This is going to be your husband?'"

"They had a matchmaker present some guys, based on the status of the families, and then my sister sat with my mother and chose six to meet. She and my mother met each one of those six guys, and his mother. Then my sister chose one to see for a second date, and I think that time the mothers came but sat at a different table. Now she has decided to marry this guy."

"So, she met him for, what, three dates before she decided to marry him?"

"I added it up because I was curious. She had seen and talked to him for 52 hours when she agreed to marry him."

"Wow."

"It's all calculated. She's well educated, so the kids will be smart. She plays violin, so she can play for her husband to help him relax after work. My family's name is more presti-gious, but his family has more money. She has a degree from Seoul National University, which is the best school in the country, and he went to Yonsei University, which is second best, and both got master's degrees in the United States. Her school was better there, too, but he has a company involved in international trade. The matchmaker decides which men are at her level, and then she just chooses one. This one had the most money and she was impressed by his father's car."

"I know what that's like," I said. "We don't have match-makers in the U.S. but we do have lots of stupid things rich people do to make sure their kids marry in their class. We have the country club, where the kids mingle by the pool or play golf. Even that wasn't good enough for my father's new family. He bought a horse farm, and these fancy-breed horses that cost as much as a house, and put my half-brothers in equestrian events. Once I had to go with them to a horse show when my half-brothers were six years old. My father gestured as we drove in. 'Look at that, Mark!' he said. 'A semi-truck. More girls ride horses than boys. Can you imagine one of your brothers marrying a girl so rich she has a truckload of horses?'"

"But not you?" she asked. "He didn't want you to marry one?"

"I'm from his first marriage, so in his eyes, I don't really count. I was cast out of that life," I said. "But whatever. I don't value the marriage market. The thing that bothers me is that my father does. He cares about money more than anything else, and he does ridiculous things to make sure my brothers get it. Anything he sends my way is only out of legal obliga-tion. It's like paying his taxes, where he wants to get away with as little contribution as possible. They get horses, and I'm a burden."

"It's the same as me," she said. "It's all based on when you're born."

"And you're next in your family?" I asked. "Soon you'll be off to the matchmaker?"

"Well, they think so. I don't want that. Right now it's nice, though. They let me have this job because teaching English is a good thing for my marriage paperwork."

"Ah. You can teach the kids?"

"Yes. My parents buy me nice clothes, shoes, handbags ... " She gestured with her fingertips at her silk suit and imported bag, and I realized how out of place she looked there in the seediest part of town. "I'm supposed to look wealthy and beautiful so everyone knows I'll marry into a great family. When I was a little kid they dressed me as a boy all the time, and I grew up wearing my sister's old clothes, but now that I'm almost marriage age it suddenly matters to them what I look like."

"They dressed you as a boy?"

"Yes. It's pretty Korean, dressing a second daughter as a boy. Some people say the evil spirits trying to curse you with daughters will see you already have a son and leave you alone. I think they were just embarrassed to have failed a second time. I was a disappointment to them the day I was born."

"I have to tell you, I'm glad to know these clothes don't represent how you really grew up," I said. "They make you look like ... someone who is really interested in money."

"It's all temporary," she said. "Like Cinderella."

"You know the Cinderella story?"

"Sure. My sister loved the movie, and I thought that was funny because she was always the one with the designer clothes and lessons."

"Except now you are, too." I smiled at her so she knew I was just teasing. Or, hopefully she did.

"I wasn't, though, growing up. My sister was always being tutored or practicing, so I just followed the maids around, wearing boy's clothes or my sister's old stuff. Remember those big tee shirts that hung down to your knees? I had those two years after they went out of style. My parents' plan was to put all their resources into her, so she would marry into a good family and set the standard for our family."

"It's fascinating," I said. "The amount of involvement parents have here is incredible. I'm not sure whether my father even knows I'm in Korea, and your family is planned out for generations. But your family's plan clearly makes *you* Cinderella, not your sister. Apparently that was lost on her?"

"I think we saw the Cinderella movie when she was nine, and I was six. She liked it because Cinderella married the prince. That's what she was raised to do, marry a prince."

"And you're supposed to marry some minor, less important character?"

"I *am* a minor, less important character. I'm not supposed to marry a prince. I never *wanted* to marry a prince. Maybe I would if he turned out to be some great guy, but I don't understand wanting to marry someone just because of his father's job."

"Or his father's car," I said.

She smiled. Or rather, slightly grinned, which was a pretty big smile by South Korean standards. "Or his father's car," she said, nodding. "Or his six factories."

"What kind of car?"

"Mercury Sable."

"What kind of factories?"

"Socks." She looked at her watch, which was some fancy Gucci model she had to tilt her wrist and squint at to read. "It's almost nine o'clock. I have to go."

We stood on the street outside the Texas Saloon & BBQ. Jennifer was looking for a taxi.

"How about we share a taxi back to the school, and you get a separate one from there?" I asked. "I think it's safer if you're not getting into a taxi alone here. The driver may think he can hurt you."

"Okay," Jennifer said. "I'm going that direction, anyway."

There were no taxis around. We walked to a four-lane street farther away from the base, and one was just approaching. She hailed it, alone, and I jumped in with her. It had become a system.

"I don't think I'd get along very well with an actual princess," I said as the taxi took off toward SNM Academy. "I'm much more interested in knowing a Cinderella, who is only dressed up for the ball, than in knowing someone who grew up with everything."

"I'm not dressed up for the ball," she said. "I'm... What do you call it, when they sell an animal and people call out what they'll pay for it?"

"An auction?" I said.

"Yes! That's it. I'm Cinderella dressed up for the auction. But this is my one chance to have these things, so why not take them?"

"I don't blame you," I said. "I'm like that in my family, too. My dad's also a doctor, a cardiac surgeon. They have the giant horse farm, sports cars—my half-brothers drive sports cars to high school. But with me, he counted out the exact penny—that's like one Korean won—that some judge ordered him to pay to my mom twenty years ago. He went to the office on the Saturdays I was required to visit, and I'd just sit there watching TV. It's always been clear to me that I was just an unfortunate intrusion in his life, and a bill he had to pay. If I had a chance to have those nice things, I would take it, too."

"You're the firstborn son," Jennifer said. "You would be treated better if you were Korean."

For a moment, I was surprised she knew the rather antiquated phrase *firstborn son*. Then I remembered where I was. It was probably the first English phrase they learned in Korea.

"You're the second-born daughter," I said. "Your situation would be better if you were American."

"But we're both Cinderella," Jennifer said.

"I think of myself as more of a 'Jack and the Beanstalk' type," I said.

We reached the school. "I think it's safer if you get a taxi without me here," I said. "I'll stand over there in the shadows and watch until you get one."

"I'd rather have you doing that than someone else," she said. "Thanks for the Texas barbecue."

"Anytime."

"I hope you had a nice birthday."

"It was wonderful."

"Tell me what you think of this idea, class," I said. It was a 104, so they had the ability to communicate in English about slightly more complex ideas than the average class.

"High school in Korea decides where you go to college," I said. "It even decides whether you go to college at all. Can we say that high school determines everything in Korean life?"

The class agreed.

"Okay. And high schools grade you on how well you do what they tell you to do, right? I think that's true all over the world. We do assignments, we memorize, and we take tests to prove we did it. That's high school."

There was more general agreement.

"So, if high school determines your entire life, and it judges you mostly on obedience, can we say that in Korea, life is determined only by how well you obey?"

I went over it again, using a few different words ("do what you're told" instead of "obey," and "future" instead of "entire lives," for example), writing on the board, to make sure everyone understood.

A young, spindly engineering student who called himself Tank answered. "Of course, all of life depends on how well we obey. This is why parents must be strict. If parents are lazy and don't punish children, they grow up to be slaves in factories, or prostitutes. Quality of life is the same as quality of obedience."

"You mean that my life—" I splayed my fingers across my chest. "My life will be good, if I'm good at obeying orders of my superiors, and it will be bad if I'm bad at obeying orders."

"Yes," Tank said.

"But can obeying also make our lives worse?" I asked. The class fell silent.

Radio, my favorite student in the class, cleared his throat. He was a married businessman who was almost thirty, working for some textile company. "Yes," he said. "After this class, I go back to my company's office. My boss take me out many nights in a week to drink soju. I get very sick."

"Your boss take*s* you out many times a week?" I asked. "Remember the '*s*' at the end of the word. It's his habit to do this, he take*s* you out."

"He…make*s* me drink a lot. I get very sick. My church says I must not drink, but drinking is very important in Korean business, for building relationships. If I don't drink, my boss doesn't trust me. I feel so bad for my body, but I must accept drinks from my superior."

"What do you think, class?" I asked. "Any suggestions for Radio?" A few recommended blood soup, a common Korean hangover cure, and two gave him names of places that sold it. Blood soup hangover-cure joints were typically the only restaurants open in the morning, because breakfast was considered a meal that should be eaten at home.

"But that's for the next day," I said. "Can he do anything to avoid having to drink so much?"

Someone suggested he start acting crazy, knocking over glasses and singing, after a few drinks. Tank, in a mocking voice, suggested that he cry, implying that Radio was a big baby for wanting to avoid the alcohol his boss wanted him to have. This got a laugh from most of the class.

"Have you heard of syrup of ipecac, Radio?" I asked. "It's for accidental poisoning, to make someone vomit so his body won't absorb it. It would be a bad feeling, to make yourself throw up like that, but it's a potential solution to your problem." Radio excitedly wrote down the word.

"Before drinking, you must eat dog soup," Bongo, who had named himself after a type of Korean minivan, said.

"Okay," I said. "This is interesting. Tell me about dog soup, please, class. Why should Radio have dog soup? What is it?"

"Soup from dog," Bongo said. "It is good for stamina. Drinking stamina, sex stamina, hangover cure."

Stamina was a word repeated by Koreans, especially Korean men, ad nauseam. It made sense that it was a big deal in a country where people almost never slept and worked nearly every conscious minute.

"Only men eat dog soup," a young woman named Liz said. Two of the other women spoke up to agree.

"Okay, why dog?" I asked. "Why not chicken soup?"

"When dog is afraid," Tank said, "he make lots of chemicals in his body."

"When dogs *are* afraid, *they* make chemicals," I said. "We're talking about all dogs, right? Dogs in general?" There were a few nods. "Okay."

"Chicken is too stupid—"

"Chicken*s are* too stupid," I said. "Again, we're speaking in general."

"Chickens are too stupid to make the chemicals. Dog...dog*s* can be made afraid enough. The chemical*s* dog*s* make are good for stamina," he said. "Like, do you know adrenaline?"

"Adrenaline. Okay," I said.

"So, number one, get a dog," Bongo said. "Number two, hang the dog with his face down."

"Number three, make a fire," Tank said.

"No, no," Bongo said.

"Oh, sorry," Tank said. "Number three, hit the dog with a stick."

"Don't kill it," Bongo said. "Just...almost kill it."

"Slowly beat," Tank said. "Slowly, slowly. Don't let him sleep. Number four, make a fire under the dog and burn off all the fur. Slowly, slowly. Number five, cut the dog into pieces, number six, make soup with garlic and red pepper."

"Sometimes in the army, soldiers make this soup if they can catch a dog," Bongo said.

Classes had gotten out for the lunch break. I encountered Jennifer in the empty hall.

"Hey, I was hoping maybe we could get together again sometime," I said.

"I don't think so," she said.

"Really? I didn't necessarily mean for lunch right here and now, you know. We saw that it's uncomfortable, trying to go anywhere around here with just us. I just meant … sometime."

"I don't think so," Jennifer said again. That end of the hall was near the back staircase, which was always unlocked so people could smoke. I gestured to it.

"Can we talk for a minute?" I asked. I held the door for her. "What's going on? I thought you had a good time the other day."

"I did," she said. "And I'm glad I went. It was a wonderful adventure, but please understand. Some Koreans here at the school may have parents who think it's okay to date foreigners, but I don't come from that kind of family. In Korea, parents have all the power. I have no choice. I enjoy talking with you, but going out together is impossible."

"Oh," I said. "Okay. I'm disappointed. Really. You're unique, and I think you and I are unique in similar ways. But I've seen enough of Korean culture to understand the situation, and I don't want you to suffer or be in danger because of me."

"We still work together," she said. "Maybe I can come out to argue with your classes for you."

"I'd like that," I said. "But do let me know if you change your mind about the rest."

"My mind is logical enough to know there is no other way."

The TV lounge was packed with three other American teachers, two Korean students, and me. On the TV, an American network news piece covered the case of Michael Fay, an 18-year-old American convicted of vandalism in Singapore and sentenced to caning, a punishment that left him permanently scarred. Half the Americans interviewed on the street after the story argued for Asian-style discipline in the United States as well. The news ended and a new show came on, and soon two sisters were punching each other in the face over some guy.

"Jerry Springer is not good for us Americans living in the rest of the world," Eric said. "I can't tell you how many classes I've had tell me how Korea is more stable than we are, because everyone in America is a kleptomaniac cross-dressing pregnant teenager in the Ku Klux Klan."

"Mm," I said. "Have they told you there are no gays in Korea? I've had three different classes tell me that."

"All the time," Eric said. "Hey Lawson, how are things going with Betty these days?"

"It's weird," Lawson said. "She's less clingy than she was before, but she gives me the doe-eyed innocent expression all the time."

"Huh. Maybe she wants you to act like she's innocent, now that she's not."

"Maybe. Hey, I'm not complaining, though. She gives it up all the time."

David shook his head.

The show broke for another AFKN public service commercial. A white man in civilian clothes met a blonde woman in a bar that looked vaguely like the Star Wars cantina. She noticed he was carrying money from a different star system, and the busboy observed that he was wearing a light jacket suitable for warmer climates. This information made its way to the back room, where three men, each wearing what was essentially a knockoff Klingon costume including bad makeup and long, bushy hair, transmitted it to their headquarters. "Make sure you're not giving away information, even when you're not saying a word," the announcer said. "Operation security is everyone's business. Practice good OPSEC."

"I tell you, though, man." Lawson said. "There's nothing in the world like that feeling, when you're pushing against her, and then that tiny opening gives, and *boop!* you're in there, where no man has gone before. A man doesn't get to feel that too many times in his life, unless he's one bad fuckin' stud, you know what I'm saying? And Betty makes these little sounds—"

"You fucking idiot," David said. "Do you know what you did to her life?"

"Hey, nobody forced her," Lawson said. "She's a big girl, she made her own choice."

"Korean guys are going to see her as damaged goods," David said. "You know how they treat damaged goods here?"

Korean Lurch appeared in the doorway. "Mark," he said. "Richard want see you right now." I followed him back downstairs.

Richard's door was open. He turned his chair toward it as he saw me in the hall.

"Jars with rotten bananas in them?" Richard said, before I even entered the office. "What the hell is wrong with you?"

"What? Oh, yeah. You mean the jars I had in my closet?"

"I guess so. Why did you have rotten food sitting around, when you know the landlady is in there all the time?"

"It wasn't rotten when I started."

Richard said nothing.

"They're kimchee jars, Richard," I said. "I was trying to make kimchee."

"A banana in a jar. That's kimchee?"

"Isn't it?"

"I don't need another headache," Richard said. "You Americans drive me out of my mind,"

"I thought you were from Baltimore," I said.

People smoked on the narrow, dirty, and poorly lit back stairs, but not many used them to travel between floors. They were perfect for avoiding Jennifer. Seeing each other would be frustrating and embarrassing.

It had been decided.

Once I'd even tried to exit at the bottom of the back stairs and make my way to the other street, but people had dumped their garbage in the narrow space between buildings, making it impossible to escape that way. I had to leave through the front door like everyone else, but I managed to avoid the times she was coming in and out of the building.

"Major Byun," I slurred. He was driving on some cratered back road outside Taegu. "I don't know how to tell you ... I don't ..."

I'd called Major Byun because I wanted to be blind drunk, completely out of my mind. Now I could barely sit up straight, but it hadn't calmed my head at all.

What Jennifer had said was right. Trying to spend time alone with her would have been as reckless as driving with Major Byun.

"I'm tired, Major Byun."

If Koreans forbade younger people from refusing drinks offered by elders, did the same apply to offers of prostitutes?

"I don't know how to tell you this, man," I said. "I'm not going to fuck a prostitute, okay? I'm sorry if that's a bad cultural thing or whatever, but I'm just not."

He reached his destination: Two little shacks sat along the roadside, with glass fronts, their interiors lit by actual red lights, each with two girls inside, reading beauty magazines and smoking cigarettes. A wrinkled little man grimaced at me and shooed the car away.

"I don't care if you fuck them," Major Byun said. "I taking you places I like. If they reject you, I know the women there are clean."

"We Korean say must always control emotion," a businessman told me, during our class discussion. "Words are very powerful, can hurt a long time."

"So, you're saying that words can damage someone for a long time, and that means we need to be very careful about using them," I said. "We control our emotions so we don't damage people with our words."

"Instead," a male college student said, "we drink. Drink is acceptable for show emotion. People forget again."

"So … we can say bad things when we're drinking, because people will forget them," I said. "Our words won't hurt them for a long time, because they will forget. But some people become violent when they drink, If we can only show emotion when we drink, maybe we're trading bad words for violence."

"Violence is okay," a female college student said. "You hit, and then over."

"So it's better to hit than to say bad words?" I asked.

Most of the class concurred.

"Hitting is instant," the businessman said. "Much better."

"But there are reasons not to hit, aren't there? Does anyone think hitting is worse?"

The class discussed the pros and cons of hitting. I took a vote. Eight of the eleven students thought hitting was better than bad words. "So, we should only use bad words when we really want to hurt someone a lot, and for a long time, is that right, class?"

The class agreed.

"Tell me, class," I said. "If we can't show emotion, is there any way we can let out our bad feelings when we're not drinking?"

"We can punish bad people," a different young woman said.

"Punish bad people," the businessman said, nodding.

The class agreed.

4

The phone rang at around eleven on a Sunday morning. Leo and Karen got calls here, mostly from their families. I rolled onto my stomach and put a pillow over my head.

Karen knocked on my door. "Mark? You in there? Phone call!"

Nobody called me in Korea. I wasn't even sure I'd given the number to anyone except Major Byun, though there was a directory at the office that was made available to everyone. My mother had believed me when I'd said I couldn't take inbound calls, and my dad wouldn't have bothered calling, even if he had known where I was.

I stumbled out to the living room. Karen had left the phone on the table.

"Hello?"

"Mark?"

It was Jennifer.

"Yeah, that's me."

"This is Jennifer. Did I wake you up?"

"Hi, Jennifer. It's nice to hear from you. What's going on?"

"I changed my mind. I do want to see you more."

The phone was on a short cord, which I was able to stretch part of the way to my room. The receiver was on a coiled cord that barely stretched enough to close the door.

"Hello? Mark?"

"Hi, sorry. Just … Are you sure?"

"You don't want that?"

"No, I do! I really do. I missed you."

"I missed you, too."

"But I'm worried," I said. "The stakes are so high for you. Do you know that word, stakes? It's like when you place a bet, the stakes are what you stand to win or lose."

"Oh, okay. Thank you. Yes, you're right. My stake is serious."

"I don't want us to do anything that would put you in danger," I said. "I think that's a real possibility. And I'm not that great of a catch, you know. I have none of those things Koreans pay attention to when they go out together. My father has money, but that'll never have anything to do with me. I grew up alone with my crazy mom, which means I grew up paranoid all the time …"

It was strange, hearing myself say these things to a woman I wanted to be with. But circumstances in Korea dictated that I could neither deceive nor omit. The words poured out.

"I failed half of seventh grade and half of ninth grade. The only job I was ever good at was selling drugs out of my dorm room. You worry about your parents not liking me because I'm not Korean, but they'd hate me just the same if I was."

"I worry about what my parents might *do* if they find out," she said, "but I don't care what they think about me seeing you. After you and I went out, I was thinking about my life, being the second daughter. I was a disappointment to them from the day I was born, and they all made sure I knew. My job, every day, has always been to sacrifice for my sister, to make sure she got the best of everything, to move the family

ahead. You make me feel like I deserve better than that. I
don't want to sacrifice this."

"I'm thrilled," I said. "But I worry about what the whole
country will do to us."

"I do, too," she said. "But I want to see you. I can tell you
are a good guy. I like that you worry about my stake."

"Let's have lunch together tomorrow in my office, then,"
I said. "Alice finished her contract, and Canada Katherine
just vanished, so I have it to myself. We can take out *mondu*."

"Okay. It will be easier for me to get food than for you," she
said. "I'll bring *mondu* to your office tomorrow at lunchtime."

My office door opened. It was only David. He stepped inside
and looked somberly from Alice's desk to Katherine's.

"Neither one's here, man," I said. "Alice's contract ended a
couple weeks ago, and—"

"I know," he said, in a low, slow voice. "Katherine's gone,
too." He entered and closed the door. "I also know why."

He paused.

"I wouldn't want to embarrass her or give away private details," he said. "But Sue and I decided to tell people
what happened because it's such an important safety issue.
We thought it was unlikely any of us would see Katherine
again, anyway."

"Okay," I said.

"Alice and Katherine were roommates, you know," he said.
"When Alice went home, Katherine lived alone, because we
didn't have a new female teacher to move in there. People

aren't exactly clamoring to come live and work in Taegu."

"Yeah," I said. "Shocking, ain't it?"

"Anyway, Katherine was there by herself for about a week and a half. Then someone broke in and raped her. She called us after he left. Sue went inside the apartment to calm her down, and I looked around outside, but the guy was long gone. The next day, Sue helped her get a ticket back to Vancouver and pack her bag. She asked us to ride along in the taxi to the airport and wait with her at the gate."

"That's terrible," I said. "I don't know what to say. Did she call the cops?"

"No point. The first thing she'd have to tell them is that she was single and living alone. She's just another bad girl."

"Yeah," I said. "That's the mentality."

"Just make sure other teachers know not to stay in one of these apartments alone," David said. "You'll still be here for a few months after Sue and I are gone, so spread the word." He turned to go.

"All right, man," I said. "Thanks for telling me."

"Oh, and did you hear Betty quit the school?" he asked.

"No. What happened with her?"

"Nobody knows."

"Not even Lawson?"

"Especially not Lawson. I asked him about it. Mostly he just seemed relieved that he wasn't going to have to deal with her anymore."

Jennifer arrived, carrying two plastic bags of food and setting them on Alice's desk. "Sorry I'm late," she said. "There was a crowd and some *ajuma* shoved her shoulder into my jaw. It took a long time to get to the counter."

Alice had taken everything from her desk when she'd left, except for the violin poster still taped to the wall above it, and the wooden *neolttwigi* seesaw model with its leaping girls trying to see the outside world. Jennifer unpacked the food, popping off covers, and laid out the same reddish plastic plates the street vendors used. "I got fried and steamed," she said.

"We need drinks," I said. "I have some teabags. Would you like green tea?"

"Yes. Thank you."

There were some ceramic cups next to the copy machine outside Richard's office. By the time I returned with the tea, Jennifer had divided the food onto the plates and sat down in Katherine's chair. While Alice had cleaned out her desk before she'd left, Katherine had not. Still, her desk was significantly cleaner and better organized than mine, every inch of which was covered with papers, books, and scribbled notes. "I left your plate on Alice's desk," Jennifer said. "I didn't know where to set it."

"Thanks," I said. I balanced the plate of food in one hand and attacked it with chopsticks.

Jennifer saw me looking at the poster. "Did Alice tell you that's my sister? My mother set up that concert right before they went to the matchmaker, and she gave me a stack of posters to put up. I gave this one to Alice. My mother had tickets printed with a price of thirty thousand won, and then she gave them all away, pretending it was because this person was such a good friend, or some upper-class contact, or whatever. Now my sister gets to marry a rich guy, and he gets to marry a concert violinist, who gave one concert. My parents could have bought a car with the money they spent, renting that concert hall just to give away the tickets."

"I don't suppose the matchmaker was any cheaper," I said. "Your sister's uncomfortable facial expression in the poster makes it look like she regrets the expense."

"Not likely. They bullied her until she became just a violin machine, so I'm sure she felt that they owed her the concert."

"Maybe she just has needles under her fingernails."

"More like someone painting her fingernails."

"A chaotic art major doing the painting, no doubt," I said. "I can see a family resemblance, but she doesn't look too terribly much like you."

"My sister and I were raised differently. My parents decided she was going to be the smart one and I was going to be the pretty one."

"You're definitely the pretty one, if I may say so."

"You may." She gave me another of her Mona Lisa smiles.

"So, is your sister the smart one?"

"Of course not. My sister is the one who got more snacks. She's an average thinker, but she's good with a violin. That's all she ever had to think about."

"What did you think about?" I asked.

"I don't know. I talked to the maids a lot, and got to know them. I taught one how to read. They didn't stay, though. Never much more than a year, and then there was a new one. Oh, I read books, though. Some salesman got my parents into a book club where they got a whole set of classics free in fancy covers, and then other books came every month. My mother put all her energy into making my sister what she was, so she left me alone to read."

"You were reading Korean literature?"

"They owned a lot of Korean literature, but the club was

all translations: the Brontës, Tolstoy, Orwell, Hemmingway, Dostoyevsky, Mark Twain."

"Maybe that's why you're so different," I said. "You were influenced by so many different perspectives."

"Yeah, I think so. That, and also because I'm the middle daughter. My parents didn't put as much effort into making me what they thought I should be. They spent all their time and family resources on my older sister and my younger brother."

"Did you hear about Katherine?" I asked.

She nodded. "David told me. I think he was right to tell the other teachers. They should know the dangers and have a chance to stay safe."

"I don't blame him for telling, either," I said. "I think a lot of that stuff happens because people want to punish anyone who is different."

"I agree," she said. "Everyone has a little box to fit in, and it's hard to be like that all the time. When people see someone poking outside the box, they get angry, because they have to work so hard to fit in theirs. They say, 'I get to go outside my box so I can put you back in yours.' They act like they're heroes for the society, but actually they're terrible people who just want an excuse to hurt someone."

"But nobody would agree with a rapist who said that, would they?" I asked.

"They say it's her fault for giving him the chance. They never think about it more than that."

"That's why nobody blames Lawson for Betty," I said.

"Right. Koreans say she made a mistake, and she has to be punished."

"I can see why parents are extra strict with daughters, here," I said. "There seem to be so many dangers for women."

"It's … what do you call it? A self-filling prophecy?"

"Self-fulfilling prophecy, yeah."

"If women are locked up all the time, then any woman alone is obvious. They talk about how she's strange and bad. Her parents must have told her to be home by ten, or not to smoke, or not to live alone, but there she is doing it. She must be disobeying."

"Yeah," I said. "But I'm thinking about how those ideas became the culture we see now, which developed over a long time. Korea has been invaded nine hundred times. I understand how those strict rules would be created, when there were always invaders outside the door."

Korean Lurch appeared in the hallway, glowering at the two of us through the rectangular window. "He thinks we're going to eat up all the *mondu* in Korea so he won't be able to have any," I said. "That's why he looks so unhappy."

Jennifer laughed, freely and with volume. It was the first time I'd seen her do so, and I wondered if it was partially to rub Korean Lurch's nose in the fact that she was having lunch with me. I hoped it was. Korean Lurch stared a while longer and then slunk away.

"Damn," I said. "He's like a raccoon getting into the garbage. Do you know what raccoons are?"

"I know the word, but only from stories and cartoons. I don't know what they're really like. They eat garbage? Are they like cats?"

"Bigger than cats," I said. "I got scratched fighting one when I was four, and I wasn't much bigger than it was."

"You were fighting one?" Jennifer asked.

"So I'm told. Once in high school I asked my mom about it, and she shrugged. 'You must've been doing something to it,' she said. You don't have raccoons here in Korea at all?"

"They might have been here once, I don't know," she said. "Korea doesn't have many wild animals. Have you heard there are no crows in Korea?"

I shook my head. "Someone decided that crows were good for stamina, and they were all eaten," she said.

"That's sad," I said. "Crows are cool, actually. They have a kind of attitude, and they're smart. I like them."

"I can watch them on nature shows," she said.

"Speaking of nature shows, how's your sister's wedding going?"

Jennifer laughed again. Her smile was natural and the laugh seemed genuine. Happy looked good on her.

"I met the guy," she said. "That means they're definitely planning to get married."

"You met him?" I asked. "Did he come to your house?"

"We met in a Chinese restaurant," Jennifer said. "Not the kind you've seen around here for lunch, but a fancy, expensive Chinese restaurant."

"How was it?"

"It was good. I don't remember which dishes we had, though. There was one with octopus."

"Actually, I meant to ask, 'How was the experience of meeting the guy your sister is going to marry?'"

"Oh," she said. "I don't like him. I told her I don't like him."

"In front of him?"

"Not in front of him, but later."

"Why don't you like him?"

"He talks like he's a really important businessman who is educating me about his complicated world, and he's not actually very smart. He asked me how my job was at SNM Junior. I said it was fine. He told me it was good that I was teaching English, because having Americans teach here is damaging Korean culture. He said we should only have Koreans teaching our children, because if they learn from Americans they could grow up to respect American values instead of Korean. I told him about how I admire the spirit of the English teachers who come here, to the other side of the world, alone, and he told me about how he got his MBA at some American school I had never heard of."

"Huh," I said. "He's traveled, then, anyway. That should mean a broader understanding of the world."

"I told him that going to a college campus and hanging around with Koreans wasn't the same thing as working in a foreign country, for a foreign company, alone. My sister was afraid I might fight with him, so she changed the subject. 'He told me he checked that about me,' she said. 'He had a friend whose friend went to my school in America, and he called the guy to ask about me. The friend said I never had a boyfriend or associated with Americans.'

"I already knew he had checked on her like that," Jennifer said, "because my sister had told our parents the night before. She was really impressed that he would do that to protect his family name."

"Where did your sister go to school in the States?"

"She got a master's degree from Notre Dame," Jennifer said, pronouncing it the French way. "There was some professor there who was supposed to be a big name, so she went to study violin performance with him. Then she graduated, came back to Korea, and asked my parents to find her a husband."

"It's all so fascinating to me," I said.

"My sister admits she went to America for two years and didn't get to know any Americans, but she and this guy were acting like they knew so much more about Americans, because they both had parents who would pay for them to go there and see only Koreans."

She looked at the clock on the wall.

"This has been an interesting and wonderful lunch," Jennifer said. "I think I should go prepare for my next class, though."

"Oh," I said. "Okay. It was definitely interesting and wonderful."

"Yes," she said. "We should do it again."

"I have my Korean class tomorrow," I said.

"Don't you spend enough time in classrooms?" she asked.

"Don't you want me to learn your language?" I asked.

"No," she said. "I don't."

The back stairs had become a habit, despite the smoke and grit. Though Jennifer still took the front stairs, I tended to get pulled into too many conversations with students there. I preferred to avoid the crowd. I'd see Jennifer soon, anyway. Today would be our third straight day having lunch together, since I'd skipped Korean class the day before.

Standing alone outside the fifth-floor door was New Clip, smoking a cigarette. He was a student in my next class, the one that I had taken over from what had been Canada Katherine's schedule. I joined him. "Hey, man," I said. "How're you doing?" I lit up.

"Hello, Mark," he said. New Clip's English pronunciation had improved significantly since he'd helped me in the open market and the motorcycle shop. "I am waiting for my inferior."

"Your inferior?" I asked.

"He is lower than me," New Clip said, gesturing with a palm pointing downward at waist height. "My junior."

"Ah," I said. "I've had students tell me stories about their friends, using *my junior* or *my senior*. It's difficult for me to understand because in my country we just say *my friend*."

"In Korea we must say junior, senior, inferior, like this," New Clip said. "Very important in Korea."

"Yes," I said. "I'm learning that almost everyone feels that way here."

"Mark, do you smell banana?" New Clip asked.

I shook my head. "I'm not even sure I can smell it anymore."

"I'm sorry, Mark," New Clip said. "What did you say? I do not understand."

"Ooh, *I'm* sorry, my friend," I said. "I have to prepare for our class. I'll see you in our classroom, okay?" I knocked off the orange end of the cigarette, which looked surprisingly like tobacco, and saved the rest of it for later.

"Okay, Mark."

The class was a 104. With so many teachers leaving, I had moved up in seniority and got to select my schedule earlier, ditching the 101s and filling it with higher-level classes like this one, though this particular class had previously been assigned to Katherine.

"I'm curious about something today, class," I said, writing on the whiteboard. "A student just told me he was waiting for his inferior. I've heard Koreans use *my junior*, when you refer in English to someone who is younger than you are, but I have not heard the word *inferior* used that way. Sometimes meanings get lost when we translate, so I feel it's important that we come to understand each other's culture on this point. In English, the word *junior* does mean *younger*. The word *inferior* is technically okay to mean *younger*, but to my ears it sounds strange, because inferior usually means *not as good*. When I think of an inferior car, for example, I think of one that might be cheaper, or less reliable, or perhaps slower. So please tell me: Is it correct to say that you are waiting for your *inferior*, when you mean to say that you are waiting for someone younger? Are younger people truly not as good as older ones?"

"Yes, this is true," one said.

"In Korea, older is always better," another said.

"Koreans must understand how to do what we are told," said another.

"Always someone is superior, someone is inferior."

"How about twins?" I asked. "They're born at the same time."

New Clip shook his head. "No. One twin is born first. Other twin is younger. His whole life, his twin brother is his superior. He must call his brother *Hyeong nym,* which means *honorable older brother.* His brother call him Dongseang. It means *little brother.*"

"Wow," I said. "But that's inside your family. How does this work when you're at college?"

"When we are college freshmen, our seniors take us on camping trip," another student said.

"Just men, or women too?" I asked.

"Everyone, men and women," a young woman said. "All college students."

"Okay, tell me about that," I said. "Do they take you on one camping trip, or many camping trips?"

"Many," one said.

"Different groups take us," another said. "Those ahead of us in our major are one group, people who graduate our high school before us are another, campus clubs are another."

"This is fascinating," I said. "But let's back up just a minute. Remember that if it's many trips, you need an *s* at the end, *trips.* People who graduate from the same high school are called alumni. Tell me more about these activities. What do you do there?"

"They make us drink many drinks, and then exercise," one said.

"Push-up, sit-up, run very fast," said another.

"Maybe we get very dirty, like push-ups in mud," another said. "Our faces must go under the mud each time. Like that."

"We must shout 'yes, sir,' many times," someone called out.

"Wow," I said. "And this happens to every university student, many times, for many different groups?"

"Yes," one said. "Many times. This is very important in Korea."

"Okay, tell me about that," I said. "Why is this important in Korea?"

"Shared struggles make us closer," one said. "Even when you dislike a person, you are close because you suffered together."

"Even when you dislike a person, there is no fighting, because you know who is superior and who is inferior," the same student said.

"I see," I said. "But what if someone just wants to go to school and be left alone?"

"Impossible," one said. "In Korea, everyone want to be close to classmates like this."

I wrote *everyone want* on the board. "Remember, class, when we're talking about every*one*"—I circled the end of the word—"we add an s to the end. It's *Everyone wants*. That seems strange, because when we're talking about everyone it seems like we're talking about a group, like when we say *they want*. But here, we're talking about *every one*. We're thinking of this one and that one and that one way over there. He wants, she wants, *every one* wants."

Some of them were writing notes. I paused to let them catch up.

"So nobody fights back?" I asked. What if someone was super strong, or maybe had a black belt or something?" I asked.

"All Korean men go into the army," one said. "Every Korean man has a black belt."

"So they do this one time in your first year, and then they leave you alone?" I asked.

"One time, but then you go for other, just social times," someone said.

"Sometimes they pretend it's social time, but then say 'freshmen forgot their place, so we must train them some more," another said. The class laughed in agreement.

"Tell me what you think of this idea, class," I said. "We said earlier that these trips are important for students, for bringing and keeping the group together. *Shared struggles make us closer*, I believe someone said. I'm wondering if maybe the hardships here in Korea, with so many wars and invasions over thousands of years, made Koreans closer to each other than perhaps people would be somewhere else. Have the shared struggles of Korean people made you all closer?

There was general agreement, and then New Clip spoke. "Mark, do you know about climbing a barley hill?"

"No," I said. "Is that a Korean saying, climbing a barley hill?"

"Yes," he said. "You know barley? It's grain?"

"Yes," I said. "The crop, barley."

"Crop, yes. We plant barley on the hill, and wait for it to be ready, in the ... in the springtime."

"Ah, you wait for the barley to be ready to harvest," I said. "In the springtime? It must be the first crop of the year, then."

"At that time, rice from last year was all gone, so there was no food. Many Koreans died at that time each year, waiting for the barley. It is a struggle. We call that climbing a barley hill."

"So, the time the barley is growing on the hill is a struggle," I said. "We're struggling, climbing the hill as we try to survive, and we call that struggle climbing a barley hill. If we don't win the struggle, we starve."

"Yes," New Clip said. "You got it."

"How are your sister's wedding plans coming along?" I asked. We were back in my office. This time, Jennifer had picked up Chinese food from the dingy little place around the corner.

"She got the ring," she said. "That was interesting. My sister saw movies of rich couples going to pick out the engagement ring together, but his family didn't do that. His father said he had already bought a superior quality diamond from a business connection. He made a big deal about how special it was. It's big, like an eraser on a new pencil, but it's not transparent. It looks more like chalk. I told her I thought maybe it's the kind they use for drilling."

"Could it be uncut?" I asked. "Diamonds don't look like jewelry when they're right out of the ground."

"I bet that's it. So it's an uncut diamond, and it looks like a dead fish eye. Some jeweler his family knows made the ring part, and it's a big lump of gold. The ring looks like a piece of gravel pushed into someone's old gum. My sister cried all night."

"You know," I said. "I think I understand why she feels that way. She gave her life to this guy so she can show off, and then he didn't deliver."

"Yeah, that's probably true," Jennifer said.

"There are probably real benefits to that materialistic stuff," I said. Everything we need comes from other people, and having them think better of you because of your jewelry, clothes or car probably helps. I bet you get treated better when you wear stuff like this—" I gestured at her outfit: A gray designer suit and an eggshell silk blouse with the collar flipped over the jacket's lapels, and a single small pearl dangling from an impossibly thin gold chain around her neck. "—than you did before, right?"

"That's true," she said.

"Since I've lived in Korea, I've come to appreciate things like that," I said. "It's not just vanity. Do you know 'vanity?' It's being very proud of yourself, too proud."

"Yes," she said. "Okay."

"I don't know how you would measure it," I said, "but say your experience walking down the street today is ten percent more positive than it would have been without the fancy clothes. I see the appeal of that, now, in a way I didn't before. I would love to have a ten percent better experience when I walk down the street here. I would feel safer."

"I don't think my sister is worried about feeling safe," Jennifer said. "I'm pretty sure with her it is vanity, like you said. She wants people to act like she's so great, because that way she can feel it must be true. She needs that fancy stuff, to tell her who she is."

"I've always felt that way about my father," I said. "He's not a nice person, he's not interesting, he's not even good looking, but he can buy Porsches. He drives them really slowly and carefully, not like a sports car at all, more like he borrowed them from some big guy who'll beat him up if he scratches them. I think he hopes that people will see the car, and not pay attention to the turd behind the wheel."

"What's that?" she asked. "Turd?"

"It's shit. It's, like, an individual piece of shit."

"Oh, okay. Yes. Koreans would never say such things about their fathers but I know what you mean."

"No, I suppose not," I said. "But I can't help feeling angry. I was considered part of my father's family until I was six years old. From them I learned that we were special people because we owned special things. When my parents got divorced,

I lived with my mother and I didn't have nice things like that anymore, and it always seemed I was no longer worth their attention."

"That was the way it was for me on the day I was born," Jennifer said. "It makes me angry, too. I'm not supposed to say that, but I always do. I make them see that I know what they're doing when they're unfair to me, and then the whole society tells me that I'm wrong and that I'm bad. But my family has always shown me that I don't matter, and I still have to do all these things to show them how important they are and how much I respect them."

"I used to try and be this loyal, loving son," I said. "I'd see that my father thought something was great, like Porsches, and try to learn everything I could, be even more into it than he was. I learned his conservative politics and tried to talk with him. Nothing I did mattered. He wasn't interested, or worse, he thought I was after his money. Once I tried to talk with him about taking flying lessons, because he had a private airplane he flew as a hobby. He told me it was a waste of time for someone my age to learn to fly and that it would cost a lot of money. Then a few years later, one of my half-brothers got his pilot's license when he was sixteen years old—much younger than I'd been when I'd asked him. My father showed me a video of my brother's first solo flight, telling me how impressive it was that he could fly an airplane at such a young age."

"My mother is always unfair like that," Jennifer said. "She promised everything to my sister, and she always gave it. Then she would tell me that if I got some score on my next test, I would get something, too. Once she even told me I could go to America and visit my sister, if I passed the exam and got into college. I did, and then she told me she'd never said it. 'How could you stay with her? She lives in a dormitory. Obviously

I never said that.' My mother lies like that to me all the time."

"But at least you had some guidance, right?" I asked. "Nobody cared enough to manipulate me."

"The guidance wasn't to help me, though," Jennifer said. "It was to benefit the family. If they had wanted me to feel loved and appreciated, I would have felt loved and appreciated. I never did. Instead, they wanted me to know that my position, my duty, is to sacrifice so that others in my family can be the stars. My grades were important because they got me into a good college, which made the family look better, which would give my sister and my younger brother better chances for getting married into a good family. They manipulated me only for that."

"I think that's a big difference between us," I said. "After the divorce, my father and stepmother had kids of their own. Nobody came to my defense when my stepmother was sarcastic and unpleasant to me. Around all of them I always felt like some unwelcome street kid who was crashing their party and being taught a lesson. Which, I suppose, I was. It was clear that I wasn't part of that family, but at least they never acted like I owed them anything."

Korean Lurch was back outside the door. There was more deliberateness to his scowl than usual. "Speaking of watching," I said.

Jennifer stared at him until he turned away again.

"Is that why you failed classes?" she asked. "Nobody pushed you?"

"That's part of it, sure. But mostly it's because of the way I lived with my mom. She's ... not predictable."

Jennifer waited patiently as I took a breath and tried to find words.

"It's hard to explain my mom without sounding whiny ... Okay, it's like this: Imagine one Saturday, you tell her you're going over to some friend's house, and she smiles and tells you to have a great day. The next Saturday, you do the exact same thing, and suddenly she's sobbing and yelling and hitting you. Nothing special about the day, nothing unusual about the announcement. Identical circumstances, but a completely different result. And not just about seeing friends. It's about everything, all the time.

"She takes something as proof that you hate her, and often that has to do with other people in your life. You're seeing them, not her, because you must hate her and love them. But sometimes it has nothing to do with anyone else. She just hears an imaginary *Fuck you, mom, because I hate you!* at the end of whatever you say.

"Most of the time, she sniffles and tells you how mean you are. And you learned early not to ask why, because that can launch her into screaming some nonsensical reason. *'We were having such a nice chat, and then you just stand there, staring into the refrigerator, because you want to show me that you don't care about talking to me at all!'* Other times, she'll stand at the sink for forty minutes, sobbing and telling you what a nasty, spiteful person you are, citing examples of things you didn't do, or things you did but that didn't mean anything, and she has this twisted way of seeing them that makes you seem totally evil. Other times, she'll be so hurt—by nothing—that she'll hit you in the face, sometimes repeatedly.

"I failed half my classes in seventh grade, and half of my classes in ninth grade, because those classes graded mostly on homework. I usually did fine on tests, and on standardized tests I was always in the top five percent, but it was impossible to focus on homework in that environment. One minute everything would be fine, and the next my mother would be shrieking and slapping me."

I scoffed. "The one person who knew what it must have been like for me, growing up with my back against the wall, was my father. He was married to my mom until I was six, and then he got away, because she started seeing this friend of his. My whole childhood felt like I was waiting for my dad to come and rescue me ... or not even rescue me, really. It never occurred to me that *I* might escape. All I really wanted was for him to tell me I wasn't mean, I wasn't cruel, I wasn't such a bad person that I deserved to be screamed at, hit, and told how horrible I was all the time. Instead, he just wrote his checks to my mother every month, and he was done. I became convinced I was a really bad kid. After that, I guess I set out to prove it."

My face was numb. I hadn't meant to say all that.

Korean Lurch appeared at the door again, and so did I, leaning at the glass, eyes buggy.

"The fuck you *want*, man?"

Korean Lurch stood frozen a moment, with his face slacker than normal and his eyes wider, and then slunk away toward his office again. Jennifer spoke quietly behind me as I watched him go.

"You're not a bad person," she said.

Major Byun finally got me into a room salon, by letting the owner announce to everyone there that I was only observing and would not be leaving with any of the women. Curiosity, and the forbidden-fruit aspect of it all, helped me put up with it.

The room salon was not what I expected, though by this point, I should have known exactly what it would look like. It was a dark basement, with a linoleum floor and black vinyl sectional pieces arranged in various configurations around tables. We all sat down, and drinks and women appeared.

Through Major Byun, the owner announced that one of his girls spoke English. I worried that I might know her, but that was ridiculous. The girls at SNM Academy were all upper-class.

Betty?

It was as if my mind had blown a fuse. I sat there, horrified at the thought, not just that Betty would be ashamed, but that my presence here would make her think I was just another asshole, doing to Jennifer what Lawson had done to her. They brought in the girl, who was not Betty, and I breathed a sigh of relief. She poured beer into my glass and haltingly said hello. She was a 101.

"Mark!" Major Byun said. "Mark!" Major Byun gestured at his restaurant-owner friend. "He want to know what American men do for stamina."

"We drink coffee," I said.

Major Byun drunkenly translated. The guy waved his hand jaggedly over the table, speaking faster. Major Byun translated back.

"No! Man stamina, with woman!" he said. "Man fuck, he want hard again, he need stamina!"

I couldn't take it anymore.

"That's an issue?" I asked. "I've never heard of that. Is that a common problem here in Korea?"

They became increasingly frustrated and angry as I continued to feign surprise and misunderstanding, until finally they each took a girl and left. The girl next to me told me that I was nice. "You know," she said. "Sometimes, I want to die."

The owner and a bouncer helped me to my feet, though my glass was still full, and out the door. Major Byun never called me again. David told me that he began hanging out with Lawson.

Jennifer and I were back in my office for lunch, this time having *jajang myeon*, a Chinese dish with black bean sauce over noodles. Someone in the office next door was moving furniture around. It shuddered as it slid over the linoleum.

"When I was fourteen, my sister had a big test coming up," Jennifer said. "My mom found these special snails for sale, and they were so expensive she thought they would motivate my sister to study harder. She bought enough for three dinners: for my sister, because of her test, for my father, because he is the head of the family, and for my brother, because he is the future honor of the family. I was with her when she bought them, and the guy was so happy to sell so many that he gave her something else for free that I could eat. I think it was fish."

"But they all had snails?" I asked. "How big were they?"

"Not too big," she said, indicating with her fingers. "About like a plum. My mother was supposed to eat mostly the extra stuff the guy gave for me, but my sister had to show she was devoted to our parents. She kept begging my mom to taste the wonderful snails, saying she didn't feel right eating such a great thing in front of her, so my mother ended up having a lot."

"But you didn't even get a bite, to try them?"

"No. They didn't want to waste them on me. Then everyone went to the living room to watch some show my father wanted to see. About half an hour after that, they were all sitting very still. My mother called me over to her, talking through her teeth. It turned out none of them could move."

"They were paralyzed?" I asked, wide-eyed. "From eating the snails?"

"Right. My mom had eaten the least, so she could still talk a little, but her mouth stayed closed. I went to find some other doctor friend of theirs on a different floor of our building and ask him what we should do. He said being paralyzed was temporary and they just had to wait. I went back to my parents' apartment and sat by myself on the balcony. They were all still frozen in strange positions, so nobody bothered me. I had never felt so peaceful. I stayed out there for more than ninety minutes, then I left them where they were and went to bed. They were stuck like that for hours."

"Why would anyone want to eat snails that make them paralyzed?" I asked.

"My family had them before, and that never happened. It was just that one time that they ate so many."

Someone began tapping lightly on the other side of the wall. The sound was not knocking but rather a soft ring of metal on metal, sounding vaguely like pins being removed from hinges.

The top of the wall tilted away, and then the bottom of the wall was dragged into what had been the adjacent room. Workmen broke it into segments and stacked them on some of the far office's desks, along with the ones they had already removed from the other side of that room. Ryan had been preparing a lesson at his desk in one of the offices, and Lawson had apparently just returned to his desk with a plastic bag of takeout in the other. The two of them sat, looking rather stunned, in what had now become a single large room. Korean Lurch stood near the stacked walls with his arms crossed, supervising the workmen and watching Jennifer and me with his lips smugly pursed.

5

The Deadbeat Club was in session again. It was still my favorite non-Jennifer part of the day.

"Here's what I have for us today," I said, writing on the whiteboard.

Book = Scholar
Money = Wealthy
Pen = Writer
String = Long Life

"My 103 class this morning told me this is a ceremony Koreans do for babies. All these things are placed on a table in front of the baby, and the thing the baby grabs first is said to be the kid's future. Is that right?"

"Yes," Paul said. "That is the first birthday party."

"Sometimes parents move one thing closer, trying to decide good things for the baby," Strawberry said.

The class chuckled slightly.

"After the 103 this morning, I was thinking about fortune-telling here in Korea. We've talked a lot about how

Korea has many strict rules that dictate the way everyone is supposed to behave. Recently I've heard a few different people say that Korean fortune-tellers are spooky because they're so accurate. I wonder if there's a connection. Would a fortune-teller's predictions come true more often in a stricter society?"

"Yes," Ivy said.

"Why?"

"There are fewer choices to make, so there are fewer outcomes," Strawberry said.

"Okay," I said. "We might say that there are fewer *potential* outcomes. Good. So, can we also say that since in a strict society fortune-tellers are more likely correct, people are more likely to believe them?"

"Yes," Sarah said. "If someone experienced that one was right for something big, maybe that person will believe in them even more."

"So they're more likely to be right, and they're more likely to be believed, in a more regulated society," I said. "Does that also mean that people are more likely to change how they behave because of what fortune-tellers say? For example, to find a doctor to marry because a fortune-teller said you would?"

"Yes," Paul said. "Maybe she would join a science club at the college to meet one."

"In Korea, your parents choose your college, your major, your career, and your spouse," I said. "That's a lot of who you are and what you're going to be, and so much of it is predictable by looking at outside factors. In the United States, people tend to think of those choices as things that define us. Even when we choose badly, we are the ones who decide, and we say that makes us who we are. What do Koreans feel makes us who we are?"

"We are not our jobs," Ivy said. "We are not our husbands or wives."

"We are the way we perform our jobs," Groundhog said. "We are our duties, and our families." He paused a moment, then added, "In Korea, we have better shoeshine men."

"Explain that, please, Groundhog," I said.

"Korea has better shoeshine men, better barbers, better bus drivers. In America, everyone can choose his own job. Everyone tries to be bigger and better, all the time. In Korea, you know you will be a shoeshine man, so you can try to be the best one. You can live as a shoeshine man, not as a doctor who must shine shoes."

"So, you're saying that here in Korea, with fewer choices to make about our lives, and fewer possible outcomes, predictability means we can do better at whatever we are assigned to be."

"Yes," Groundhog said. "A rule is that I must obey my father. My father wants me to be a banker. I predict I will be a banker."

"Good," I said. "That's a powerful prediction, covering most of the hours you will be awake for the rest of your life. But we have talked about your career a few times, Groundhog, and I know you feel that banking is a boring job, and you're not happy about having so many managers above you. Don't you think maybe you would work harder at a job you felt passionate about?"

"No. I would enjoy that much more, but I will work the same way at any job."

"And that's as hard as you can, almost every conscious minute, pretty much every single day, right? Even though you don't want to be a banker?"

"Yes, as hard as I can."

"I'm curious, Groundhog. Do you know what you chose at your first birthday party? Was it the money?"

"No. It was the string."

The new office/workroom always had people in it, working or eating alone at their desks. There would be no more private lunches there. Today Jennifer and I had taken the motorcycle to *Susung Mot*, pronounced like moat, which was pretty much what it was. Though *mot* is the Korean word for lake, the small, rectangular *Susung Mot* had about as much water as the moat around a castle.

"What item did you choose at your first birthday party?" I asked. "When they put everything in front of you on the table."

"I didn't have a first birthday party," Jennifer said. "Nobody cared about my future. There are pictures of my sister and my brother at their parties at my parents' house, but not of me."

The idea in coming here was that the restaurants were expensive, and therefore they would have to be nice to us. We walked by a few of them, coming to one with flower boxes on the windows and wrought iron decoration on the doors. "Maybe this one?" I said. "It looks vaguely European. Maybe they won't mind someone of European ancestry."

"Sure," Jennifer said.

A young man stood at the front desk, dressed in black, his longish hair in Korea's trendiest style for men, a kind of bowl cut that made him look like a mushroom. He stared at us for a moment without speaking. We approached. Jennifer began speaking to him in Korean. A gray-haired man in a suit came bustling up from someplace, gesturing at us as if shooing pigeons, speaking loudly in Korean. Patrons turned their heads to watch as he scooted us back out the door.

"He said his restaurant is exclusive and romantic for

Koreans, and he doesn't want it to get a bad reputation. He said we should go back by the military base."

"Let's do that," I said. "This was a mistake."

"There's no time to go that far today," she said. "It would even have been difficult to get back to work after lunch from here. I guess we have plenty of time now."

Neither of us wanted to try our luck at another place, so we stood by the lake, looking out at the cold, patina-green water. It was cold enough to justify turning up the collar on my overcoat, but the real reason I did it was to hide my face. Two trucks of American troops rolled past, escorted by three Humvees, one of which had a man perched at a machine-gun turret on top of it.

"It's strange to me, to see all the soldiers and war machinery here, among the high-rises and designer suits," I said.

"I have never known anything else," she said. "It's how we live, here. I was the fastest in my middle school class at putting on a gas mask, and the best at first aid. Does it bother you, all the military stuff?"

"I'm used to tension, growing up the way I did. In college I was dealing drugs, and when you're a criminal there's no higher authority, no judge to complain to if you got cheated or whatever, so I'm used to having guns around all the time. But the actual military stuff—the uniforms, bases, and salutes—that stuff does bother me. It's just so creepy, having thousands of soldiers ready to kill on one man's word."

"That's Korea," she said.

"This *feels* like a country at war," I said.

"Always," she said.

I climbed back to one of the oddly-angled single seats in the lounge, balancing a Styrofoam box of *mondu*. Jennifer was teaching her afternoon classes and I was fueling up for my evening ones. Jessi and Lawson were there, watching the TV, which was playing a Toad the Wet Sprocket song called *Walk on the Ocean*, over video of U.S. Navy ships crashing through waves.

"We're not allowed to eat in here," Jessi said, sounding annoyed. Jessi stood out in Korea because she was a natural platinum blonde just this side of albino, and her left eye was severely cocked inward. Her other eye was glaring at me.

"Fuck this company," I said, eating.

"See?" Lawson said in his most obnoxious *boy-let-me-tell-you-what* Southern drawl. "That's your problem, right there. What's good for your company is good for you. You go badmouthing your employer like that, and the people who could've helped you are going to turn away. That's why you have such a problem with Richard. I just got my contract extended for another year, and a bonus, even, because I'm not going around biting the hand that feeds me."

"Fuck this company," I said again, "and fuck you. You think I want etiquette lessons from someone who ruined Betty's life on a whim?"

"Betty made her own choice," he said. "I'm not ashamed of fucking her. If she has a problem with it, that's between Betty and her higher power."

"The higher power here is the society," I said.

"Wait," he said. "Let me get this straight. *You* are telling me I ought to play by Korean rules. You think the Koreans approve of you?"

"It's not about their approval or their dehumanizing rules. It's about you thinking you're somehow superior because you're willing to kiss ass, yet you've knowingly destroyed the life of someone who trusted you."

"And you're doing better by Jennifer? How many students have seen you two coming and going together? Probably a few hundred, with eight classes a day and each lasting only a month at a time. They see you in the halls, getting in taxis, riding off on your bike. At least I was honest with Betty. I'm not gonna be responsible if she didn't believe me when I said I don't want a girlfriend. What lie are you telling Jennifer, that love will conquer all? She's as stupid for believing in you as Betty was for believing whatever shit she made up in her head about me."

"You're both assholes," Jessi said. "If you're going to live in this country, you have to respect its culture and follow its rules. A society's rules aren't dehumanizing just because you disagree with them."

"Oh, I'm culturally insensitive because I don't buy into the idea that Jennifer is a whore who should be beaten up and raped because she sits with me in a coffee shop? Fuck you and your high horse, Jessi. I'm not trying to win any popularity contests; I'd just like to walk down the street without being attacked."

"If you don't like being here, go home," Jessi said.

"I can't."

"Why?" Lawson asked. "Because you've been on like three dates with Jennifer?"

"If you two are having a great time here in Korea, that's wonderful," I said. "Maybe you can publish a travelogue about your warm and fuzzy tour of duty respecting the local culture. None of it invalidates my experience."

"What happens when she finds out you hate her country?" Jessi asked.

"It hated me first," I said, "and she hated it before I got here."

"It was a good idea," I said. "Worth trying."

It was Saturday. Jennifer had suggested trying to go to the movie *Philadelphia*, in which Tom Hanks played a character who had AIDS. She had thought that perhaps it would draw a more tolerant crowd.

It was at the *Han-il* theater, which was an enormous place with multiple balconies and a few hundred people in attendance. I was the only non-Korean. The lights had stayed on well past the scheduled start time. Everywhere I looked, it seemed that people were staring at us, or perhaps laughing, or even taunting us. Jennifer sat stiffly with her face pointed at her lap.

When the lights finally dimmed, the screen showed public service announcements reminiscent of the ones on AFKN, featuring brave South Korean soldiers driving tanks and storming beaches.

The movie was censored beyond intelligibility. It wasn't even clear that Tom Hanks was supposed to be gay, and the plot made no sense. Voices still seemed to come at us from the crowd. We managed to hang in there for about forty minutes.

"I don't want to be here at the end, when all these people come spilling out together," I said.

"Where can we go?" Jennifer asked.

Jennifer and I carried the groceries up the concrete outdoor steps. "I think they left cooked rice in the refrigerator," I said.

"If we can't do fried rice, we'll make all this into an omelet."

"It's Saturday," Jennifer said. "I have time. We can make rice and then fry it, if we want."

"I want to try this *makgeolli* in it," I said, unlocking the door. "Welcome." We unpacked the groceries. Leo and Karen had indeed left cooked rice, and the two of us set about prepping garlic, peppers, and green onion to sauté. Jennifer added some kimchee to the pan, pulling it apart with her fingers and dropping in a few shreds at a time. We worked together well, asking each other's advice about how many cloves of garlic or how much soy sauce, and maneuvering easily around each other in the tiny kitchen.

"Trust me, just one spoonful of *makgeolli*," I said. "It'll make it taste better."

"Okay," she said. "I heard French people use wine in cooking. I guess *makgeolli* is technically rice wine."

Our fried rice was steamy and salty. The *makgeolli* rice wine blended well with the tangy kimchee flavor. We filled our plates and sat down at the table. "I think we have one beer left. Do you want to split it? I've tried actually drinking this wine before and it gave me a headache right away."

"Beer sounds better to me, too," Jennifer said. "*Makgeolli* is known to cause terrible hangovers."

We emptied the bottle into two glasses. A dog was barking outside. "Is that your landlady's dog?" she asked.

"I don't think they have one," I said. "If they ever did, it probably escaped while they were beating each other senseless. Do you have any pets?"

"No," she said. "I used to, but my mother got rid of them."

"Really?" I said. "That's another thing we have in common. Right after the divorce, my mother gave away Abigail, the dog we'd had when I was a little kid. Some guy came to pick her up. I was six, living in a new town, with no dad and no dog, and I didn't know why."

"She didn't tell you why she gave the dog away?" Jennifer asked.

I shook my head. "I think it was mostly my father's dog. He was into dog shows, and Abigail was some champion."

"Why didn't he keep Abigail?"

"Abigail was old by then. He had a new show dog, a bull terrier named Dolly. My dad isn't sentimental. The guy who took Abigail seemed like a nice old guy who wanted to have a dog around. She was better off with him than with my dad, who twisted her ears and hit her when she didn't fetch or go over jumps right. Dolly, the new one, made this terrible sound when he did that stuff to her."

"I know that sound," Jennifer said.

"Every minute of Dolly's life was spent in a kennel where she could only run three steps, unless she was training or in a show. When I was a kid I would go to my father's house every other weekend, and he usually had this guy come to help him train her on Saturday nights, with the twisting of ears and all that. My dad worked on Saturdays and then drove me back to my mother's house on Sundays, so I hardly saw him except when he was training the dog. The room I stayed in when I was at his house was full of Dolly's trophies."

"Your only dogs were your father's show dogs?"

"No. When I was in fifth grade, my mom was single and going on dates on the weekends, and she bought a dog so I could stay alone without being lonely. He was big and goofy, and I wanted to name him Barney, but my mother named him some weird-sounding, fancy, official thing that short-ened to Brandy. She sent in papers to register him with some group because he was a purebred dog. That was really impor-tant to her; she must've learned it from my father. Then she got remarried when I was sixteen, and we moved into a new house. She thought Brandy would be bad for the carpet. My new stepdad knew some guy who would take him, and we drove out to this trailer where the guy lived, and dropped him off there. That was that."

"I've never known anyone with a stepdad."

"It was better than living alone with my crazy mom," I said. "After the divorce, my mom had a series of guys she dated, some for a few months, some for a few years. I got to know them, their kids, their families, and then they'd disappear. There was Dave, who had been my dad's friend. He had two older boys and a girl close to my age. Then Larry, who was a mechanic my mom met once when she had car trouble. He had two grown-up kids, one son and one daughter, and a younger girl who was a year older than me. During the time my mom was with him, I felt like I had actual siblings. I even went to Larry's mother's house for Christmas. Then there was this guy Jon who was a friend of one of her work friends. He was into sports, and his son was a state champion wrestler. My mom didn't date him very long, though, so I didn't learn much about sports from him."

"You don't know what happened to any of them?" Jennifer asked.

"Nobody ever said anything about it, they were just gone. Finally there was one guy who stayed, my stepdad, Floyd. It was nice, but he never really stood up to her like I'd imagined a stepfather might. He drank and smoked and mostly let my mom do whatever outrageous stuff she was going to do. My mom started all these big fights with his family, and his daughters hated my mom, so there was a lot of drama like that."

"I can't imagine my mother with different boyfriends," Jennifer said.

"Why did your mom give your dogs away?" I asked.

"She didn't give them away," Jennifer said. "She sold them. Most of them we had when I was little, so I didn't understand. But when I was eight, a dirty, skinny dog followed me in the street one day. It was friendly but I was afraid of what my parents would do if I got my clothes dirty, so I tried to—" She waved her hands, palms down.

"To shoo it away," I suggested.

"Yes. I tried to shoo it away, but it wouldn't go. It followed me back to my parents' house, and I gave it some food."

"And let me guess," I said. "You asked your parents if you could keep it, and they said you had to take care of it by yourself. A classic tale."

"I had to convince them he would be a good watchdog and keep the house safe," she said. "My preferences don't matter."

"Ah."

"The maid taught me to feed him and clean him. I called him Baby. His fur was gone in spots when I got him, but it all grew back. He got bigger around and became more energetic. My father worked and my mother was busy with my sister's lessons and practice, so I had a lot of time alone to sit with him outside and read. Do you know what Children's Day is in Korea?"

"Yes," I said. "A few classes have described it to me. Instead of every kid celebrating a separate birthday, and then having Christmas or Hanukah or whatever, Koreans have one day for all the kids to celebrate. All holidays in one."

"Yes. I woke up on Children's Day, early because I was excited. A man knocked on our gate, and behind him I could see a truck with a few dogs in a cage on the back. The man told my mother he would pay her extra because Baby was so healthy and clean. I cried and begged, but my mother said this was a great opportunity. We could always get another stray to guard the house."

"Wow," I said. "Was that for dog soup, then?"

"Yes," she said. "Even at eight years old, I knew what they did. That's the only reason anyone would drive around buying dogs. When the dogs go into the cage, they know what's happening. They all made horrible, sickening cries. Baby whined and thrashed but the man was used to handling dogs. I ran behind the truck, crying. The man drove off, and I could see Baby jumping up against the cage door. I got too tired and couldn't run anymore. I stood in the street, crying, and then I tried to run again..."

"There are so many terrible people," I said. "Dogs are better than people, you know? They're so simple. If you're not terrible to them, they won't be terrible to you."

"Yes," she said.

I took her hand. Our eyes met. "I can't promise much," I said. "I have nothing, and no power, especially here, but I can promise this: I won't be terrible to you."

She gave me that alluring slight smile again. "I won't be terrible to you, either."

I sat like that a moment, taking in her eyes and her smile, and then I kissed her.

"And I won't ever tell your secrets," I said.

Even decades later, writing a book, I still wouldn't.

"Swallow your pride, man," Leo said. "Ask your dad to wire you money for a ticket home. No way the contract is keeping me here after Karen's done."

"I'm not leaving Jennifer here," I said.

"What're you going to do if Richard fires you?" he asked.

"You may not have a choice. Better to have some cash ready, I'd say."

"Besides," I said. "I don't come from that kind of family. There's no court order that says my dad has to help me get out of Korea, and that's the only way he'd help."

"A plane ticket isn't too expensive. I bet your mom would be able to send you a few hundred bucks. That plus the envelope from work would get you back."

"Yeah, that's just not the way my mom is. She gets really paranoid, and there's no way to ask her for stuff. I went back for Thanksgiving break my freshman year of college and ended up sleeping in my car by Friday night."

Jesus. What the hell did you do? Shoot the dog?"

"I did laundry on Thanksgiving morning. She saw that I was using her washing machine and freaked out, screaming about how I was just taking advantage of her and how inconsiderate I was. Then at the actual dinner, when we went to my stepfather's sister's house, I was talking to his relatives instead of paying attention to her. That pushed her over the edge, and it degenerated from there. By the next morning I was gone, but I had nowhere to go. I couldn't get back into the dorms yet."

"She must've been having a bad holiday," he said.

"It's always like that. I went to college in my hometown, because that was what the divorce decree had said I was going to do. That Christmas break, I only lasted three days at her house, but I'd gotten a key to a frat house from some guy on my dorm floor, just in case. The next year I didn't even try going back. I stayed in friends' empty apartments when the dorms closed over break. Once I could afford a security deposit, I started getting my own apartments and never had to go back."

"So if you leave Korea, where will you stay?" Leo asked.

"I don't know. I've never felt welcome at my father's house, and when I graduated from college and got my ticket to come to Korea, my mother literally made me burn the furniture from my room. Pretty clear message, I'd say. Anyway, believe me, I'm getting out of here as soon as I'm able. I just can't be stupid about it."

Leo turned his attention back to what he'd been watching.

"What's this?" I asked. "Cop show?"

On the screen was a lone white Ford Bronco, driving alone on a wide freeway, followed by a mass of police cars.

"It's OJ Simpson," Leo said. "His ex-wife is dead. They think he did it. This might be the end for the Juice."

"From now on, we'll have only Sac-Sac," I said.

Richard and Mr. Pock, the boss of the Korean staff, with whom I had never before spoken, were both waiting for me in the lobby after class. This time they wanted to speak to me in the conference room that was intended for counseling incoming students, rather than Richard's office like my usual chastisements.

Observing Richard and Mr. Pock trying to enter a room together was like watching a nature show about avian mating dances. Each bowed and gestured the other toward the door. Then Richard opened the door and held it, sweeping his hand invitingly through the empty frame. Mr. Pock came around behind Richard, taking possession of the door handle and making a similar gesture. None of this seemed to have come from either culture, as far as I could tell. My best guess was that each of them was trying to follow the customs of the other's home country, but neither had learned what those were. They both took cues from the other's behavior, copying each other into ever more bizarre and complex patterns. Through trial and error, they managed a strange equilibrium that let them slip through the door together, bowing and gesturing the whole way.

"I'll get right to it," Richard said, taking a seat. "You are in South Korea, and you will heed cultural norms here. Teachers should set the highest standard."

Mr. Pock spoke. His pronunciation was shockingly bad for someone running an English school. "You must stop!" he said. *Must-uh stoop!*

"Good golly," I said. "What is it this time?"

"Your landlady called again," Richard said.

"I'm shocked," I said. "Lemme guess. She doesn't like the way I fold my socks."

"She said she saw you bring a Korean woman into your apartment on Saturday."

"So?"

"So, you are a teacher with this company, and you are expected to uphold the moral standards of the community."

"I'm not doing anything immoral," I said.

"In South Korea, you are. Dating between white men and Korean women is offensive here. You can't go insulting your landlady. She's worried about what her neighbors will think."

"Is she worried that her neighbors will see her and her husband beating the shit out of each other in the yard a couple times a week?" I asked. "How's that for moral standards? Fucking hypocrites."

Richard's eyes widened. "That is none of your business. Whatever you saw—"

"See," I said. "It's not something I saw, it's something I see.

All the time. They scream and kick and slam fists into each other's faces. All. The. Time. They wake us up—"

"That is inside their family and it is none of your business."

"My personal life is none of their business."

"You don't have a personal life with respect to them. They are older than you, and you live in their property. And you certainly don't have a personal life with respect to dating another of our teachers. Oh, are you surprised that Mr. Shin let us know it's Jennifer? He understands duty and why it's important to protect our reputation. We're talking to her next."

Mr. Pock leaned toward me, speaking gently. "You landlady think Korean woman her family. All Korean. She think she must stop what will hurt her parents."

"Wait, though," I said. "I thought we're not supposed to interfere with each other's families in Korea."

"You're not Korean," Richard said. "This is not your country. What you are *supposed* to do is be respectful."

"I think this has a lot more to do with the fact that my landlady has a shitty life and no power to change it, so she wants to lord whatever stupid power this society gives her over me."

"Think whatever you want," Richard said. "But follow the rules. We brought Lawson in here just like this after his mistake, too. That one cost us a paying student. You're here to teach English. That doesn't give you the right to rub everyone's nose in your sex life. The bar girls are fine, as long as you stay near the base. But Jennifer? That ends, right now."

"You are not yourself," Mr. Pock said. "You are teacher of SNM Academy. Be proud. Act like proud man."

After Jennifer emerged from her own special meeting with the dancing bosses, the two of us had settled on Cujully. After our last visit there together, however, I was in no hurry to arrive. We had warm coats, and the cold gray day kept the sidewalks relatively free of people as we walked along. My chest was tight with helpless rage, but I managed to speak, and even remain somewhat analytical. Jennifer, as always, was calm.

"If they could easily have fired me, I'd already be gone," I said. "They have a hard time getting Americans here. Nobody wants to come to Taegu. It does seem like they'll try to replace me and then give me the boot, though. How concerned are you about their threat to fire you?"

"I don't know," she said. "I'm their success story, because I learned English here and became a teacher. It's no secret I'm the best speaker and the most popular of the Korean teachers. It would hurt them to get rid of me."

"According to them, it hurts them to keep us," I said.

"It's hard to keep circus elephants, too," she said. "But nobody buys tickets to see dogs."

We walked past Cujully and kept going, not yet ready to go inside. "Let's go around the block again," I said. "Then you go in first. I'll wait a few minutes and come in and order something to go. I'll act like I ran into you unexpectedly."

"Sure," she said. "It's worth trying."

"We can't talk about any of this in there," I said. "Too many SNM students hang out in the place, and it's too dangerous. No relationship stuff, nothing about my landlady."

"Right," she said. We walked together the rest of the way around the block, separating a few paces from the door. "Okay, see you in a minute." I did another lap around the block.

She was seated at a table near the back when I entered the place. "Jennifer?" I said. "Is that you?"

"Oh, hi, Mark," she said. "Are you meeting someone?"

"No, I was getting a cup of this good Cujully coffee to take back to the office. I'd rather drink it here, though, actually." I realized it might be obvious that both sentences were lies. Cujully had terrible coffee made from Korean tap water, and I had no intention of drinking it, there or anywhere. Patrons bought it just to have a place to sit.

"There's a seat here," she said. "You're welcome to sit and finish your coffee."

"Oh, thank you," I said. "Are you sure it won't disturb you?"

"No, it's fine."

The music was louder than the last time we'd been there, but there were several tables nearby with nobody talking. Many of their occupants blatantly stared at us.

"My class this morning told me there are 120 boys for every 100 girls in Korea, at every age, going back for decades," I said. "This country must be starving for women."

"That's why they lock us up and watch us," Jennifer said. "If they find that one of us has escaped, they devour her."

I narrowed my eyes in a sly smile. "Impressive," I muttered quietly.

"Doctors aren't allowed to tell parents whether they're having a boy or girl," she said. "There were too many abortions. In the old days, parents would keep having kids until they got a son. A lot of people still do that, so there should be more girls than boys. I guess a lot of doctors are still telling."

"Wow," I said.

"Once when I was four, my mother was pregnant, and my aunt came to the house with this giant fish, as big as I was," she said. "A carp, I think. It was thrashing around, and they nailed it by its tail so it hung upside-down in a doorway. Then my aunt attacked it, rubbing down the fish from tail to head, bending all the scales backward, over and over again. Even at four years old, I could tell that it was really suffering, flopping and jerking in pain. After a while the scales were coated in some white stuff, like snot. My aunt scraped it off into a glass, and my mother drank it. It was supposed to make my mother have a boy."

"They thought they could determine the baby's gender after she was already pregnant?"

"Yes. I'm sure she did gross things like that during all her pregnancies. I remember thinking that it must be really important to have a son, if they would torture a fish and drink snot. I think that time with the fish was the first time I understood how unwanted I really was."

"Yeah, that'd probably do it," I said.

"That's the same aunt who forced her daughter to marry this policeman," she said. "My cousin is a few years older than my sister, and the guy my aunt made her marry is really controlling and unfriendly. Now he's a police chief in a suburb near here so my aunt is proud that she made her daughter marry into power. My cousin was just a tool to be used."

"It does seem that people get used a lot by their families here," I said. Some of the people in the crowd bristled. There were apparently at least a few Cujully customers who spoke enough English to understand. Pointing out injustices wouldn't fix anything, but it felt a little like fighting back.

That touch of a smile was on her lips again. "In college," she said, "I volunteered at an orphanage. It was mostly girls. I used to wonder how many of them were second daughters like me. The only boys in the place had physical or mental problems. I saw a lot of kids like that there, kids who couldn't walk, kids who couldn't learn. Many of those kids had parents who came to visit them and gave money to the orphanage."

"They … had parents?" I asked. "The parents didn't want them?"

"A lot of families feel they have to hide every weakness," she said. "Especially genetic things; that would hurt the other kids' chances of a good marriage. Some of the parents loved the kids and wanted to be with them, but they couldn't find anywhere to live. Koreans mostly live in complexes and tall buildings, and those places wouldn't let the children move in. The building managers were afraid prospective tenants would think there was something wrong with the building."

"But I thought Koreans couldn't mess with each other's families," I said. "It's a pretty big intrusion, deciding who can live with the family."

"Usually Koreans don't mess with each other's families," she said. "But it's really about authority. They don't interfere with a family's authority over its weaker members, but they also don't question the authority of landlords."

"Is authority always so absolute?" I asked. "Even if there's something terrible going on?"

"I think all of our maids had been beaten by their husbands. I was usually at my parents' house alone with them, so I heard a lot of stories. One of them had been unconscious in front of her building for more than a day. Nobody helped her because it was a family matter. That's how much Koreans respect the hierarchy. They'll attack strangers for doing something they think an authority figure would disapprove of, but they won't help an unconscious woman," she said.

"I've seen that, the attacking strangers part," I said. "Maybe it was better for you, growing up with maids instead of being so controlled by your parents."

"I wasn't as free with them as you may think. The maids all knew my position in the family and treated me differently from my siblings, too. When I was three or four, there was a maid who beat me and shook me all the time, and once she held me upside-down inside a well because I talked back to her. She would never have tried it with my more valued siblings."

"I'm ... so sorry," I said. "That's horrible."

"We had a new maid every year or two," she said. "They were usually young wives who had run away, and they were willing to cook and clean for almost no money, just to have a place to live. Nobody else in my family cared to know anything about them. The husbands always came to ask my mother to send their wives back to them again, and she always did.

"One was very young, though, barely out of high school. Her father was a bus driver, and he had lived alone with her. I was about twelve, and I used to go shopping for groceries with her. She got really nervous whenever we walked down the street. Her father eventually found out where she was staying. He told my mother that he needed the girl to come back, because he had nobody to do housework. The maid didn't make a sound, but her eyes were leaking tears and her whole body was shaking as her father talked, but my mother sent her back with him."

"If she was being abused, couldn't she call the police or something?"

"Police in Korea bring wives and daughters back to men who beat them all the time," she said. "It's family business, they say, not police business. The police are always on the side of whoever has power in the family, and that's never an unmarried woman. In Korea people say that a woman first obeys her father, or if he's dead then she obeys her older brother, then she obeys her husband, and then, after her husband dies, she obeys her grown son. The police support that because it's about family harmony."

"Did you ever see any of the maids again?" I asked.

"No. Except the bus driver's daughter. My mother wanted to ask if she could hire her back for a few hours a week. Maybe she felt guilty. Maybe the girl did better work than the older ones had. I don't know. She took me to visit them where they lived, in a little shack. The girl answered the door with a scarf on her head. The father called her stupid and ordered her to make tea, and then when she brought it, he pulled the scarf off. She was bald. 'Let's see her sneak out of here again now,' her father said. She sat there with us, tense and very still, and she didn't speak at all. The father turned down my mother's offer, and we left. I never saw her again."

"He had shaved her head?"

"Yes. Parents can do that, in Korea. When I was in college, I didn't understand that. There was a salon near campus, and I got my hair cut into one of those Sassoon styles, with the angle." Jennifer ran a finger near her jawline, illustrating. "When I came back to my parents' house, both my mother and father screamed at me. I went into my room. My sister was visiting from her college, and she came in and told me I was wrong to get my hair cut without their permission. 'Your body and your hair are gifts from our parents,' she said. 'You have no right to change them without their permission.'"

The two of us talked on, sharing little tidbits with our staring, sneering audience, until it was time for Jennifer to return to work.

Jennifer and I went to lunch with Leo and Karen. Chinese again, but a different place than we usually went. With them along, I thought we might resemble a more ordinary group of coworkers.

"So what's this news you said I'd like?" I asked.

"Karen is officially going to be my roommate," Leo said. "They're going to move you out to a different place. Some new guy will be your roommate when he arrives. Say goodbye to Sluggo and Sluggette forever!"

"Hey, that is good news," I said. "Was that your idea?"

"After you told me about what happened when Sluggette saw Jennifer at the house last weekend, I thought it was time to suggest it."

"And they have no problem with Karen living with you in sin?" I asked.

"I'm a dirty foreign slut," Karen said. "They don't care what I do."

"When are they moving me?"

"Dunno," Leo said. "Richard likes me, but I'm still a peon unworthy of being told much."

The restaurant was darker than the other Chinese place nearby, though still with the omnipresent yellow linoleum and plasticized tabletops. Since coming to Korea, I'd learned to appreciate darker spaces. This particular place was packed, though, which was never good for Jennifer and me. There was a short wait before a table opened up. When one did, Jennifer and I sat down across from each other, businesslike and professional. Leo and Karen squeezed in between us on one side. We both glanced quickly at the crowd before shifting slightly closer together to accommodate them.

"How did you like Seoul?" Jennifer asked.

"It was okay," Karen said. "There's a good Indian restaurant near the shopping area in *Itaewon*. It has carpet, and wooden furniture instead of this Formica stuff. Sometimes I think I'll forget what it's like to eat in a real restaurant, living here. The food was good, too, if you like Indian."

An *ajuma* came to take our order. She had no menus. "Oh," Leo said. "Okay. What should we get? I only know a few things."

"This kind of place usually only has the typical stuff all Chinese restaurants have," Jennifer said. "We could get a big order of *tangsooyook*. That's my favorite Chinese dish, and it's good to share."

"Sounds good," I said. *Tangsooyook*, the sweet and sour pork dish common to these joints, was mostly tasteless goo, but if it was Jennifer's favorite, it was good enough for me. The *ajuma* waited. Leo and Karen agreed.

"Can you help us order, Jennifer?" Leo asked. Jennifer paused, rolling her eyes as if trying to remember the words, and then haltingly told the *ajuma* what we wanted.

"It looked like you had trouble ordering." Leo said. "Is *tangsooyook* an unusual order to place?"

"No," Jennifer said. "I'm trying something new. I'm hoping that people will be nicer if I pretend to be Korean-American when I'm around you guys."

"Is it working?" Karen asked.

"Not yet. What else did you do in Seoul?"

"We went to the demilitarized zone," Karen said.

"Really?" I said. "Is it worth seeing?"

"Eh," Leo said. "I guess so. I mean, it's weird, seeing the most heavily armed border in the world. You look through this barbed wire fence, like fifteen feet high with coils of wire and razor tape, and you know there are a million live land mines there. And they tell you all this stuff, about this fake village the North Koreans have where nobody lives, with the world's tallest flagpole..."

"They said the big North Korean flag flying there weighs 600 pounds," Karen said. "And we learned about the tunnels."

"The North Koreans have been digging tunnels under the DMZ for years, apparently," Leo said. "The south has found three tunnels so far, and each one could let, like 20,000 troops—"

"30,000," Karen said. "30,000 troops per hour, through each tunnel. But why would they do that when they could just send five guys to plant chemical warheads or something?"

"Or spies," Leo said. "You know North Korea has spies all over, right? They have lots of them here in South Korea, but there are even some in the United States. In Japan, they kidnap random people off the street, take them to North Korea, and force them to teach new spies how to pass for Japanese."

"Yeah," I said. "I've heard there are hundreds of North Korean spies in the U.S. I wonder if they try the kidnapping thing there, too. Sounds like once they got the victims into North Korea, they'd never get out."

"Everywhere you go up there, you see weapons," Leo said. "They want to display them so the North Koreans see they mean business. Machine guns, tanks and giant howitzers everywhere, and those big square things with missiles in them. They kept telling us how North Korea has a million-man army right there, though. I didn't see anything that made me think they can stop a million soldiers."

"Oh, and you can't gesture at North Korea," Karen said. "You can take pictures across the border, but not point at them. Apparently the North Koreans will take that as an attack."

"That's kind of funny," I said. "One guy points and says, 'hey, look at that bird!' and a million soldiers come charging at him with bayonets, blowing up on landmines…"

"Tanks start rolling, howitzers firing," Leo said. "Yeah, it really feels like that."

"I think there really are birds there," Jennifer said. I realized I hadn't seen a bird in Taegu.

The food came. It was a huge platter with more than enough battered pork on it to feed four people, drowned in a clear, starchy sauce with a few slices of carrot and onion mixed in. Everyone took chopsticks and napkins from a tray at the center of the table, and Jennifer also collected a small shaker of red pepper, a bottle of soy sauce, and a bottle of rice vinegar. "I like to make a dipping sauce for it," she said. "Would anyone else like to try?" We all said we would. She took four little sauce dishes and put a little mound of pepper flakes into each one, then moistened them with vinegar. Then she mixed them with a chopstick into a paste, which she diluted to a liquid with soy sauce. She passed the dishes around to everyone.

Dipped in the spicy, tangy sauce, *tangsooyook* didn't taste boring at all. "I've never heard anyone in Korea say it that way," I said. "'*I like to make a dipping sauce.*' Most people I meet here say *in Korea we do this,* or *in Taegu we do that.* I think it's interesting that you didn't say it that way. Is this dipping sauce not a Taegu thing to do?"

"I think it probably is a Taegu thing to do," Jennifer said. "I don't usually say *we* do this or that. Maybe it's because I don't fit in."

"Probably," I said.

The food went fast. Leo leaned back and said he couldn't eat another bite. Karen patted his stomach. He put his arm around her. She kissed him on the cheek.

6

'd been given only one day's notice to get my stuff ready so it could be moved to the new apartment. Fortunately, most of my possessions still fit into a single suitcase. It had been two and a half weeks since Leo had told me the company had decided to get me a new apartment.

When Jennifer had returned to work after lunch, I used my extra afternoon time to check on the move's progress. I no longer had my key to the Sluggo/Slugette building, however, and the gate was locked. Slugette saw me through the bars and approached, speaking gruffly and gesturing up and down the street in a series of hostile stabbing movements that may have indicated that someone had come and gone. From her hostile tone and aggressive body language, I gathered she was blaming me for the interruption they'd caused. Leo had already shown me where the new apartment, Alice and Canada Katherine's old place, was located. It had apparently been empty since Katherine went home.

I kick-started the bike, and Sluggette raised her voice so her rant could be heard over the chainsaw buzz of its engine.

"I hope you and your husband kill each other, you horrible cunt," I said, in English.

My suitcase had been delivered to the new place, which was nearly identical to the old place. The landlady was another *ajuma* who looked like the first, but she seemed to take no particular interest in me.

Some basil plants were wilting at the top of the stairs. Canada Katherine had written her name on the terracotta pots. Basil was not used in Korea so she had probably brought seeds from home.

The new guy was already in there, sitting on the vinyl sectional, expressionless, smoking a cigarette and reading the Bible. He was probably in his late twenties, and skinny in a way that made him look deflated, with deep wrinkles in his drooping face, despite his youth.

"Hey," I said. "I'm Mark. Looks like we're going to be roommates."

"Yeah," he said. "I'm Shane."

"Did you just arrive?"

"Yeah."

"Where from?"

"Iowa City, Iowa. I just finished my MFA in creative writing there."

"Ah," I said. "I just graduated from there. That's a world-famous writing program. How'd you end up here in the 'Gu?"

"Teaching jobs are hard to find, especially in poetry."

"Mm," I said. "Well, welcome, for what that's worth."

"Thanks. It seems pretty intense, here," he said. "Teaching eight classes a day, early mornings and late nights, all different levels. This is like boot camp for teachers."

"But we get Saturdays off," I said. "Koreans think Americans are too weak to work like they do, so they don't try to make us. They even give the Korean teachers Saturdays off, I guess so they'll look like foreign experts, too. We don't work anything like regular Koreans do."

"Jesus," he said, blowing smoke. "I hope you don't mind the smoking, by the way. I can go outside, I guess, but that'll mean I'm out there all the time."

I took out my own cigarette pack and pointed at his lighter, next to the red Marlboro pack and the TV in the bay window. He nodded. I grabbed it and sat down next to him, lighting my own. "I hope *you* don't mind," I said.

"What the fuck is that?" he asked, once the smoke had hit him.

"It's a mild hallucinogen I make from banana peels," I said. "I call it Jamaican kimchee."

"It's like pot?"

"I wish. It's more like airplane glue."

"Sounds great."

"Probably not the word I'd choose," I said. "But sobriety is overrated, especially living here, as an absolute minority, in what might be the world's unfriendliest nation."

He snubbed out his Marlboro, which he had smoked right up to the filter. "You trying to make me regret coming here?"

"Nah. Koreans'll do that. Jamaican kimchee?" I offered him the pack. He took one and lit it.

"Ugh," he said, grimacing as he exhaled. "This is preferable to sobriety?"

"And, lucky you, I make enough of it to share." I nodded at the Bible, which he had set next to his cigarettes. "You a Bible guy, Shane?"

"I'm a literature guy," he said. "I didn't bring it so it can tell me how to live. I was trying to think of how to bring a lot of stories and good writing in a compact package." He took a long drag. "Lot of damned good writing in the Bible."

Jennifer and I sat in one corner of a traditional Korean tea shop. Half of the seating area consisted of mats on the floor, but we'd chosen a spot in the other half, which had tables and chairs. Along one wall were shelves with perhaps a hundred different teapots and tea sets for sale.

A surly Korean man with a shaved head appeared next to our table, dressed in bulky gray robes. He neither smiled nor spoke. Jennifer ordered for both of us, and the man turned silently away again.

"Why did you think of this place?" Jennifer asked. "He's not friendly at all."

"Yeah, but watch him," I said. "I think he's a real Buddhist monk. He's the same with everybody. My class brought me here yesterday, and I noticed he grimaces at everyone and never says a word. We're all equal in the eyes of the Scowling Monk."

Around the room were traditional black and white paintings. A few were abstract portrayals of animals like fish and tigers, but the majority were single Chinese characters. "Do you think he paints these himself?" I asked.

"I'm pretty sure he does," Jennifer said.

The paintings were unframed, done on flimsy traditional rice paper which had then been glued to a stiff scroll backing. The bottoms of most of them curled upward. "That one's my favorite, I think," I said, indicating a huge scroll bigger than a door. Its single character was comprised of lines over a foot wide. "What do you think he used to paint it? A mop?"

"Maybe."

The Scowling Monk returned. He had wide, low, bowl-like cup of plum tea for Jennifer, with a few pine nuts floating in it. I had ordered green tea, which came in a squat little cup with a lid. Inside was a ceramic strainer, containing tea leaves. Jennifer motioned for me to put the lid back on. "Leave it for a little while," she said. The monk disappeared again.

"This is an interesting design," I said "Tea for one. I should buy one of these and make tea for myself at work. Probably twenty thousand won for it, though."

"My parents are giving two of them to each guest at my sister's wedding," Jennifer said. "All handmade, ordered special. Pairs of them in little wooden boxes, with the names and the wedding day in Korean calligraphy. Would you like one?"

"Yeah," I said. "Thanks. They won't miss it?"

"They have 230 guests, but they bought extra to be safe. I think there are 250 sets of two. Nobody will notice."

"The wedding is soon, isn't it?"

"Yes. It's getting stressful," Jennifer said. "Weddings are negotiations between families. You say things like, 'When you provide a food basket for grandma to take home, make sure it has this certain type of rice cake, because that's what she likes best.' It's always back and forth, like that. His family is all businessmen, so they know how to do it. Now that they've decided to get married, my sister and her future husband go on dates together. Every time they meet, he mentions some gift he wants my parents to buy him. My mother was prepared to get expensive luxury stuff here in Taegu, but he only wants things imported especially for him."

"But they didn't negotiate for that," I said. "And I thought you said that your parents' gift to them was enough cash to buy him his own Mercury Sable, anyway."

"Yes, plus everything inside the house, like the refrigerator, stove, washing machine, and all the furniture," she said. "That was all worked out with the parents, but this is him putting pressure on my sister. It's not part of the official negotiation."

"And that's how he's spending his dates with the woman he's going to marry," I said.

"He's a businessman," Jennifer said. "He's doing his business."

"So your sister goes to your parents and says, 'He wants this, he wants that?'"

"She cries. 'It's bad enough I have to get married in Taegu,' she says. 'My wedding is already second-class, compared to my friends. You can't compare my wedding to other Taegu weddings because my friends are all from Seoul.'"

"Her friends are snobs, huh?"

"One of them got married last year to the son of the sitting president. My sister's friends are the richest, most powerful people in Korea. My family has nowhere close to that much money, but we have a prestigious family name."

"So your mother is okay with all that the groom is demanding?"

"Not okay, but she feels she has to do it. She won't talk to my sister about it but she complains to me about how obnoxious my sister and her future husband are being. It's almost over now, but it's been happening for months. They've been to Seoul for shopping three times already. Everything has to be the best in Korea, made by the most famous people who make traditional foods, clothes, teacups and all kinds of things. My sister will change clothes four times during her wedding day, and my parents have to provide Korean traditional clothes for all the groom's close relatives."

"Can you imagine if we had that money?" I asked. "Just what they're spending on your sister's wedding. We'd be set for life." I realized she might not understand the idiom. "We wouldn't have to be afraid about money again," I said.

"I would just like the two plane tickets to Hawaii," she said.

"Last day of class," I said to the Deadbeat Club. "Why so glum, chums?"

I was prepared to explain the relatively obscure words glum and chums, but the room's atmosphere wasn't conducive to silly teaching techniques.

"I got a job," Groundhog said.

"At a big bank," Paul said. "Very prestigious, very respected bank."

"Congratulations," I said. There was a long pause. "I guess you'll be working a lot."

"All the time," Groundhog said.

"We won't have our class anymore," Sarah said.

"Well, we won't see Groundhog, but I'll still be here," I said. "Anyone else coming back for the next session?"

They all shook their heads.

"It's time for everyone to go to work, or get married," Strawberry said. "Groundhog was the first to get a job, and Sarah was second."

"Sarah?" I said. "Really? Congratulations, Sarah! Where will you be working?"

"You'll still see me," Sarah said. "I will be teaching English downstairs, with your girlfriend."

"She beat me for the job," Ivy said.

"Oh, really?" I asked. "Did you interview for it, too?"

"They chose Sarah because she is prettier," Ivy said. "They said maybe I can apply again."

"None of us are coming back for the class, Mark," Strawberry said.

"I will miss you all very much," I said.

"I think it's through this door and up the stairs," Jennifer said. We had parked the bike some distance away and wound on foot through twisting, narrow paths among tin shacks to reach this ramshackle brick building. In the day's glaring sunlight, it was easy to see that most of the bricks had begun to disintegrate from age.

"Does the sign say there's a coffee shop up there?" I asked.

"No. It just says Van Gogh, but that's the name I remember."

The window in the old wooden door revealed a rickety staircase. Jennifer pushed it open and started up toward the single bare lightbulb hanging from a wire at the top. The L-shaped hall upstairs had several unmarked solid doors, but Jennifer confidently strode to one and tried the handle. "No reason to pretend to meet each other here," she said. "Nobody would believe you found this place by yourself."

It opened, admitting us to a dark, windowless room with a counter and cash register on one side. A small desk lamp illuminated the cash register, but otherwise the room had no electric lighting. Jennifer said something to the young woman behind the counter and paid, and I followed her to a table.

"What do you think?" she asked. "Dark enough for us?"

"I guess we'll see," I said. "Do you mind if I take that chair instead of this one?"

"Sure."

I scooted past her and sat down. "It's stupid," I said. "I'm sorry."

"I don't understand," she said.

"I know it'd be better for me to sit with my back to the door. I'd be less obvious that way, if nobody saw my face, but I can't do it. When I try to sit with my back to a door, I keep twisting around to see who's coming and going. I try not to, but I always end up facing completely away from the table."

"Oh," she said. "I noticed that before. I wondered what you were doing."

"I would tell you if I knew. It's this strange habit I have. I always feel like I'm about to be attacked. Did you ever get a terrible feeling of dread, like in a bad horror movie where the audience is shouting at a character, telling him not to open the door? You know something awful is about to happen, and you have to brace yourself for it. That's the way I've felt every day of my life. I feel like I need to know where everyone is so I can be ready for whatever's coming. Does that make sense?"

"Yeah," she said. "I've heard of that. It must be difficult, to feel that way.

"It's stupid," I said.

"It's not," she said. "Usually I don't notice who is around me or what they're doing. I feel safer, knowing you are so alert."

I smiled at her. "Okay," I said. "Sure, you do."

"I do. I know you understand dangerous situations. That's always good to have around."

The woman brought the coffee, in a setup that seemed better suited for a chemistry lab than a coffee shop. It was a metal frame holding a round-bottom Pyrex flask, with another flask inverted over it, forming an hourglass shape. The bottom one had water, and the top one had a screen holding dry coffee grounds. The woman lit an alcohol lamp under it and went away again, leaving us illuminated in flickering light.

"Speaking of dangerous situations," I said, "how was your visit to the American Center?"

"Okay. I got information about a few programs and found out how to register for the GRE. My TOEFL score is fine for any of the schools I saw."

SNM Junior had made Jennifer supply an official score from the Test of English as a Foreign Language in order to be considered for employment. It was the same standardized test required by graduate schools in the United States for candidates from non-English-speaking countries.

"How likely do you think it is?" I asked.

"I'm pretty sure I can get accepted to a school. I don't think it's very likely that my parents would pay for it or fly me there."

"Would they actively try to stop you from attending graduate school in the United States?"

"They wouldn't think of that," she said. "I don't have any money, so how would I do it without their approval? Now that my sister is getting married, they're already starting to focus on my brother. His marriage will be the big one, and it's going to take a lot of their energy. They might think it would make my brother look better if I had a master's degree, but even then, they'd just tell me to get one in Taegu. They already proved they can send a daughter to the United States for graduate school, so repeating that with me wouldn't get them extra points. The only reason they would accept is that it might help me marry a little better and raise our family a little higher before they find my brother a wife."

"School's worth trying, anyway," I said, without sounding particularly convincing. Every move we considered had already been blocked, not as in chess by a player of superior skill, but by a rigid system that had evolved over thousands of years. My eyes closed involuntarily, and I envisioned myself popping the top of my head off with a screwdriver and scraping black, tarry stuff—symbolizing pain, perhaps, or frustration—off of the surface of my brain.

"I didn't know it would be this hard," I said. I opened my eyes and found hers, sparkling in the blue firelight. "For either of us. This is insane, trying to spend time together in this country."

Her eyes welled with tears. "And so what are you saying?"

I reflexively grabbed her hand. "Nothing," I said. "Nothing at all. I'm not going anywhere. I love you, and you're the most important thing that has ever happened to me. Okay?"

She sat bolt upright. Her eyes darted from table to table as she slowly pulled her hand away.

I realized my mistake. My gesture might have put the two of us in danger. Nobody challenged us or called us out, though, and we both relaxed a bit. She leaned closer and said quietly, "I know you love me. I'm glad, because I love you, too."

The woman returned and extinguished the flame, removing the top flask and lifting the frame and bottom flask, into which the coffee had drained. She poured the coffee into our cups and carried the syphon apparatus and lamp away again. The service was unremarkable, which made this one of the most pleasant places we'd visited together. It was, however, terribly inconvenient to reach from our workplace.

"I want to be with you, wherever we are," I said. "But I don't know how much longer we can do this. People say love conquers all, but that's not really the way it is. An angry mob can conquer two people in love by beating them to death. Love just gives us a reason to fight like hell."

"I agree," she said.

"Graduate school could be the answer," I said. "We might be able to get loans, and we could live on campus, which isn't as expensive."

"We have to try whatever we can," she said.

"We could start tutoring, for private clients," I said. "That might get us some extra cash. Our students at SNM Academy pay a lot of money to see my little circus act."

"It would be illegal," she said.

"We have to do something," I said.

"You made pancakes?" Shane asked, emerging from his room.

"We did," Jennifer said.

"Hi, Jennifer," Shane said. "Did you stay here last night?"

"Of course not. I just got here about 20 minutes ago. It's almost noon, you know."

"Really?" Shane said.

"Here, have some," Jennifer said. She gave him a plate with the last two from the batch we'd made. I had been looking forward to them, myself, but the mix was too precious to make another batch.

"Wow," he said, moving the Bisquick box to sit down at the table. "Thank you. I didn't know I'd miss things like pancakes. They smell good." He squeezed the plastic bottle of Hungry Jack syrup onto them. "How did you get this?"

"Black market," I said.

"There's a black market in Taegu?" he asked.

"Yeah, but they're super suspicious of white boys. It's a weird conglomeration of folding tables in a ... where is it, hon? A basement?"

"Just a building, I think," Jennifer said. "I've only been there once, though, and I think it moves around."

"I remember going down some stairs," I said. "Anyway, it's dark. Most tables are walled off on three sides with black fabric, so you can only see what's on them when you're standing right there, and each only has one lamp on it. The aisles are so narrow you almost have to turn sideways to move around. I think it's intentional, to slow down cops and let the sellers escape if they get raided."

"My first illegal cuisine," Shane said. "This is great."

"We're going to ration it so it will last," I said. "It's tempting to gorge on it, but the black market's difficult to find, stressful to shop in, and expensive as hell. Mix and syrup would be about four bucks back in the States. Here I paid 15,000 won, so that's, like, $18.00."

"Jesus. How'd you even find it in the first place?"

"I was saying how I missed American foods, and one of my students said he could take me there. I gave him a ride and bought him a jar of spaghetti sauce to say thanks."

Someone buzzed the gate. "That's Leo and Karen," I said, pushing the button to admit them. "They're heading out today."

Leo lugged a giant plastic bag up the stairs. It might have been the one he'd gotten on our trip to the open market together. "Hey, guys," he said. "Hi, Jennifer. We just wanted to say goodbye, and to drop off all the stuff we're leaving behind. Better than Sluggette taking it all."

"There's some of Leo's camping stuff, like a pad to sleep on and a sleeping bag, all the pots and pans, sheets, blankets, towels, and a few dishes," Karen said. "Keep what you need and pass on the rest to whichever poor bastards move in there next."

"Sounds great," I said. "Thanks. Good luck, friends."

There was a flurry of hugs and handshakes, and Leo and Karen were gone.

"Yes, I have the knife, still," my student Ricky said in our 103 class.

"How did you get it into Korea?" I asked.

Ricky had been to New York City, he said, which was rare for someone his age. Usually, Korean males who hadn't yet performed their military service weren't allowed to leave the country. Ricky apparently came from a powerful family. Somehow he'd brought back a butterfly knife he'd bought for $15 in a pawn shop.

"I put it into my suitcase," Ricky said. "Nobody bother me."

"But they're illegal here, aren't they?"

"Illegal, yes," another student, Dominic, said. "Big trouble if you have. Ricky is lucky he is not catched."

"Caught," I said. "He's lucky he wasn't caught."

"Wasn't caught," Dominic said.

"Do you know how to work it?" I asked Ricky.

"Of course," he said.

"Do you think you're fast?"

"Yes, I am very fast."

"I'm sure you are, for a Korean," I said, goading him. Getting him to part with the knife wouldn't be terribly difficult, as long as I took it step by step.

"You think you are fast, Mark?" he asked.

"Faster than you, my friend," I said.

"I bet you 10,000 won that I am faster than you," Ricky said.

"If you win, I'll give you 10,000 won," I said. "But if I am faster than you, you give me the knife."

"No," he said. "Knife is too valuable."

"Okay, then," I said. "If you bet the knife, I'll bet 100,000 won."

"Okay."

He brought it to class with him the next day. The class judged. He was good, using the traditional swing-pivot-swing technique that brought the blade out at the top of the fist. On my turn, I swung it upside-down by the tab, making the blade appear at the bottom of my raised fist in a single motion, easily twice as fast. Ricky nodded graciously in defeat, and I flicked it closed again, slipping it into my pocket.

It was early afternoon and Jennifer was back at work. One of my 103s, Jim, had brought me to a place he knew that served real American beer. I had barely enough time for one before I had to get back and start my next block of classes.

"You see, Mark?" Jim said. "It's an American bar!"

Neither Jim, nor apparently the proprietors of the place, had ever seen an American bar. This establishment, called JaRaLa, with its pastel mint walls and dainty, modern halogen track lights, looked much more like a Korean coffee shop than any bar I'd patronized in the States. Mariah Carey's *Vision of Love* was playing on the stereo, driving home the coffee shop ambiance. The place did, however, serve Miller Genuine Draft, which I hadn't had in a long time. "It's great, Jim," I said. "Thanks for bringing me here."

Most of the seating was at little two-person tables, but they did have an actual bar, with five stools. Jim and I sat down at the bar. On the wall in front of me were palm-sized gold letters spelling out the name of the place, with some smaller, thumbprint-sized ones spelling out gibberish underneath.

The bartender, an unusually tall and angular Korean guy with hard-gelled hair and a goofy smile, came over. "An Gel!" he said, extending his hand. I shook it. He turned to Jim and said something in Korean. Jim spoke with him a little bit.

"He is one of three owners," Jim said. "Many bars have this kind of guy. His job is to drink with customers. He want everyone call him Angel, like Angel city. He ask did you go to Los Angeles."

I nodded. "Hi, Angel. I'm Mark. Yes, I have been to Los Angeles."

"He ask if this bar is like Los Angeles," Jim said.

"Um, yeah. There might be a place like this in Los Angeles." It was then that I realized the little gold English letters on the wall behind the bar actually attempted to spell something. Together the big and small letters read:

JA RA LA
JASS & RACKNROLL LASANGELS

Angel wanted to be my friend. Through Jim, he told me he wanted me to patronize his establishment, because having a real American there would make it look authentic. As Jim and I drank with him there at the bar, I learned that he was able to get all kinds of black-market American goods, not just beer, and he even had a connection who could change Korean won into US dollars at a good rate.

"Thanks, Angel," I said. "I'll definitely come back. It's nice to feel welcome."

Jennifer and I boarded the train early on Saturday morning. It was a two-hour trip each way, which meant we could have some time together in Pusan and still get her back to Taegu on time.

"This is as close to a weekend getaway as we can manage, I guess," I said, settling into our seats.

"There's no DMZ in Pusan," Jennifer said, "but let's try to have a nice time anyway."

"Yeah," I said. "I'm sure there'll be tanks and guns and stuff, in any case."

"I'm glad we're doing this," she said. "It's an adventure. I missed you last weekend." Jennifer's mother had said she needed a break from the sister's relentless wedding-related demands for attention and expenditure, and sent Jennifer to go with her, instead.

The train started rolling.

"I took my sister to a little coffee shop I used to go to sometimes in college," Jennifer said. "The owner is a nice lady who does fortune-telling as a hobby."

"The book-kind of fortune-telling, or the ghost-kind?" I asked.

"Book-kind. She looks up dates, mostly. She's the one I saw a few years ago who told me that I would be happy once I changed my name."

"Changed your name?"

"When my sister was born, my parents took her to some fortune-teller to get an auspicious name for her. They named her Ji-Young. When I was born, they just chose something to match her name, so they called me Eun-Young. This fortune-teller saw something in her book saying that the name was bad for me, and that I had to change it to be happier. I got a job at SNM Junior, and they asked me to have an English nickname, so I became Jennifer, and now I'm happier." She smiled in that way she had that seemed only to involve her eyes. It always made me want to kiss her. I sat still instead, glancing around at the other passengers.

"I wanted to ask the lady about you, but I couldn't with my sister there. I told her my sister was getting married soon, and she said she'd be happy to look them up in her book. My sister gave her both birthdates, the wedding date, and the date they got engaged. Some other stuff, too, but I don't remember it all. Then the lady looked in the book, and told my sister that all the fortune-telling was only for fun and she shouldn't pay attention to it. She tried to close the book but my sister wanted her to go ahead and tell her. The lady said my sister and her husband were a terrible match and they would cancel out each other's energy, making each other weak and unhappy."

"So I guess the matchmaker didn't consult the same book, huh?" I asked.

"I guess not. My sister acted like she didn't believe in it, but I could tell it upset her."

"My class took me to a fortune-teller once," I said. "She told me I had to stay in Korea because there was something really important I had to do."

"So you stayed in Korea, because of a fortune-teller?"

"No. I stayed because I couldn't afford a plane ticket. But it was nice to hear that there was some reason to be here. And then you and I went out for my birthday."

It was an enjoyable and uneventful train ride to Pusan. Nobody bothered us. Trying to decide where to go once we got there was difficult, however. There were shopping areas and nice restaurants, but upon discussing it we decided it wasn't worth inviting the harassment those areas tended to bring. We ended up down by the docks, which looked a lot like the sleazy areas next to the military bases back in

Taegu, except that the signs were mostly in Russian instead of English.

"I heard a lot of Russian sailors come to Pusan," Jennifer said. "It's their favorite port."

I bought a pair of shoes, a box of tea, a pair of black plastic wrap-around sunglasses, and a pair of fingerless leather gloves for riding the bike. Jennifer bought some socks. We hid out in some dark bar full of Russian sailors.

"This isn't any better than Taegu, but at least we tried," I said.

Jennifer had a schedule card from the train station. "We can take an earlier train back to Taegu," she said.

"Yes, let's do that."

At the train station, a group of five young men jostled roughly past us. "Ooh, baby!" one said, in drawn-out, mocking, bad English. "I love you!"

He grabbed her ass.

The world came into hyper-focus. I would never fix this place, but I could fix this guy. All this awful shit would continue to exist, but I could ensure that this one asshole would not. Slowly I slid the knife out of my back pocket, keeping it folded and hidden in my fist.

Jennifer didn't grab me or even touch me. She did not stand in my way. There was only her voice, coming from somewhere beside me, parting the fog.

"Please don't let these turds take you away from me."

I stayed frozen a moment, then slid the knife back into my pocket. They moved on.

Jennifer and I made the train and it rolled out of the station.

"So much for Pusan," I said. "I don't think we'll be coming back here."

As it turned out, we would soon be desperate to return to Pusan.

It was another first day of class. A 104. The students were introducing themselves to me by their nicknames—the usual array of professions, baptismal names, and hobbies—until one student introduced himself as Shutter Man. The class laughed.

"What's funny about the name Shutter Man?" I asked the class.

"My wife is pharmacist," Shutter Man said.

"Your wife is *a* pharmacist," I said.

"Ah. Yes. My wife is a pharmacist. We have a small pharmacy."

"And are you also a pharmacist, Shutter Man?"

"No," he said. "I am shutter man."

"Hmm," I said. "I think you might mean that you are *a* shutter man, here. You weren't saying shutter man as a name that time, right? You were saying that you are *a* shutter man, whatever that is. It's a job?"

The class laughed again.

"Best job in Korea," one of the other men said.

"Koreans say best job is having wife who is pharmacist," another said. "In the morning, you open the door." He acted as if he were raising an overhead door. "Wife work all day, then in the nighttime, you shut the door. We say he is shutter man."

"I see!" I said. "So, Koreans say that *the* best job is being married to a pharmacist, and opening and shutting the door."

"Yes," someone said.

"So, pharmacists are the best husbands and wives to have?" I asked.

"Only pharmacist wife is like this," one said. "If woman marry pharmacist, she still have baby, cook, clean the house, like that."

"Oh, so it's only when a man marries *a* pharmacist that he can be a shutter man," I said. "There are no shutter women. I see."

I leaned toward him and gave Shutter Man a comically dramatic raised-eyebrow, Groucho-Marx-esque sideways look. "So tell me, Shutter Man, my good friend," I said. "Can you get me a gigantic bottle of Valium?" I smiled, returning to the front of the little room. "What do I mean when I say gigantic, class?"

"Really, really big," someone said, pronouncing it *beeg*.

"Yes! Like a giant." I spread my arms out, miming a few big steps. "Fee fi fo fum, I'm a great big giant." I mimed picking up an insect. "Hello, little human, I am going to eat you!" I mimed dropping the tiny human into my mouth. "Mmm, humans." I rubbed my stomach. Turning back to him, I asked, "So, Shutter Man, my good friend. Can you get me a gigantic—that is, like a giant—bottle of Valium?"

Shutter Man smiled and played along, giving me a quick nod. "Yes," he said.

I clasped my hands over my heart, looking up at the ceiling. "My hero," I said. "Now, class, tell me more about why it's always the woman's job to raise the children."

They told me all about the woman's duty to be a wife and mother. It was the same discussion I'd had with classes, probably eight or nine times by this point. Each discussion was nearly identical. Each time, a few students insisted that women with jobs were selfish and made their husbands look like they couldn't support their families. As with every other class to have discussed the topic, this one had a student who explained, kindly and slowly, to me, the foreigner who would not otherwise guess: "In Korea, mothers love their children."

"He says that this is the one you want, if you need to be able to record messages," Jennifer said.

We were standing in a tiny electronics store, the kind common in Korea, with a brightly lit front window jammed full of glittering electronic crap, mostly Samsung, and more of it stacked to the ceiling inside. Next to the cash register on the counter at the back was a board with various pagers attached to it. There was a model that merely beeped or vibrated, a model that allowed callers to leave a number that would be displayed digitally across the top of the pager, and a model that had all the features of the others but also allowed the leaving and retrieval of voice messages.

"Are you sure you want to do this?" she asked. The slight tremor in her voice was barely noticeable, but Jennifer was not easy to rattle. In this case, that was to be expected, though. In spite of her intelligence and her independent spirit, Jennifer had been sequestered for all her life. She'd never committed a crime before.

"We need the money," I said. "Or we'll never get out of here."

She filled out the paperwork, using Katherine's name, spelled out in Korean *hangul*, and our office address and phone.

Shutter Man had brought me a gigantic bottle of Valium. It was the size of a pickle jar, and brand new.

Julie, a teacher from the UK who had previously hung around mostly with David and Sue, had wanted to try it. "Let's go shopping on it!" she'd said. "Like 'Mother's Little Helper.'" David and Sue had completed their contracts the month before, and the coming weekend was to be Julie's last before she returned home as well.

The entire basement of the upscale newly-constructed Dongdaegu Department Store sold gourmet groceries. Now Julie and I were browsing around, drugged into a nice, comfortable state, with Jennifer making sure nothing bad happened to us while we were incapacitated. Jennifer and I drew the same old stares, the same murmuring comments.

"Are people always this shitty to you two?" Julie slurred.

"Yeah," I said.

"Always," Jennifer said.

"That's awful," Julie said. "Fucking people!" She sneered at a few staring housewives nearby.

"We're used to it," Jennifer said.

"We find tranquility however we can," I said.

"Valium is nice," Julie said.

"Beats the hell out of banana peels," I said.

For the second Saturday night in a row, Jennifer and I went to JaRaLa. Both times, Shane had come to meet me there when she went back to her parents' place at 9:00.

"You did exactly the same thing when she left last week," Shane said.

"What?" I said.

"You walked to the door and watched her as she waited for a taxi. Then you sat with a white-knuckle grip on your beer, staring at the street with your jaw locked. It's sweet that you miss her, but, I mean, Jesus, man."

"But you must know why I'm like this," I said. "I'm sure you hear it in your classes. Don't they tell you those not-so-funny jokes about kidnapping and rape? Since she's a young woman, Jennifer is constantly watched and monitored, and most of the country feels that strangers are entitled to severely punish her for indiscretion. She works for our school, so there are hundreds of people out there, strangers to her and to me, who know who we are. They talk to each other. She might be in serious danger right now, just because some-one saw us walking down the street together. That's where she lives, all the time. That's what she returns to when-ever she goes away, and it's more dangerous than ever now because of me."

"Yeah, but there are rapist assholes everywhere," Shane said. "It's not an exclusively Korean problem."

"True, there are rapists everywhere," I said. "But here it *is* different. It's structured. It's ... *institutional*. In Korea, it's about the entire society, the way it functions, not just some guy attacking her. Koreans have been constantly invaded, looted, kidnapped, raped, and starved, for hundreds of years, and this society developed in that environment, with no room for error. Everything is about making the family stronger, bracing for the next famine or invasion or whatever, and they're all threatened by anything that might rock that boat. They punish every little variance, and you and I are huge, glaring variances here. We're invaders."

"Oh, I see, and they think you're an invader, taking her against her will," Shane said.

"No, not against her will. Against *their* will. The collective values of the society are more important than her will. What she wants is irrelevant."

"Even regarding her own life?"

"Yes. They say their interest in how she runs her life is more important than her interest in running her life. From their perspective, I am stealing her from *them,* especially from her parents."

"And so they treat you like a criminal."

"I'm used to being treated like a criminal, Shane," I said. "I'm used to being excluded and feeling unwelcome. I've been a hoodlum my whole life. They want to tell me I'm stealing her? Fuck it. Okay, I'm stealing her."

"Just marry her and take her home, then, Mark," Shane said. "Fuck the contract."

"Can't afford it. With my savings so far, I might be able to buy two tickets to the States, though I doubt it. Even if I could get us there, we have nothing, and nowhere to stay. I have to be able to pay for tickets, first month's rent, and a security deposit, even if we don't need a car. I have to complete the contract, get that return plane fare and that other couple of grand that'll pay for her ticket. I need to save cash, like she's saving her insulting salary, so we'll be able to rent a place. I'm going to need to land a job there before I can even sign a lease. Or maybe we can apply to grad schools. I don't know."

"Wow," he said. "Speaking of money, how's the tutoring going?"

"It's my first attempt at teaching elementary school kids. They haven't made up their minds about me," I said. "They're not sure whether I'm more like a father or a birthday clown. I have to keep them entertained so they'll talk, because I know their mom listens outside the door, but that leads to me being treated like entertainment. I need this job, and if mommy hears them screeching and talking to each other in Korean, I'll be gone. I have one trick, though. When they start to get wild, I start talking in a John Belushi, angry-samurai voice. I put my chin down and puff up my chest and kind of growl in a low tone. Then I start my sentences with long, drawn-out sounds and then rush everything together at the end. *Whaaaat doooo you think-you-are-DOING!* Like that."

"That scares them? I don't think their fathers actually talk like that."

"It was the best impression of an Asian authority figure I could manage," I said.

"They don't find it funny?" he asked.

"No. They totally buy it. Simmer right down."

"How many do you have now?"

"Two sets of kids and one group of college guys. If you ever do this, don't tutor college brats. At a Korean school, they're in class with a bunch of other people, and it's run by Koreans so they feel like they have to be sort of civilized. When it's just a group of their friends in a coffee shop, they're fucking awful. Today one of them pinched the hair on my arm and said *'Hairy, like animal, ha, ha, ha!'*"

"I wouldn't do what you're doing for all the dogs in Korea," Shane said. "Do you know what they'll do to you if they catch you?"

"I don't."

"Well, you know our visas don't allow it," he said. "And Richard and Mr. Shin have repeatedly warned us against doing it since we got here."

"They don't want the competition," I said. "Doesn't matter, man. I need the cash."

"Have you figured out what to do about the visa?" Shane asked. "You know SNM isn't going to renew your contract."

"If I even last there until this contract ends, that is," I said. "I'm working on some ideas."

"You don't have much time left to figure it out," he said, shaking his head. "Everything you do here is so damned scary."

"It's what I have to do."

"You've got posters all over. There's no way to know who is calling. If one of them turns out to be a cop, you're fucked." He lowered his voice. "I don't envy you, my friend, living on the wrong side of the law in South Korea."

"Not easygoing people, Koreans," I said.

The Scowling Monk brought the tea. It was jasmine, this time, made in a tiny terracotta teapot. First, he set down what appeared to be a ceramic casserole dish, except that it had glazed latticework across the top. At the center of the lattice, he placed the little teapot, shaped like a miniature version of Aladdin's lamp. He opened the lid, the size of an American quarter, and poured hot water over the dry tea leaves inside. After waiting a moment, he poured the water out the spout and through the lattice.

"He's rinsing the tea, to get rid of bitterness," Jennifer said.

The Scowling Monk filled it again, put the lid in place, and then poured hot water over the pot. It steamed up around the teapot from under the lattice. He left more hot water for refills and disappeared. Jennifer and I watched the steam swirling up and around the pot as it steeped.

"So, tell me about the wedding," I said.

"I'm exhausted," she said. "Two days before the ceremony, my mother asked me what I was going to wear. I showed her some things in my closet but she said they weren't good enough. She had to get me something out of my sister's closet."

"With all they negotiated for, I would have thought they'd demand clothes for you."

"I think they forgot. The wedding took all day, and I had to wear this designer original skirt suit made for my sister, who is fatter than me, so I kept getting poked by pins. The wedding had three separate parts. The first was a church-style ceremony, where my sister had a white dress with that part that drags on the floor."

"A train, I think it's called," I said.

"Train. Right. That part took more than an hour. Then they had to change into Korean *hanbok* for the traditional Korean part where they bow to the relatives. The bride and groom have to bow all the way down, get on their knees, and put their heads to the floor, in front of all these people who come sit in chairs in front of them. Then they have to get up again every time, because the people they bow to are higher status so they can't stay seated when they come in."

"That sounds exhausting."

"My sister had two friends dress in *hanbok*, too, and they helped her stand up all those times. It's supposed to be the younger sister's job, but she wanted her fancy friends to do it instead. It usually takes two to three hours to bow to everyone, but people from the groom's family kept coming up, wanting to be bowed to, so we had more than four hours of that. The guests were all at the reception, eating expensive food and drinking the whole time. Then my sister and her husband changed clothes again, into suits, and went to see everyone at the reception. After that, they changed again into travel clothes and went to their honeymoon in Hawaii. They'll be there for a week, and then move into his parents' house."

"I thought his parents bought them a house," I said. "Wasn't that part of the negotiation, that his parents bought the couple a house in the fancy part of Seoul, *the Korean Beverly Hills*?"

"Yes, but it's empty now. First they have to move in with his parents. My sister has to wake up at three in the morning to make breakfast for his parents every day, and wait outside their door with a tray and her forehead on the floor until they wake up and take it from her."

"How long will she do that?"

"Until they tell her to stop it. Maybe a few days or a few weeks."

"Korean weddings don't sound like much fun," I said. "In America, they tell girls that their wedding day will be the happiest day of their lives."

"That's what they say here, too. But it's supposed to be bad if the couple smiles on their wedding day, so they're always really serious, with no expression."

"Let me guess," I said. "If they smile on their wedding day, they'll have a daughter."

"Yes. I think that's it."

Shane came back from a weekend trip to Cheju Island, which students had told me was "Korea's Hawaii." A connection of his from the Iowa Writers' Workshop had arranged a meeting for him with a prominent writing professor at the university there.

"How was your tropical vacation?" I asked.

"Cheju is about as tropical as St. Louis, but whatever," he said. "They hired me. I'm going to miss you."

"Congratulations," I said. "When do you leave?"

"My flight is tomorrow afternoon at 2:18. I'm here to pick up a few things, and that's it, man." He went into his room, sifting through his few possessions. "Here," he said. "I got this at a bookstore near Taegu University a while ago. It was the only book the store had in English and I was sick of the Bible. You can have it."

The book was two inches thick: *The Edgar Allan Poe Anthology.*

"Thanks, man," I said. "I'm going to miss you, too.

Then Shane was gone. He had lasted exactly two months.

A few weeks later, Korean Lurch showed up at the apartment with Michael, a new arrival, who dragged in two suitcases. One was full of clothes, and the other contained vitamins, a velvet bag of crystals (which he later placed in strategic locations around the apartment to channel energy), and a juicer. Michael both looked and talked like a taller, pudgier version of magician Doug Henning, except that his hair and mustache were closely trimmed. When he talked, he tended to draaaaw ouut his worrrrds like Henning used to do when he talked of the "worrrld of illuuuusion." He had eyes that always seemed wide open, and a perpetual half smile that should have been creepy, but wasn't, because his demeanor was so non-threatening. He offered me the use of his juicer. I offered him some Valium and explained the black bananas in jars, which I continued to process in anticipation of the day the Valium ran out.

7

We were back at the Van Gogh, illuminated by the alcohol lamp beneath the coffee syphon. The hot water had flowed from the lower flask into the upper part with the coffee grounds. It boiled and churned, cycling the little specks of coffee around and around.

Even this hidden coffee shop had someone at nearly every table. "One thing I'll never get used to in Korea is the population density," I said. "In terms of area, Taegu is about the same size as Des Moines, which is a city near my hometown, but Taegu has ten times the population. To me it feels kind of suffocating. The fact that everyone lives on top of each other is probably one reason the society has evolved to be so strict. Koreans need more rules, because every individual's behavior can impact so many others."

"I agree," Jennifer said. "Being so crowded is an important part of why Korea is this way. The Americans I have known seem to believe that they are free because they decided to be free. They think they can teach Koreans how to be like them, but it isn't that simple."

"It's obvious to me that Americans can be freer because we have more space and more resources," I said.

"Yes," Jennifer said. "And invaders have come again and again to take what Korea does have. Koreans had to learn to sacrifice individual interests for stability. Freedom isn't some skill people need to learn."

"All over the world, resources keep dwindling as it gets more crowded," I said. "Other places are becoming more like Korea. We're not stuck in the past, here. This is the *future*."

The coffee shop woman smothered the fire and poured the coffee.

"I think you're right," Jennifer said. "The whole world will follow the Korean example someday. Now I'm depressed."

We hid in the Van Gogh's relative peace for a long time. Eventually, we got tired of sitting in the dark and went back out into the day.

We made our way through the warren of shitty little shacks and had nearly reached the main street, when Jennifer's shoulder came slamming backward into my chest like she had been launched from a giant howitzer. I ended up partially backed into a doorway.

"What—"

"Let's stay here a minute," she said.

"Okay," I said. "Why?"

"I saw a relative. She was across the street. I don't think she saw us, but if she did, she'll definitely tell my mother about you. She's probably already gone, but let's wait."

"What relative is she? Like an aunt or something?"

"She's my ..." Jennifer's voice trailed off as she thought. "My mother's brother's wife's ... brother's wife."

In my mind, I tried to map out that relationship. "How do you even know who that is?" I asked.

"In Korea, we know."

"So, everywhere we go, we have to watch out for the possibility that some distant relative will pass us on the street?"

"Yes. I think her family might have a business near here. We can't come back to the Van Gogh again."

"Hey, Eric," I said. "Did you say you were getting your hair cut today? I'd like to get mine cut more like yours. Would you mind if I tagged along?"

Eric, another SNM Academy teacher, had been U.S. Army Airborne before college, and still looked the part. "I thought you liked to keep it longer so the Koreans can tell you're not military," he said.

"Didn't help," I said. "They treat me the same. Anyway, I've been spending more time down by the American bases, lately. I'm going to stand out in Korea no matter what I do. Might as well fit in somewhere."

"Mine's not regulation, you know," he said. "But I have a guy who cuts it like this without me having to explain what I want, now."

"Great. That's all I want. Well, that, and I'm also hoping you can show me what the ranks look like so I don't piss off the wrong people."

"Most'll be in civilian clothes off base, but sure, I can do that."

"Hello, New Clip!" I said. "How are you today, my friend?" New Clip and I had encountered each other on the back staircase again, but this time New Clip wasn't smoking. He appeared to have been waiting for me.

"I'm fine, thank you, and you?" he responded, in the rote, monotone, Korean way. "Mark, I want to talk to you about Jennifer."

"Oh?"

"Mark, Jennifer is from a good family. What you are doing is wrong. You must leave Jennifer alone."

To amuse them, I had informed my early morning 102 class that I knew how to cook, since I'd held a few shitty restaurant jobs while I was in college. As a general rule, men did not cook in Korea, so the class had been intrigued by this news, as well as the concept of having separate, special foods exclusive to the morning. Soon the students were volunteering to bring in dishes, utensils, and napkins. "My office is across this street," the Old Man in this particular class announced. "Mark can cook there."

Fine.

Over lunch, I'd driven back to my neighborhood to purchase and assemble the necessary materials, like eggs, pan and spatula, and even a few loaves of a bread so spongy and nutritionally deficient that it rivaled American white bread. The next morning, I realized it was too much to carry on the bike. Because getting a taxi was an uncertain proposition, I started walking toward work by 5:00 in the morning, with heavy plastic bags in each hand. No taxi stopped, so I had to walk the entire 45-minute trip.

Old Man had said he was a doctor. The oily, fishy odor of his office made me wonder if perhaps he was a traditional herbal medicine doctor, who perhaps had a hangover cure he could administer to me at that moment. "No, I'm an MD," he said. "My practice is limited to proctology."

I made a few sample eggs; scrambled, over-easy, and over-hard, and some toast, which I made in a dry pan. I tried to explain what American bacon was like. I had estimated breakfast for 16 people, but failed to consider that people trying new foods from other countries tend not to eat much. This turned out to be especially true when they were sampling greasy fried eggs using metal chopsticks in a fishy-smelling proctology office.

Jennifer had scheduled me for a tutoring gig that after-noon, so I had to miss lunch with her. When I returned to the school, there was a big poster on an easel in the lobby. It had my coworker Ryan's picture on it, and announced that he would be the new director at SNM Junior, which would be moving to a new, separate location as soon as construction was finished. Ryan was Richard's favorite teacher because he could speak Korean and had no plans ever to return to the UK, so the choice of director was not surprising. A student translated the Korean for me, and I learned the new SNM Junior location would be out by Susung Moat. It was the first any of us had heard of it. Korean Lurch would be transferring there, too, so at least he would be out of my face. Jennifer, however, would be far away. There would be no more lunches together.

A little after 10:00 that night, I was again carrying heavy plastic bags in each hand, heading back to my apartment. I hadn't even looked for a taxi. I passed a line of closed and darkened storefronts, sealed behind heavily padlocked rolling overhead doors or rusty accordion-fold latticework. A lone bulb left on inside a store gave off enough light to reveal my non-Korean face to four drunken young men, who took an interest in me. When I tried to step around them, they moved back in front of me.

I set down the bags and stood, holding my frying pan in one hand and tapping it once against my other palm.

Everyone froze for a moment, and then they continued on down the street, shouting insults to prove that I hadn't intimidated them.

At the apartment, Michael turned from the TV. "Took you a while," he said. "Bike broke?"

"Couldn't take it. Had these." I set down the bags.

"Ah." On the screen, a nervous-looking guy stalked around, shoplifting from the base PX as the Police song *I'll be Watching You* played. "Heh. This was on last weekend, when Joon-ho was here. He asked me, 'Why army must tell soldiers do not steal?'"

"Oh, no," I said. "That high school kid from downstairs again? Look, man, I don't need another landlady sniffing around in my business, okay?"

"Mark, I'm telling you, it's better to be on friendly terms."

"Landladies are a serious threat," I said. "You don't know because you're still fresh from the world. They are nosy and they meddle. They can get us fired and kicked out of the country. They can get Jennifer fired. If any of those things happen, I'll never see her again. Don't fuck around with the landlady or her family. Please."

"No, no. I'll show you what I mean, okay? The son told me his mother wanted to know about Jennifer. 'She worries for her parents,' he told me."

"Yeah!" I said. "See? This is the kind of shit I don't want them poking around in!"

"I told him you're both orphans," Michael said.

"What?"

"I said, 'Oh, you mean that girl who comes to visit sometimes? She has no parents. She has no parents, and Mark has no parents. That's why they are friends.'"

I shook my head. "What … ?"

"Then he came over here," Michael said. "He pointed to your jars of black, slimy bananas, and made a face. 'Those are Mark's,' I said. 'Mark is from Iowa City. That's the way they like bananas in Iowa City.'"

I laughed. "Michael," I said. "I'm glad you're here."

The new single office/workroom was full of teachers doing last-minute prep work before the afternoon block of classes began in 20 minutes. There was more space than there had been before, since the SNM Junior teachers had moved out, but the noise level hadn't diminished much. Most of the SNM Junior teachers were local Koreans, and their behavior was more subdued than that of their foreign counterparts at SNM Academy. I sat at my desk, leafing through the *Korea Herald*.

The paper had printed a picture of its annual English-language speech contest winner, a 16-year-old high school girl, along with her essay arguing that Koreans should never marry non-Koreans. In it, she assumed that all parents on all sides would be horrified by such a union, and insisted that anyone marrying outside his or her own race was selfish, reckless, and childish. Further, the girl argued that since their children would never be accepted by either culture, interracial couples were negligent parents, even before they had kids. She urged such couples to grow up and become more responsible.

Reading it felt like someone was trying to drown me. I wanted to thrash, to fight, to do something to set them all straight, but there was nothing to do. I didn't even have a coworker with whom I could discuss the article or commiserate about the persecution we felt. The next class was another *fuck you* vibe class.

I washed down another Valium with some lukewarm green tea and went to the back stairs to smoke.

"I wasn't seeing you much on work days, anyway, now that I'm tutoring all the time," I told Jennifer over the phone.

"I know. It's no fun staying here with my sister, though," Jennifer said.

Because the last term had ended before the new building was ready, SNM Junior had been forced to postpone the start of classes. Since the school found itself paying teachers to do nothing, the leadership had decided to mandate the teacher training in Seoul that Jennifer was supposed to have taken when she'd been hired. She had arrived in Seoul the previous day, Saturday, and this was the first opportunity she'd had to call me. The training schedule and the proximity of her family meant we wouldn't get another chance to talk before the next weekend, when I would be visiting Seoul.

"Tell me all about it," I said.

"My sister's toad-faced husband is back here in Seoul now," Jennifer said. "He just got back from some business trip overseas."

"Where'd he go?"

"He doesn't tell her. She never knows where he goes, and she usually doesn't even know when he'll be home. Most of the time my sister is here alone with two maids, who she calls stupid and lazy all the time."

"Couldn't she ask him?"

"Koreans say that it would be disrespectful to demand more information than the husband wanted to give. My sister thinks it's not her place to know his business, anyway."

"A year ago that would have surprised me, but not anymore," I said.

"Yesterday, he was lying on the couch, watching TV. I was in the kitchen, and I heard him start yelling my sister's name. She was in the shower. He kept shouting for her. She ran out, in a bathrobe with a towel around her head. She stood there, dripping on the marble floor in front of him, and said, 'Yes, husband?' He shifted his position to see the TV behind her. 'Bring me an ashtray,' he said."

"He sounds charming," I said.

"She deserves it. When she went to college here in Seoul, she stayed with our cousin, who was a modern Korean career woman. She worked at some British bank and I think she made a lot of money, for a woman in Korea. She would wake early, make breakfast, wash the dishes, and take a bus for an hour to work, work all day, and then come home and make dinner. Once when my sister was staying there, our cousin bought a bowl of prepared fish to make into soup. It wasn't a packaged meal, but just different kinds of fish and shellfish, skinned and opened and ready to cook. She still had to add vegetables and spices. Her husband found out she'd bought the seafood that way and shouted at her, saying if he wanted to eat mass-produced food he would've gone to a restaurant. My sister told my family the story when she came back from Seoul, because to her it was a big scandal. They all agreed that my cousin was wrong for buying it."

"So, do you get along with this guy at all?"

"I don't try. Before they married, he told my sister that he hates chicken. He said that if he came home and smelled chicken cooking, he would turn around and leave again. I've already brought takeout chicken here once. I know he also hates it when I wear shorts because it's not modest—he's like Mr. Shin's friend who stomped on the woman's sandals. Every evening when I come back from work, I change into shorts."

"But why doesn't he stomp on you? He sounds like a guy who would try to fix your behavior."

"He still has to worry about what my parents think."

"Why? He got your sister. They're married, and she can't ever leave. Why not do whatever he feels like?"

"He's the oldest son. My family is more prestigious than his. He can do whatever he wants to my sister, but if he convinces my family he's a bad guy, my family is powerful enough to lower his family's reputation, and his younger siblings won't marry as well. His family has money, so they got to marry up to my sister. He has to behave."

"Except when he's calling your sister out of the shower," I said.

"That was like making a dog roll over," Jennifer said. "He brought her out to show me that she'll do whatever he says. If I tell my parents about that, they'll think he's being a good husband, taking control of his wife. It's not the same with me."

"So you're tormenting him because you can get away with it."

"No, not just that. Also because he's a liar. Before the wedding, he and his parents told my family that they would support my sister to get a Ph.D. in America. He said he'd buy her a better violin, some fancy one like famous concert players have, and he would set up a room in their house so she could practice for auditions to get back into graduate school. Now she's married to him and all those promises are gone. There's no violin, no practice room, and no more talk of going to the United States."

"But it's your sister," I said. "I would think it might feel good for you to see her experience a little disappointment, for once."

"I had to sacrifice my whole life so that she could be at the top of the marriage market," Jennifer said. "Now she's married to this guy who lies and cheats. That's all my sacrifice was worth, to get her this ugly, dishonest man. I asked him about those promises when I got here, and he had no answer. I'm going to keep asking forever."

"That's a hell of a way to start a marriage, lying to her like that," I said. "Won't your parents hold that against him like they would if he did something to you?"

"Technically, he didn't break the promise. As long as my sister is still alive, he has time to give her all of that, even though in reality she's losing her talent every day she just sits here. Everything he promised to give my parents was due at the time of the wedding, and he delivered those. These things I'm bugging him about were just for my sister, who is now his property. My parents gave her up completely when he married her, so they don't get to complain about what he does with her, including breaking promises to her that he made before the marriage. Complaining would look like they don't know their place. For me, it's different. I look concerned about my sister."

"And at the same time, you're pointing out to her that you were right about this guy all along," I said. "Korean society has so much going on beneath the surface. It's interesting to watch you navigate all of it. Oh, and speaking of navigation, I'll get into Seoul around mid-afternoon on Saturday, according to my train ticket."

"You're still going to stay in *Itaewon*?" she asked. "You don't have to, you know. It's like the places near the military bases in Taegu."

"Yeah, I know. Dirty and sleazy, American G.I.s, whores, and Korean thugs. But it's cheap. If you were staying with me, I'd check into the Hyatt or someplace. Hey, maybe we could meet at the Hyatt when I'm in Seoul. I'm sure they have a bar. A place with international clientele like that would have to treat us decently."

"I can take a taxi there. I've seen it, right downtown. Maybe five o'clock? We'll have a couple hours before I have to be back to my sister's."

"Great! That'll give me time to find a *yogwan* and check in. I'll meet you at the Hyatt bar at five on Saturday."

"I will be there."

"When does your training start?"

"Six tomorrow morning. I'm observing a class. We were supposed to prepare a—"

The line went dead. Even if I'd had the number, I wouldn't have been able to call her back. My phone didn't ring again.

It was now early July of 1994, and my year-long contract would be ending soon. It was already clear that SNM Academy did not want me back for a second year, and my visa would expire with the contract. I had to figure out a way to stay in Taegu, when all I really wanted to do was take Jennifer away with me. The need to escape was at odds with the need to stay with her, and the disconnect was making my head hurt.

The military bases were too far away from SNM Academy for them to be practical lunch destinations when Jennifer was around, but they were fine for my longer lunch break alone. With Jennifer in Seoul, this was my chance to dine with other Americans, so I had chosen to visit a little food stand just outside Camp Henry. It had a total of four tables, plus a shelf along one side where people could stand, like I was doing, when the tables were full. It mostly served the cheap, nasty, deep-fried stuff that old ladies sold from carts downtown, like fish cakes and hot dogs, always on sticks. The menu had a few items that could almost be called food, like omu-rice, which was a thin shell of scrambled egg filled with a scoop of fried rice and drizzled with ketchup, but for the most part it was all toxic garbage.

Only idiots would eat here.

With one hand, I fumbled with the strap of the neck pouch ID holder I'd bought at a little shop a few doors down. It was black nylon with a clear plastic window the size of a standard military ID, and it was now pressed against my shirt under my tie. Inside were my Iowa driver's license and my green SNM Academy ID card, which was handwritten in Korean and included a black-and-white photo of me. On the shelf in front of me was the plastic bag I'd gotten when I'd bought it, still containing the other ID holder I'd acquired at the same time.

The *ajuma* brought me my meal of Korean ramyun, which was basically ramen noodles with hot sauce.

A table opened up and I snatched my bag and hard plastic bowl of steaming soup, splashing it over my thumb as I scrambled for one of the chairs. I held a napkin to the stinging thumb.

"Can we sit with you, sir?" a young man said. There were two of them, in civilian clothes, but both were clearly new recruits, probably not yet out of their teens. I nodded and gestured at the seats across from me. They nervously sat down, and I realized my clothing might be contributing to their deference to me. I was probably the only white guy they'd seen wearing a suit in Korea. This was good to know.

"Is this place any good, sir?" the other one asked, sitting down directly in front of me. "I haven't been here before."

I gave him a knowing smile. "New here, huh?"

It was a safe bet. There were only about a dozen of these stands selling to soldiers outside the American bases in Taegu, and this one was closest. Americans never ventured beyond these few streets.

"Yessir," the other one said, sitting next to him. "Both of us."

I looked at them sideways, feigning doubt about my own words. "Not DOD are you?" It was the only thing I knew to ask that would make me sound like I belonged.

"No, sir," the one directly opposite me said sheepishly. "We're both privates."

"Mm, that's what I figured," I said. "I'm supposed to have some new people working with me soon, is all." I poked at the ramyun, hoping to make it appear as if there were few noodles left while leaving the mass of them submerged. They introduced themselves as Troy and Jamie. I gave them my real first name.

The *ajuma* brought their food. They had each opted for cheese ramyun, a dish created exclusively for Americans who didn't realize there was no such thing as Korean food with cheese. It was the same bowl of greasy noodles in spicy water, but with a whitish slice of artificial American cheese floating on top of it. Troy jabbed the cheese with chopsticks, separating it into globs that bobbed like Crisco in dishwater.

"You work here at Camp Henry, sir?" Jamie asked.

"Can't tell 'ya," I said, rolling my eyes. "OPSEC."

"Ha!" Troy said. "Always OPSEC."

"I'm glad for all that," I said. "Really, my job's boring and stupid, and I'd be embarrassed because it's so completely non-Rambo. Instead, I get to say I can't tell you because, you know, OPSEC. Now I sound mysterious."

We had a nice conversation about the silliness of AFKN commercials, the dirtiness of the establishment in which we were dining, hometowns, and other trivia. It was my second such lunch that day.

Jennifer and I both had the code to get phone messages from the pager, so at least we could communicate that way. She had kept the actual pager, so she could still get notifications and arrange my tutoring appointments from Seoul.

"Hi, it's me," her message said. She had probably left it over her lunch time. There were traffic noises in the background. "Sorry I had to hang up. My brother-in-law came into the room. Later, he told my sister he'd heard me speaking English on the phone. I don't know if it will become an issue, but I shouldn't call you from her house again.

"Remember that you are meeting a new tutoring client tomorrow at 2:00, in front of the Ariana Hotel. She drives a silver Sonata and she'll honk at you. Follow her on your motorcycle. She and a neighbor lady will have their kids together for you to teach at an apartment.

"I'll leave messages when I can. I love you."

I called the pager number again, this time to leave a message.

"Hi, it's me," I said. "I'm glad you're okay. Do me a favor, would you? Paint your toenails red and let your sister's husband see them. If he thinks he has something on you, it's better to make him angry so maybe he'll tip his hand now."

Jennifer probably wouldn't know the idiom *tip his hand*.

"If it's going to become an issue," I said, "let's make sure he makes it an issue now. We don't want him to be able to plan anything devious.

"I'll be in front of the Ariana Hotel tomorrow at 2:00, so don't worry about me making the appointment. I'll see you Saturday at 5:00. I love you."

When I arrived at the Hyatt, I discovered our chosen meeting place wasn't so much a bar as it was a coffee shop that also served alcohol. It took up much of the hotel's main floor, and had real wood tables, dark green carpeting, and carved stonework from the floor to the high ceiling more than two stories above. Jennifer was already there when I arrived.

I walked right up and sat at her table. There was no need this time to pretend we'd accidentally run into each other.

They served Heineken. She talked about her week, her training program, and the new tutoring client she'd arranged for me to meet. I paid the shockingly expensive tab and we went out through the hotel's back door. We walked around the grounds a while, looking down at the sprawling city below.

Even here, neither of us would ever have considered touching the other. We stayed together like that, quietly talking as the sun went down, and then she had to go.

"So we'll try TGI Fridays tomorrow?" she asked.

"I would really like some passable American food," I said.

"Noon?"

"Yeah. I'm sure I can get a taxi there by noon."

"You have the paper I wrote with the address for the taxi driver?"

"Yes. And you can help me get back to the train station after that?"

"Sure. See you then."

Jennifer got a taxi by herself. I made my way back to *Itaewon* and spent the evening sitting on a low concrete wall outside my shitty *yogwan*, watching prostitutes approach American soldiers and ask them, "Short time?"

I spent many of my solitary hours with the Poe anthology, eventually reading the entire book a few times through. I came to think of the stories as my heritage, the dark voice of my people. I took comfort in the murders and maelstroms and premature burials, and Shane's scribbled notes and underlines made me feel less alone.

Angel wanted my help in making his bar feel more American. Together we found artists to redecorate, using broken bits of electronics and spray-paint. He brought me samples of American beers he could get, and I advised him on which ones to stock. Cellophane in soup cans opened at both ends gave the halogens shades of red, green, and blue, but they got too hot so we had to pound holes into the cans, producing a disco-ball effect as little pinpricks of light appeared around the room. The place had an edge to it now; it was dark and gritty, and unlike anything else in Taegu. The illegal imports gave it credibility, as did my presence.

I got him to ditch the Mariah Carey and Boys II Men, in favor of the Spin Doctors. I had learned from my classes that Koreans believed African-Americans were at war with Korean-Americans in America's ghettos, and so out of a sense of solidarity they tended to shun black rap artists. I did, however, introduce Angel to white rap songs like "Jump Around," by House of Pain, and "Informer," by convicted criminal Snow.

The crowd swelled. JaRaLa was a success. South Korea would never be home, but really, no place was. At least I could try to make the best of it.

8

I was a hoodlum cliché, literally standing on a corner, smoking a cigarette, though perhaps the suit and tie made me look like a particularly successful one. The post I was leaning against had an advantage over every other place on the street, though: It allowed me to see who came in and out of the guard station, but gave the armed men inside it no view of me.

The week before my trip to Seoul, I'd met seven Americans here in this area outside Camp Henry on the two days I'd had off from tutoring and met seven Americans. So far into this midday break, none of them had passed by. I was ready, though, with my ID pouch around my neck, the plastic window pressed against my shirt again, hiding the fact that I didn't actually have the credentials people bought the holders to display. The pouch did contain my United States passport, however, as well as a hundred U.S. dollars I'd exchanged with Angel's help from Korean won.

I lit one cigarette with another. If this plan was successful, I would have a lot of things to do, all of which would need to be taken care of before I had to return to work.

If this plan was unsuccessful, I might be imprisoned or shot.

I saw Jamie, one of the Army privates I'd watched slurp up globular cheese *ramyun* the week before. He was walking toward the guard station with some other guy I hadn't met. I walked slowly, pacing myself to intercept them about five yards from the gate.

"Oh, hi there, Jamie," I said.

"Hello, sir," Jamie said.

I waved a hand. "Just Mark, please, Jamie."

"Thank you, Mark. This is John."

"Hi, John," I said.

"Hello, sir," John said.

"You guys headed back on base?" I asked.

"Yessir," Jamie said. "You, too?"

I showed him the cigarette. "Gotta hang out a minute," I said.

They proceeded into the guard station and produced their IDs. From my new vantage point where our paths had crossed, I was able to see when they'd been cleared and allowed onto the base. I ran after, calling out, "Jamie!" as I passed the three MPs without looking their direction. My peripheral vision showed a rack of M-16s along one wall. "Jamie! John!" I held up the other ID pouch I'd bought. "One of you dropped this, I think!"

The MPs didn't bother me.

I was on the American military base.

I held up the pouch. "It was lying there in the street when you walked away." I stood breathing heavily, in hopes it would convince them I hadn't given myself time to actually look at the pouch.

"Not mine," Jamie said.

"Maybe you can check and see whose ID it has, sir," John said.

I turned it over, revealing the scraped plastic and the seam I'd ripped out. "Oh," I said. "I guess someone dropped it in the street. Fucking people. We're guests in Korea. We shouldn't go leaving our garbage around like that." It was another lesson from AFKN.

"Yessir," one of them said.

"Apparently I came to Korea to pick up American garbage," I said. "Well, back to work with me, I guess. Have a nice day, soldiers."

The base was huge. It had a movie theater, a bowling alley, a convenience store, and several restaurants. In a cluster of office buildings, I found what I was looking for. The sign read Civilian Personnel Office. On the bulletin board in the hall were postings for crappy part-time jobs like dishwashing and flipping burgers at the bowling alley. One ad stood out: "Test Examiners Needed. Proctor written examinations. Set your own schedule. No minimum hours."

I went in. A tired-looking middle-aged white man in civilian clothes sat behind a desk. "Hi," I said. "I thought I'd sign up to be a test examiner."

"Oh, really?" he said. "They're always looking for those." He handed over a couple of forms and I filled them out. There was a spot for some number from a military-issued ID. I pointed at it with the tip of my pen. "What am I supposed to put here?"

"That's for your ID number."

"I have a passport with me," I said. "Should I use that?"

"No," he said. "You should have a military ID."

"I don't have that," I said.

He looked from me to the paper. I decided my best move was to remain silent.

"We'll have to treat you like one of the Korean contractor employees, then, I guess," he said finally. "Gotta get you a temporary work pass. Come with me." He put a sign in the window and locked the door, and I followed him to another building. I got my picture taken and was handed a blue laminated card, with words in Korean and English. I followed the guy back to his office and finished the paperwork. He gave me a piece of paper with a name and phone number on it. "Call these guys to get on the list. They'll call you when there's a test, and you'll come in to hand out pencils and watch the time. Pays minimum wage but it's easy money."

"Sounds great," I said.

My next stop was the base post office. The girl behind the counter, with one stripe on her uniform I knew from Eric meant she was another private, told me she needed to see my ID before she could rent me a mailbox. I showed her the blue thing but she said that wasn't the right kind.

"But this is all I have at the moment," I said. "I was told to make this arrangement by someone pretty high up, and I'd hate for either of us to piss him off. Can't we just leave that part blank, private? I'm sure neither you nor I want to waste a lot of time dicking around with forms."

She guessed we could, in fact, leave that part blank. She took my paper and issued me a receipt for my cash payment.

I had one more stop to make before I could head back to SNM Academy. The bookstore was near the bowling alley, but it didn't have many actual books. One wall was glass, facing out into a food court area, and the other three walls were covered from floor to ceiling with magazines, three-quarters of them in tinted plastic wrappers to hide their pornographic covers. In a small section near the register were the ones I was looking for: military themed ones like *Soldier of Fortune, American Survival Guide,* and *Gung Ho.* I got one of each.

It was the second Wednesday of Jennifer's training course in Seoul, and I had a rare two-hour block off in the middle of the day. It wasn't enough time to sleep, but at least I could return to the apartment and hide from the crowds a while. I told myself I might as well get used to the separation; when she returned, we'd be working in different parts of Taegu and it would feel like this most of the time. Grabbing the phone, I punched in the pager code and checked the messages. There was one all in Korean that sounded like a housewife calling to make tutoring arrangements, and then there was one message to me from Jennifer.

"Red toenails and sandals, and he still didn't do anything to me," she said. "I don't think he plans to cause any trouble about me speaking English on the phone. They all know I teach English and work with English speakers. Maybe it's okay?"

Her message continued. "There was a message today on the pager from a professor at Shinho University medical school." This made sense, because we had targeted that school with our posters, assuming that doctors and medical students would have both the need and the funding for tutoring in English. I hadn't expected a professor to answer, though. "He teaches medical English and he would like to have you assist. I'll set up a meeting for you and let you know where to meet him. It's not the school where my father works, so don't worry.

"Have a good week. I love you."

North Korean supreme leader Kim Il-Sung had died on Friday, leaving a potential power vacuum. Nobody knew what would happen next in North Korea, and every base in South Korea was on high alert. It was now Tuesday, and the military activities were still ratcheting up. I had stayed away from the U.S. bases to avoid scrutiny, but convoys of military transports and giant weapons prowled around the streets. Tiny specks that were obviously fighter planes streaked overhead, crisscrossing the sky with long contrails. Uniforms and guns were everywhere, and daily tests of the air raid sirens had begun. There were reports that the North Korean military was exhibiting signs of increased vigilance, but we were told the intention behind North Korean troop movements was hard to interpret.

Jennifer was still in Seoul, just a few miles south of the North Korean border. American news on AFKN presented an endless stream of experts commenting on likely outcomes if the Korean peninsula flared into hot war again. Some of them estimated that Seoul could hold out as many as four hours against North Korea's million-man army, but most said North Korea would overrun the city sooner than that. Taegu was a four-hour highway drive south of Seoul.

Jennifer and I had been exchanging worried messages on the pager. She would have no way to get out of Seoul if there was an attack.

I'd paid a visit to Motorcycle Row over my Monday lunch break. My bike was too small to be allowed on the highway, but nobody would be enforcing that if bombs did start falling. With a series of gestures and a lot of cash, I'd accomplished some modifications. The bike now had a removable welded frame along the back wheel that could hold two jerry cans of gas. I had gotten the guy to change out the stock springs for ones that lifted the back end an extra few inches. The new tires had the biggest knobs that would fit between the forks, in hopes of keeping them from being punctured by debris. With his own gestures, the guy had suggested modifying the exhaust, opening it up to reduce the back pressure and thereby provide a little more horsepower, but I had decided against it. Keeping it quieter might prove more of an advantage.

It was now Tuesday, and I was spending my afternoon break on the paving stones outside the duplex, sanding the metal parts of the bike and hitting them with flat black spray-paint. A taxi dropped Michael at the corner, and he came walking up as I finished putting the first coat on the new tank.

"This is really scary," he said. "It's war."

From somewhere in the sky there came a loud, cracking boom. Another jet breaking the sound barrier.

"Just now in the taxi, I passed two trucks full of soldiers," he said. "They were all clutching machine guns. I couldn't see their faces because they were wearing gas masks."

Discovering a spot I'd missed, I shook the can again and sprayed, adjusting the angle of the can to reach the bottom edge of the new tank.

"Why are you doing that?" Michael asked. "It's like rearranging deck chairs on the Titanic."

"Jennifer is in Seoul," I said. "If there's a war, she'll be trapped there. I'm going to go get her."

"That's crazy," he said. "Even if you didn't die on the way up from chemical weapons, which you would, you'd never find her."

"We've got it all worked out," I said. "She knows how to get to the Hyatt hotel, from work or her sister's place. She could even walk it if she had to. I found it on a map and plotted the route. I stuck a copy of the map on the living room wall so I see it all the time. Hopefully I'll have it memorized, but I can take it with me too, in case I need to find a different way to get there."

A formation of jet helicopters flew directly overhead, close enough to read their numbers. Each was the size of a bus and had rockets and machine guns pointing everywhere. Windows rattled and the ground vibrated as they passed.

"Here," he said, pushing a paper at me. "I picked one up for you at the American Center. It's the number of the American Embassy and a contingency evacuation plan from Pusan."

"Can you leave it on the table for me?" I asked. "I've got my hands full with this right now."

"Why are you doing that?" Michael asked.

"Oh, you know," I said, without looking up. "I figure it's safer to drive a flat black bike into a war zone than a bright orange one."

"It's the same," he said. "That bike can't make it to Seoul, anyway."

"It can," I said. "I tested it yesterday on some country roads outside town. I could hold a steady speed of over 80 kilos, which I think is around 50 miles an hour. It shakes a lot and it's hard to keep it going in a straight line, but it's doable."

"You're going to go 50 miles an hour on inch-high knobs, for four or five hours, directly towards North Korea." He gestured at the streaking contrails. "Where they're going."

"Yeah."

"And then four or five hours back. Or ten. Or a hundred."

"I got lots of gas." I began painting one of the jerry cans.

"Mark, you know that thing people say, about losing the battle and winning the war?"

"Yeah," I said. "I think there's a lot of wisdom in that, actually."

"Well, I think you may have to lose this battle, but win the war of staying alive."

"Doesn't apply in this case," I said. "If I lose this battle, my war is over."

"There's brave," Michael said. "And then there's just stupid."

"It's only stupid if I'm giving up something," I said. "Everything I care about is in Seoul right now, and I'm not leaving here without her." I focused on the paint as it coated the can. It was a pretty even coat, but there were a couple places where it had bubbled or dripped.

"But, Mark, seriously," Michael said. "What could you possibly—"

"I'm not leaving her here!" The panic in my voice surprised me, as did the sound of the spray can clattering against the brick wall across the street.

Michael flew out for the United States the next day, taking his crystals but leaving his juicer behind. I never saw him again.

A postcard arrived for me at SNM Academy. It was postmarked Taiwan but had a picture of a university on Cheju Island.

> *Dear Mark* ~~and~~
> *I'm leaving Korea now,*
> *but I don't know where I'm going.*
> *Shane*

The North Koreans didn't attack. The issue of Jennifer having spoken English on the phone was never raised again. Jennifer began working at the new school, which was so far away that we weren't able to see each other during the week. Saturdays and Sundays were full of tutoring jobs, some of which Jennifer had arranged for herself to teach. If we were lucky, we saw each other for one date a week.

I made decent money from tutoring, which Angel converted to dollars. I stored the cash in an envelope I kept inside my locked mailbox on the military base.

One Saturday, I took Jennifer up to the guard shelter at the gates of Camp Walker.

"How do I sign someone onto the base?" I asked. The MPs presented me with a form to fill out. "You need your ID," one said.

I pulled out my blue card and wrote down the number, though the space was clearly made for numbers from actual military IDs. The MP took the form back and stared intently at it for a moment, but he didn't challenge me. Jennifer passed through the gate.

"Welcome to the United States," I said.

Together we went and got burgers and sodas at the bowling alley. Nobody harassed us. Nobody stared. It was, however, a military base in a country at war, and there was a constant feeling of being monitored and watched, even when we couldn't see the guard stations or surveillance cameras.

A few weeks went by like that, seeing each other for one date a week, spent at one of the bases. We visited the movie theater and the bowling alley on Camp Henry, or the bar next to the Camp Walker golf course together when we could, and the rest of the time we worked. We missed each other, but the brown envelope in the mailbox got thicker. Sometimes, to break the monotony, we took the motorcycle out of town and climbed up into the mountains, but there were always judging eyes and rudeness from others around us, even there.

One day, as we were eating together at the base's Burger King, I slid a small package across the table. "Here, take this," I said quietly. "I found the ad for it in a magazine. I used a post office money order and had it shipped here."

Jennifer opened it, reading. "Pepper spray? Is it for cooking?"

"It's a weapon," I said. "It's made by taking the spicy part from hot peppers, and concentrating it into a spray. If someone tries to hurt you, you spray them in the face with it."

"I think I could get in trouble for having this in Korea," she said.

"That's true," I said. "It's your choice. I worry about you out there, though, every time we're apart. It makes me sick to think you could be in danger because someone might have seen you with me."

"Thank you for worrying about my safety," she said. "I'll keep it."

"I think that's the right choice," I said. "I hope it is. Oh, and there's more." I dug in my jacket pocket, producing a plastic box the size of a bag of airline peanuts, with about six inches of cord. "You plug it into the phone line, and the phone plugs in at the other end. This little green light stays on when everything is okay, and the red one comes on if someone is listening to your conversation."

"Why did you buy it?" she asked. She slipped the pepper spray into her purse and piled the padded envelope and plastic blister packaging onto the tray with the other garbage.

"It was twenty-five bucks, from the same store where I was ordering your pepper spray," I said. "About 20,000 won. I thought it might not be a bad idea, since our tutoring enterprise is becoming more popular. Korea is the kind of country that would spy on us."

"Yes, it is," Jennifer said. "Will it work with Korean telephones, though?"

"I think so. The phones have the same connectors we do in America. I think it's likely that the Korean telephone service was initially set up by the United States back during the war. A class told me about the emergency number here. It's 119, right? That's just like what we have in the States, except there it's 911. It seems to all be one system. I'd bet most of the world's phones are interchangeable, actually."

"We're all taught the 119 number, but I don't know anyone who has used it," Jennifer said. "I couldn't compare it to the American one."

"I've never used it here, but it's a pretty good system in the United States."

"Have you seen it used there?"

"Yeah. My mom called it during some big fight with a boyfriend when I was maybe nine years old. I remember he took the phone from her and tried to hang it up, and she said, 'It won't hang up, it's 911!' He lifted the receiver, and the police dispatch was still on the line."

"I don't know if it works like that here," Jennifer said, picking up the tap detector and inspecting its wire and connectors. "It does look like phone equipment is the same, though." She handed it back to me.

"I think you should have this, too," I said. "You're the one who answers the messages."

"I don't do it from my parents' apartment, though," she said. "I call from a payphone because I can't have my family hear what I'm doing. It was bad when my brother-in-law heard me speaking English on the phone, but if my parents heard me speaking in Korean to make arrangements for you to tutor, they'd know too much."

"Oh. Well, you could keep it in case they're out and you can return calls from there someday."

"But if I return a call that turns out to be the police, they would know the number I'm calling from. They would just come straight to my parents' house. It's better if I just always call from a payphone. I'll keep the spray, but I don't think this would help anything."

"I guess you're right," I said. "Twenty-five bucks I could've saved."

"South Korea doesn't trust foreigners, you know," she said. "It might not be a bad idea to put it on your own apartment phone."

When there were just two months left on my contract, Richard disappeared. As wartime scavengers had done for thousands of years, Eric and I let ourselves into his office and went through his desk, which had apparently been hastily abandoned. There was nothing of value except a book on English idioms called *The Elephant in the Room*. Eric didn't want it, so I kept it.

In a drawer full of jumbled papers, we found a letter from the United States Department of Justice, addressed to Richard at some address in Pusan. It was a curt answer to his inquiry about proper channels to follow when seeking presidential pardon for a crime.

I discovered that the tap detector plugged right into my phone. So far, the green light had always illuminated whenever I used it.

I got a new roommate, one William Tucker, from Idaho. He was perhaps in his 50s, though so weathered he looked ready for the nursing home. Fat and saggy, with thick eyelids, a mostly bald head, and a hoarse voice, Willy lumbered up the stairs with an open bottle of gin while Korean Lurch lugged his bag upstairs. He offered his hand. "Looks like we're going to share the apartment, young man," he said. "I'm Mr. Tucker."

"You introduce yourself to your roommate as *Mr. Tucker*," I said.

"Of course I do. There are reasons that protocols and formalities exist. One is to reveal people with attitude problems."

"Shit," I said. "I just got rid of Richard, and now they bring in another one?"

Korean Lurch dumped the bag at the top of the stairs and turned to leave. The landlady intercepted him, gesturing up at the apartment. Korean Lurch kept looking at me as he answered her question, narrowing his eyes with a self-satisfied grin.

Willie tried to drag his bag into his room, but failed to do so. He muttered something about being old, but it probably had more to do with the fact he still hadn't set down the bottle. I went into my room to read Poe.

The first guy I'd met behind this counter at the base Immigration Office had said they couldn't issue a military visa for someone with just a blue ID card, so I periodically passed by until there was a different guy. This second guy said the same thing.

"But I don't know how I'm supposed to do my job, then," I said. "Everybody knows bureaucracy is a nuisance, but stuff like this makes me think it may compromise our readiness."

"I wish I could help you," he said. "You'll have to ask your supervisor."

"I understand we all need to remain vigilant, and I understand your deference to the chain of command," I said. "But it's hard to imagine maintaining a policy that could weaken our operational capabilities. It's just a paper snafu."

Every time he spoke, I stared at his forehead until he finished, and then responded with strings of goofy AFKN phrases and buzzwords like that. This went on for twenty minutes.

Finally, he gave up. "I'll give you 30 days to get your paperwork straightened out, if you'll just leave this office now," he said.

Now there was a new stamp in my passport. It had numbers and dates, and the English part read: VERIFIED UNDER SOFA ROK-USA. It was only valid for 30 days, but with the money I was making from private tutoring, I wouldn't need to do this for very long.

I met with most of my adult tutoring clients at JaRaLa. Jennifer met me there sometimes on the weekends between gigs. I'd be leaving my job, and therefore company housing, soon, so Jennifer asked Angel if he knew any places that rented apartments by the month. Monthly rentals were rare in Korea because young people tended to live with parents even after marriage, but it turned out that Angel had just rented such a place, and he had an extra bedroom.

"He says you can move in with him," Jennifer said. "I think you should do it. It's in *Bongdeok-Dong*, right by Camp Henry, and we could walk to the Texas Saloon. People will assume I'm a prostitute and leave us alone."

"Sounds like paradise. Did you say *Bong Duck Dong*?

"That's close."

"I can't wait to write to my friends with a return address reading *Bong Duck Dong*," I said.

"I don't know if it will have a mailing address," she said. "It might be more like … a shack."

Richard's replacement was a woman named Anne, who had been teaching English in the United States and overseas for more than ten years. Middle-aged, professional, and confident, she gave me the impression that she would be a good leader. Anne arranged to meet one-on-one with each of the school's teachers, and on my last day there, I became one of the first to sit down with her.

"It looks like you're on your way out of here," she said. "I heard that you didn't get along with Richard. I would offer you the option to stay, but they made it clear that I'm not allowed to do that. Oh, and I guess I'm supposed to chastise you for bringing your girlfriend to your apartment. Mr. Shin said the landlady complained."

"Yeah, after he told the landlady all about her," I said. "But whatever. Fuck him. I have other plans. You seem like an okay person, Anne, so I might suggest you make other plans for yourself, too. This place sucks."

She nodded slowly. "When I arrived, I met with my boss, who is also Mr. Pock's boss," she said. "He saw that I have a master's degree in teaching ESL, and felt the need to explain that he didn't think women should be educated, and that he wasn't planning on educating his own daughters. It seemed like an odd thing to say, for someone running a chain of schools."

"Not so odd here," I said. "Sorry to be the one to tell you."

"You finished your contract, in any case," she said. "Apparently, that's rare. This is your last envelope, with a sheet, in Korean, describing how much you got for each part, like salary, value of plane fare back to Iowa as of yesterday, and the severance money. Good luck to you, Mark."

"Good luck to you, Anne."

My room in the apartment Angel had rented was only big enough to lie down in from corner to corner. Unlike the shack Jennifer and I had expected, this place was a two-story poured concrete structure with eight units.

Much of my time at the new place was spent in a fog. Angel believed that the thick, tarry smoke from Jamaican kimchee was good for keeping mosquitos out of the apartment, and he loved to partake of my Valium. After a while, we figured out that the banana stuff worked much better when we soaked it in alcohol for a while and then drank it.

The tap water was unheated, so I had to warm it in a pot on the two-burner tabletop stove and mix it into a big bowl of cold in order to sponge off. The front door was actually an old sliding shower door, with a folding lattice outside it that locked with a combination padlock. The ceiling was two inches above my head, and I had to crouch to get through every doorway. The kitchen had roaches the size of cigarette lighters, and the prostitutes who lived above and on either side of us came back drunk and loud at all hours of the night, though they probably said the same about us. Angel didn't own any furniture, and obviously neither did I, but I did have the camping mat Leo and Karen had left behind. By first layering about two hundred used plastic grocery bags flat against the poured concrete floor and then taping the camping mat on top of them, I created a bed. With the sleeping bag on top of it and the sheets on top of that, it was comfortable enough for sleeping, or at least for sedated sleeping.

Jennifer was welcome there all the time, so it was paradise.

Angel knew all the best speakeasies and after-hours joints. After he closed JaRaLa at 2:00 in the morning, he'd take me to frequent these unlicensed establishments. We became regulars at a night club in a dry cleaner's basement and a butcher shop that turned into a pub. Both served until 5:00 in the morning.

I met a friend of Angel's who had a business delivering liquid propane gas tanks on the back of a motorcycle, who introduced himself to me as "Mr. LPG." Once, at an illicit bar in the back of a stationery store, I turned around to discover that Angel had disappeared. It became clear that he had enemies in the crowd, and around a quarter of four they began acting on their animosity toward us. It started with shoulder checks and harsh words, and progressed into yelling and shoving. There were at least five of these guys, and

Mr. LPG and I barely escaped to our bikes amid shouting and breaking glass.

They had found Angel before that. He spent the next three days in his bed, covered in bruises and mostly unable to move.

It was my first day teaching at the medical school. There were 120 medical students in the lecture hall. Dr. Kim, my new boss, had given me a stack of papers to review, each with a single handwritten paragraph in English. It was their first assignment, so before getting into actual medical English he'd asked them to write about their most recent vacation.

Dr. Kim called on a few students he'd selected, bringing them to the front of the room to read their paragraphs aloud. After they did, he asked me for comments. I wrote out the problem areas on the chalkboard, sometimes acting out why there was something wrong.

"We wouldn't say 'I stayed in the ocean for six days,'" I said. "I think you mean that you were at the seaside for six days. Or, if it were me, I might just say that I was *on vacation* for six days. If you were *in* the ocean—"

I stepped down from the short stage at the front of the room, raising my fingertips up under my chin.

"—it means you were in the water." I scrutinized my fingertips as if shocked by their pruniness. "Six days!"

The class laughed.

Afterward, I walked back with Dr. Kim to his office. "Mark, you are the best teacher for this class ever," he said. "I would like you to meet some other professors. They would like your help with teaching and copywriting for publication."

"That's great, Dr. Kim," I said. "Thank you. I'm getting busier every day. Pretty soon I'll be working like a Korean."

"Yes," he said. "I think so."

We were having lunch at Camp Henry's bowling alley. I was getting used to the new routine of tutoring and teaching at the medical school, but I still hadn't figured out how to finagle another visa and this one was almost expired. I'd passed the office a few times hoping to see a new guy, but I only saw the same two who already knew me.

"I noticed there's a travel agent here on the base," Jennifer said.

"Yeah, with posters of palm trees and all that," I said. "These guys have everything."

"I was thinking that we could go somewhere," she said.

"We tried with Pusan. There's no way to do anything interesting and still be back in time."

"What if we didn't have to be back in time?"

"Then we'd be free. Comparatively, at least."

"I think I can tell my parents that our company is taking us on a team-building exercise, like college kids," she said. "They work in education, so they don't know what companies do. We could fly to Cheju Island, where Shane used to work, and have three meals a day together, and swim in the ocean. We could be together for more than an hour or two."

"A few days would be magical if we could get away with it,

especially now when we're not seeing each other much. Do you think they'd buy it?"

"I won't give them much time to think about it, and I'll act like it's an ordinary thing. I think we need to do this. Our first date was on your birthday, and that's in about six weeks. It's been almost a year of hiding and pretending to meet accidentally, and now we barely see each other at all. I have just enough of my own money to pay for the whole trip. It won't hurt our savings too much."

I signed her onto the base. The travel agent was a cheerful, middle-aged American lady with a dishwasher blonde ponytail and bangs. She found us two tickets for that coming weekend.

"Let's do it," Jennifer said.

The travel agent entered our information into the computer. "Make sure you stop back to the Immigration Office before your trip," she said. You'll have to get a new stamp so your visa stays valid. I've never seen a stamp like this; you must have some weird job. You've only got until next Friday, September 30."

can't believe we're actually doing this," I said.

"We are," she said. "It wasn't easy, though. My parents demanded the hotel name, the phone number there, and the name and phone of everyone going. I stalled until it was time to go and then just slipped out."

"And that's it?"

"They want me to call them when my flight lands, but I'll just tell them I forgot."

The plane lifted, and we were free.

Cheju Island was sunny and warm for Korea in September, though not actually tropical. We stayed at the Hyatt and walked the grounds like real guests. It had glass elevators and an indoor koi pond. We swam together in the ocean. Afterwards, we made plans to dine in the hotel restaurant and went upstairs to get changed.

"I'm starting to worry that my parents are going to do something bad if I don't call," Jennifer said.

"Like what?"

"I don't know. Call the police and report that I'm missing, maybe. Something crazy like that."

"Whew. Well, we don't want that. Maybe you'd better call."

She called from the room, but told them she was standing at a pay phone. She started talking faster, with increasing interruptions and louder volume.

She set down the phone. "They sent my sister here to meet me," she said. "Her plane lands in 20 minutes. She's staying at an expensive Korean hotel on this same beach, and I'm supposed to meet her there. What should I do?"

"I don't know," I said. "I can't predict how your family will react."

"I can't, either," she said. "But I'm not going to see my sister. We deserve our escape today."

All the hotels were on the same stretch of beach and there was no telling where the sister might appear. The Hyatt's restaurant was too dangerous. I ran downstairs and found a little store that sold beer and dried file fish, and together we sat on the balcony most of the night, watching the fishing boats baiting squid with stadium lights.

We took the hotel's shuttle bus back to the airport, arriving an hour early for our 1:26 p.m. flight Sunday afternoon. We checked in, got our boarding passes, and looked for seats at the gate.

"It's my sister," Jennifer said.

There was no time to react. A slightly heavier, spoiled, sheltered version of Jennifer was coming at us, with a self-satisfied, toad-faced man behind her. The two women met and spoke briefly in Korean, and then the sister went away again. We boarded the plane.

"What happens now?" I asked.

"My mother will be at the Taegu airport," Jennifer said. "I'll have to go back with her."

"No," I said. "Fuck that. They can't get away with this bullying. You're a 23-year-old woman with a full-time job. You've done nothing wrong. If anything, they owe us for wrecking our trip."

"They *can* get away with this bullying," she said.

"Just come to my place with me instead," I said.

"I can't. If you try to interfere, the police will take you to jail. You've seen the way the school treats us for going against what people *think* my family wants. You've seen the way people are on the street, the way the landladies are. What do you think it will be like if you and I are fighting my mother in an airport, with all the security and police and soldiers around? You have to leave the plane first, and let me meet her alone."

"No way," I said. "I won't let that happen."

"We have no choice. This is my fault. I thought we could go to Cheju. I bought us the tickets. Now I'm going to have a bad night because I made that mistake. As long as you are not involved, we'll be able to see each other again. It's like Michael told you: Lose the battle to win the war. We can't fight here and now. We just can't. If the police take you, you'll be gone, either in jail or kicked out of Korea. Then all of this was for nothing. Please, just get off the plane and go back to *Bongdeok-Dong*. I'll leave you a message when I can."

I sat silently for a long time.

"I don't think I can do that," I said. "I see what you mean, but I just don't think I can do it, letting you face ... whatever it will be, alone."

"Please."

"You're worth it to me," I said. "The fight, the cops, even jail. You're worth it all to me. I need you to know that."

"I do know."

The plane landed. I grabbed my bag and looked into her eyes. "And I think your family is shitty," I said.

She smiled at me, but this time her eyes showed sadness and worry. "Thanks," she said. "That's nice to hear. I think your family is shitty, too."

"Thanks."

I stared a while. I put my hand on her shoulder.

"Go," she said.

In the airport, hundreds of Koreans were waiting for passengers, milling around, and sitting at gates. I felt their eyes following me as I exited the airport alone and slunk into a taxi. In the rearview mirror I caught my reflection. My father's eyes mocked me.

It was now Monday, a little after noon. I picked Jennifer up at work and took her straight to Camp Walker for lunch, making the long drive in record time with sheer recklessness and aggression.

I parked the bike outside the base and helped her off. She winced. "My mother kept hitting me when I talked to her," she said. "I have bruises on my face, neck, and shoulders, but I covered most of them with makeup."

We sat in a booth at the base Burger King, trying to figure out what to do.

"My mother kept saying that she didn't want my father to know how she had failed with me. She's trying to make it so she's the keeper of the secret, but she has been lying to me and cheating me my whole life. She'll get some advantage from it, and she'll try to get rid of you one way or another. I'll be her prisoner, worse than now."

"What can she do, really?" I asked.

"I don't know," Jennifer said. "But whatever it will be, it will be bad. She won't give up and she doesn't play fair. If I tell my father right now, I will take that power from her. She won't be able to use the secret against me. I'm going to tell him."

"There has to be some better option," I said. "It's like running straight into a minefield, telling your father. Maybe we should have your mom meet me. If she sees us together, she'll see that we really love each other."

"Even if she does, it won't matter," Jennifer said. "Marriage isn't about love to them. I don't *want* to tell my father. It's scary, and it will be unpleasant, but my mother won't tip her hand about what she's going to do, and he will."

"I'm scared of this plan," I said.

"It's just another bad night," she said.

"I don't know how many more bad nights you can survive," I said.

"At least one more," she said.

I sat on the idling bike, about a dozen blocks away from the cluster of high-rises where Jennifer's family lived. I'd dropped her off in this spot a few times after our dates, so that she could walk back to her building without anyone seeing her with me. It was as close to her Korean life as I had ever been.

It was a little before midnight on Monday night. There had been no messages from her. I'd decided to come here, though I had no idea what I could do. Maybe I could take her away from this place. I'd removed the metal jerry can frame from the back of the bike to make it easier for her to jump on, in case I got the chance to help her escape.

Jennifer's family lived in a brand-new luxury high-rise that was some distance outside the main area of the city. It was one of eight identical gigantic buildings, each fifteen stories tall, all surrounded by a single sprawling parking lot and segregated from the street by a tall fence. There was nothing behind the development except a narrow dirt road for vehicles being used in construction of the last building, which as yet had no lights and only Dumpsters in its parking lot.

I rode slowly along the construction road. The bike's engine was small enough that its stock exhaust wouldn't draw much attention at this distance. I found a dark place to park near one of the Dumpsters and walked toward the lit buildings.

There was a payphone at the edge of the parking lot. I considered using it to check for any messages she may have left during my 40-minute drive from my apartment, but its location was well-lit, and much too close to one of the buildings. I'd be seen, for sure.

I didn't even know which building she was in.

I walked around the edges of the parking lot, trying to find a vantage point where I might see someone running out, trying to escape into the night, but the place was too big.

Someone was following me. I could hear hard shoes hitting the concrete with heavy, purposeful steps, and the sound was growing steadily louder and more distinct.

Near one of the buildings was a darkened bench. I added a stagger to my walk and raised my hands to my face, flopping down onto it. The footsteps drew closer. I kept my face hidden and rocked my body as if I were trying to find balance, just another intoxicated businessman returning from a tough night drinking with the boss. The footsteps slowed, then stopped. I stayed like that, hunched over with my white face out of view, until the steps receded again.

This was stupid. Jennifer and I should have discussed what to do. As it was, she had no way of knowing I'd even come. My chance of being accosted by security guards was much higher than any realistic hope I would encounter Jennifer.

I made my way back to the bike and drove to my apartment again.

At least I could check messages from the payphone at the end of my street.

I got there around one in the morning. There were no messages from her.

At 3:44 a.m. Jennifer barely tapped on the glass front door and I was up, reaching out through the folding lattice and unlocking the padlock.

She was wearing a red sweatshirt, gray sweatpants, chunky black high-heeled pumps, and glasses, which I'd seen her wear only once before, at the Cheju Hyatt. I tried to hug her but she shuddered and backed away. "Sorry," she said. "It hurts."

"Another bad night," I said. Even her breathing was labored.

"I told my father," she said. "My parents both screamed at me and hit me. My mother choked me and pulled me to my knees by my hair, and they kept hitting me."

"I'm so sorry," I said. I helped her sit down against the wall.

"I shouted back at my father. I asked him why he thought he had the right to beat me. He hit me again and said because he's my father he could kill me if he wanted to, and I should be happy he had not yet. He asked me how I could be so inconsiderate, to damage his reputation by seeing an American." She squirmed against the floor. "This hurts too much."

The only soft place to sit was my bed of plastic bags and the camping mat. There were bruises on her face and both sides of her neck. She curled one arm against her as I helped her move to the bedroom and lower herself onto the bed.

"I went to the complex where you live," I said. "I wanted to be there in case you needed me, but I stood out too much to be useful."

"I don't think you could have helped," she said. "My parents pushed me into my room and closed the door. They said I was quitting my job, and they were going to arrange a marriage for me right away, before anyone found out about you, and they were going to keep me in the house until then. When I heard them talking to each other in their bedroom, I ran out. I put on shoes and ran outside, and I thought you might be there. I looked for you but I didn't see you. There was a delivery truck on the street, and I ran to it and climbed in. The driver was surprised, and I just kept saying 'drive, please drive,' until he did."

"That could have been dangerous," I said.

"I kept the pepper spray hidden in my hand," she said. "The driver kept talking to me. 'Whatever you did to upset your husband, it will be okay. Just go back, make him a nice breakfast, and say you're sorry. He will probably forgive you.' The truck was going in the wrong direction but I rode until there was a train station with taxis. Then it was more than an hour to get here."

A few hours later, I went out to the closest payphone and called the school for her. "I saw Jennifer yesterday and she was really sick," I said. "I told her I'd call in for her this morning because I'd be up early anyway, and she should sleep. She says she'll be in tomorrow."

I called my tutoring clients next, cancelling everything for the day.

It was now Tuesday afternoon. Jennifer and I had spent much of the day sleeping. I'd made a run for Chinese food, and the two of us sat in a corner of the living room, picking at it.

"I need clothes," she said. The swelling in her face made her sound like she was talking with her mouth full. "I have to go to work tomorrow, and I can't work in sweat pants."

"You can't go to work tomorrow, dear," I said. "You can barely talk. The bruises have darkened since last night."

"I should be a little better tomorrow," she said. "I have makeup for the bruises."

"You do?"

She dumped out her purse. Among the contents were her makeup bag, her passport, the pepper spray, and the paper with her TOEFL score. "I got the most important things," she said. "Just no clothes. We don't have enough money to leave Korea yet, but we do have jobs. We have to keep them."

"If you go to work, your parents could show up."

"They're worried about their reputation, how they look to the community. I'm sure my parents will not show up at my job. They would damage everything they're trying to protect."

"All right," I said. "We'll get you some clothes."

Together we shopped, staying in my neighborhood, moving slowly and awkwardly from one little store to another. It was difficult to find anything suitable for work because they catered mostly to prostitutes. The reception we got was colder even than we'd had in the other parts of Taegu, and we realized what story the bruises seemed to tell. Eventually she found a pair of pants with a wide belt, and a passable flimsy blouse.

We spent the rest of the day in and out of sleep.

By Wednesday morning she was still talking strangely, but she was quite skilled with makeup so at least the bruises were mostly hidden.

"I have my class at the medical school today," I said. "But maybe I can call in sick. I don't like you being so far away today."

"Don't call in sick," she said. "It's strange to do that in Korea. You get most of your writing and tutoring work from that job, and you need to keep it."

"But—"

"There isn't any other way," she said. "Money is the only way we can fix anything; we can't spoil our sources of income."

She was right.

"I'll take the pager," I said. "If your parents do show up, call it and enter all ones across the screen. I'll come running."

"My parents are not going to the school," she said. "I will be fine."

I dropped her off and went to work. I was preparing for my class at a desk I sometimes used in the urology department, and two young urologists came in, both named Dr. Lee, with whom I'd worked closely in preparing a paper for publication. They wanted to know why I looked like hell. I needed someone on my side, and these guys knew me. They would be powerful allies to have, so I told them all that had happened with Jennifer and her family.

Both doctors became irate, demanding to know why I thought I had the right to help Jennifer disobey her parents' will. "I'm going to marry her," I said.

"Marriage is what her parents decide," Dr. Lee #1 said. "It doesn't matter what you do."

"They beat her black and blue," I said. "That's what her parents decided."

"That is proof her parents love her," Dr. Lee #2 said. "You are only interfering in their family. You are too stupid to see."

I stood up, inches from #2's face. "Fuck you," I said. I turned and leaned in even closer to #1's face. "And fuck you, too. I'm too stupid? You do what you're told, say what you're told, and *think* what you're told. Neither of you has ever had an original thought in your lives, but you're programmed to believe this sick shit is right. There's nothing human about either of you, and there's sure as hell nothing human about anyone who would marry you out of some twisted sense of duty. You're machines, bound to other machines, producing machines, at the command of machines! I would pity you both, if I didn't have such contempt for you."

I snatched my bag from the desk and shoved past them, heading down to the lecture hall early.

Dr. Kim found me sitting on the riser, staring at my pager. "Oh, you are here," he said. "I had been waiting for you in my office."

I didn't respond.

Students began filing in. I began teaching two minutes early, in hopes of getting through the day's material as fast as possible.

I taught for about 25 minutes, checking the pager constantly. Maybe it would be all right, after all.

I was in the middle of writing a sentence on the board when the pager sounded, in a startling series of loud beeps like a smoke detector. I yanked it from my belt. Rather than the "1111111111" I had dreaded or the regular local telephone number I'd hoped for, it was jumbled, unreadable pieces of digits.

I had already kick-started the bike when I realized I still had a piece of chalk in my hand. I raced toward Jennifer in high gear with the power rolled all the way on, passing rows of cars on both sides as I navigated the space between the lanes. Giant knobby tires on concrete made the bike shimmy at high speed, but the constant feeling that it was about to slide away from me helped me focus on what I was doing instead of dwelling on what might be happening to Jennifer.

No one at her workplace would help her.

The light changed at an intersection with four straights and a turning lane in each direction. I was going too fast to stop but was still too far back to catch up to the last cars running the red as the opposing traffic started to move. I shot across, leaning down over the handlebars in hopes of coaxing a little more speed. Tires screeched and horns honked but I made it across. At another intersection the cars were stopping but the turning lane was empty, and so was the opposite one. I shot from one to the other as a truck began to pull into the turning lane, but I cocked my head to the side just in time to avoid having its mirror take my head off.

No one there would help her.

My fastest trip from the medical school to Jennifer's workplace under normal circumstances had taken about 40 minutes. This time, it took about 15. The new SNM Junior building's parking lot hadn't been poured yet, and I skidded to a stop in the gravel, breathless, with my face hot and my pulse pounding.

Jennifer's sister was standing outside with some *ajuma*. "Where is she?" I asked. The sister responded with a bemused half-smile, but otherwise the pair of them seemed completely unfazed by my arrival.

I set the kickstand where the bike had stopped and ran upstairs to the lobby. The Korean receptionists both knew me, but neither responded when I asked where Jennifer was. I had never taught in this building and I didn't know the layout.

"Jennifer!" I shouted. "Where are you?"

Ryan came out from his little office behind the reception desk. "What's happening here?" he asked. His heavy English accent with notes of frustration and shock sounded to me like a Monty Python sketch.

"Jennifer paged me," I said. "There's some problem."

"That's impossible, Mark," he said. "Jennifer has been teaching all morning."

"Don't bullshit me. Where is she?"

"I just told you. She's teaching."

"I need to talk to her right now."

"Her class has five minutes remaining."

"I don't know if I can wait five minutes, Ryan," I said. "Look, man, you and I have never had any problems between us, but I don't know who I can trust right now. Maybe she's here, or maybe she's been carried off already and every minute I waste talking to you is taking her farther away."

"Just wait five minutes and she'll be down, I promise," he said.

Pushing any farther wouldn't help anything. "All right," I said. "I'll wait."

"And I have to tell you this, Mark," Ryan said. "This is the second disruption in two days, and both had something to do with you. She's the best teacher we have, but there's a limit to how much the school can tolerate. If there's another incident, I won't be able to put her on the schedule anymore."

"If she's not here in five minutes," I said, "I'll have nothing left to lose. Remember that."

I waited five minutes. Jennifer came downstairs.

"I got the page," I said. I showed her the unreadable display.

"Who sent this?" she asked.

"You did. Right? Because your sister is downstairs?"

"My sister is downstairs?"

"Yes. With your mother, I think."

"Come with me," she said. She left the lobby and climbed the stairs, all the way to the roof. She leaned over the edge, peering down to the front door four stories below. "I was right when I said my parents wouldn't come here," she said. "But I forgot that they could send others. That is my sister, and the other one is that evil aunt I told you about, the one that nailed the fish to the door."

"The one who married off her daughter to the police chief?" I asked.

"Yes."

"Great. Let's just get out of here."

"Okay."

She already had her purse with her. We went all the way down, passing the lobby and heading straight out of the building. The sister and aunt ignored me but stepped in front of Jennifer, shouting and waving their arms. The aunt grabbed Jennifer by the wrist and shoulder and tried to push her toward a car. Jennifer shook loose and shouted at her. The sister stepped between them and lowered her voice. Jennifer scoffed and said something back. The sister shook her head.

"Let's go," Jennifer said.

"Mark," the sister said in the halting 101-level English I'd have expected from one who'd studied in America but had avoided talking to any Americans. "If you love her, you should give her good advice. You know she should be with her family."

"I'm not so sure," I said. "Does your father still think he has the right to kill her if he wants?" The sister's eyes widened but she had no response. "I can see from your face that your father isn't the only one who thinks that," I said.

I started the bike and Jennifer climbed on. I gave it as much gas as I could without bringing up the front wheel. The aunt grabbed Jennifer's belt as we passed, jerking her off the bike. The taillights hooked under Jennifer's knees and tipped her backward so that she fell straight onto her shoulders in the gravel. I jumped off the bike and ran back to her. Jennifer was unconscious.

10

Jennifer!" I said, kneeling down and taking her hand. "Jennifer, can you hear me? Are you injured?"

She mumbled something unintelligible. Then her eyes opened a little, and she managed to raise herself up enough to lean on one elbow. I put a hand behind her back for support. The aunt squatted down behind Jennifer's shoulders. She forced one of her hands under Jennifer's arm and hooked the other under her chin. Then she stood, ripping Jennifer away from me and hoisting her to her feet.

The aunt pushed Jennifer toward the car. I scrambled up from the gravel and grabbed Jennifer around the waist, sliding a foot in the gravel to wedge myself between her and the aunt. The woman seized Jennifer's arm and jerked on it as hard as she could, but I held tight. Jennifer moaned and went limp. The aunt planted her feet and bent her knees, pulling like Jennifer was the rope in a tug of war match. Without letting go, I shifted position and was able to pry Jennifer's wrist from the woman's clutches. Her body fell into my arms. As I was lifting her, the aunt came at us again, seizing fistfuls of Jennifer's hair and shirt and yanking downward, trying to rip her out of my arms. The shirt tore. I spun halfway around, bringing Jennifer's chunky high heels level with the aunt's face. "One more time, bitch," I said, in English, "and it's your turn to get knocked out."

I carried Jennifer back into the building, which had a long, straight staircase leading up to the main floor. I struggled up stair after stair, then stumbled across the lobby into the conference room, where I settled Jennifer into a chair and locked the door behind us.

She slowly regained consciousness.

"How are you?" I asked. "Is anything broken?"

Her eyes were partly open but she didn't answer.

"Jennifer! Do you know where you are? Do you remember what's happening?"

"My purse," she said.

"Just tell me if you're okay."

"I don't have my purse," she said.

"Forget about the purse," I said. "Tell me how you're feeling."

"It still has my passport in it."

"Shit." Through the glass wall I saw the sister and the aunt, standing at the counter with their backs to us. The aunt was on the phone. The sister was holding the purse.

I opened the conference room door as quietly as I could. The sister didn't turn toward me. I took a few quick steps and snatched the purse out of her hands. Returning to the conference room I showed it to Jennifer, but Jennifer didn't react. She was deathly pale.

"Jennifer? Hon, I'm worried you may be going into shock. Can you hear me? Talk to me."

Her eyes remained unfocused, but she spoke, in a faint and distant-sounding voice.

"My aunt was talking to her son-in-law," she said. "The police will be coming now."

"I know you shouldn't stand," I said. "But can you stand?"

"I don't know," she said. "Can I lean on you?"

"Always."

I helped her to her feet. She was too small to put an arm around my shoulder, so instead she wrapped it around my waist. I opened the door to the lobby, which now contained a few parents waiting for their kids to get out of class, as well as Korean Lurch, New Clip, and some other male Korean employee I'd never seen before.

Jennifer and I moved toward the stairs. Korean Lurch and the two others stepped in front of us.

"That is enough," Korean Lurch said. "This school is responsible to her family. We will not allow that you go."

"Look around," I said quietly. "Parents are gathering. Little kids will be pouring out of classrooms. There are three of you, and I bet more will come out of the woodwork. You can probably beat me, but before that, I promise you we'll paint this place with blood, and that will greatly embarrass your employer. To whom are you most responsible, to her parents, or to the job you'll have for the rest of your life?"

Ryan emerged again from his office. The sister and aunt stood next to him behind us with their arms folded.

Korean Lurch didn't move. I pushed past him and helped Jennifer down the long flight of stairs. They all followed.

We made it to the bike and I got it upright. The driveway was the only part of the parking lot not walled off by buildings, and the half-dozen people that had followed us out of the school formed a wedge that completely blocked the exit to the street.

Fighting us here in the parking lot would be less embarrassing to the company than fighting us in the lobby. Though
they'd let us down the stairs, they had no intention of letting
us leave.

I couldn't put Jennifer in front of me and drive well
enough to navigate through all these people, so she had to
perch behind me. The bike's new height made balancing her
difficult, especially when kick-starting it. I managed to get
the engine turning and knocked it into first gear. Gripping
her hands at my waist with my left hand, I gave it gas with
the right. The bike launched toward the crowd but I turned
it around, heading for the row of buildings that penned in
the parking lot.

My mind became a torrent of frenetic thoughts and shitty
realizations. There were three times as many people there
to grab at Jennifer this time. She was still wearing that belt.
She was semi-conscious and needed my help to stay upright,
which meant I had no hand to fend them off or even work the
clutch. If I rushed at the crowd and hurt someone, the cops
would have more reason to ... What would the cops do? Did
they need any reason at all? *Red Rover, Red Rover, we'll run
them right over.* How fast could I be going when I hit them,
given that I would have to turn the bike 180 degrees first?

As the bike accelerated, a bright spot appeared to our right.
Daylight showed between the SNM Junior building and the
adjacent one. I let off the gas.

There was a narrow space there. I put a foot down and
turned toward it.

The gap was littered with broken cinder blocks, heaps of
construction debris, and other garbage. It appeared to be
wide enough to accommodate handlebars, though barely, so
I aimed for it. The crowd shifted toward us as the bike's front
tire hit the first piece of debris, tipping us forward as the

shocks compressed. I rolled on the gas and the bike jerked forward, raising the wheel slightly off the ground. It hit another, bigger obstacle, and we tipped forward again.

The gap was slightly wider than the handlebars, but up close the piles of debris were taller than I'd anticipated. The trash was knee-high in some places, and much of the material was solid and jagged, like broken bottles and a shattered toilet bowl that pointed a razor edge toward the center of the space. The bars scraped against one wall and then the other as the bike wobbled. The crowd behind us was closing in.

Jennifer slumped sideways. I gripped her left hand tightly in mine, tugging brusquely. "Hey! Jennifer!" I said. "Stay conscious, now. I need to feel you grab my waist."

Slowly, weakly, her forearms tightened at my sides.

Something slipped under the rear wheel and sent it sliding up against the left wall, slamming my right forearm and shoulder into the SNM Junior building. All I could do was give it more gas, so I did, and the bike shot forward, still leaning sideways, dragging me along the wall, shredding my sleeve and scraping away a lot of skin. The forward momentum and a hard kick against the ground got more of our weight under us again, but then the back wheel spun in broken glass, throwing shards and threatening to tip a second time, but I kept the gas on.

The bike, modified for war as it was, made it through.

We turned left onto a sidewalk and then left again onto a street.

I pulled the War Machine all the way inside our tiny living room, closing the opaque glass door so nobody could spot it. The two of us sat down on the mat in the bedroom. Jennifer bandaged my arm using a tee shirt and some of the tape from the floor. We both passed out for a while.

We woke to the pager's obnoxious beeping. The apartment was dark. I flicked on the light and we sat against the wall, staring at nothing.

"We should check the page," Jennifer said, sitting up.

"How are you feeling?" I asked.

"I hurt everywhere," she said. "I'm dizzy. Did somebody pull my hair?"

"Your fish-nailing aunt."

"I'm not surprised." Jennifer gingerly lifted her shirt, revealing bruises on top of bruises. She took off the belt.

"What can I do for you?" I asked.

"I need to eat. I think that's why I'm dizzy."

"There are probably a lot of reasons, but I'll go to the store."

"I'll come with you."

"I don't think you should. First of all, you can barely sit up. Second, we stand out more together, and we don't need to draw attention to ourselves."

"We don't stand out so much here in *Bongdeok-Dong*."

"Right now, we stand out everywhere. You rest, and I'll bring back something for us to eat." I stroked her hair at the right side of her face, seemingly the only part of her that wasn't bruised or abraded.

"Okay," she said. I helped her lie down again. She was almost instantly asleep.

I scooted past the bike and undid the combination lock on the front door, relocking it from the outside. There were only a few street lights, so I was able to move around mostly in the dark. A little convenience store had three Styrofoam trays of *gimbop* in plastic wrap, so I got all of them, a few cans of Sac-Sac, and a case of Bacchus F energy drink. On the way back, I stopped at a payphone and checked the pager message. The display worked normally, showing that someone had left a voice message from an ordinary phone number. I punched in the code and the message played. It was a woman, speaking in Korean, which I had expected. Probably just some tutoring inquiry.

The voice switched to well-spoken English. "Mark? I will leave this message for you, too. This is Sarah, from SNM Junior. After you and Jennifer left here today, the police came. Mr. Shin told them a former student had seen you often when he drove through *Bongdeok-Dong*. He suggested they should look for you there. Be careful."

I walked back to the apartment, hyper-aware of the blank, staring faces I passed on the street. A siren sounded a few blocks away. I walked quickly, ducking my face whenever I passed under one of the area's few street lights.

Jennifer was awake when I returned. "I'm tired but I can't sleep," she said. "Too many bruises, and the floor is hard."

I told her about Sarah's message. "We have to leave Korea," I said. "Right away."

"Yes," she said. "We can go to the travel agent on the base when it opens in the morning. Tonight, we should pack."

Together we spent most of the night filling the cracked brown vinyl suitcase I'd brought with me to Korea. Jennifer changed into the pair of her sister's old jeans she'd kept at my place for mountain climbing. She folded and packed her sweatpants, but that was all she had. The rest of the bag would be for my clothes. "Most of this other stuff will have to stay behind with Angel," Jennifer said. We made a pile in the corner of things he might want: the pots and pans I'd bought in the open market with Leo, the Jamaican kimchee, the Bisquick mix and Hungry Jack syrup, the Poe compilation from Shane, what remained of the Valium from Shutter Man, Michael's juicer, Katherine's basil plants, and Richard's copy of *The Elephant in the Room*. We packed one of my suits and left the others hanging from the window bars. Jennifer rolled and folded everything, arranging it all to fit neatly inside. There was a little extra space, so I threw in the butterfly knife and the tap detector. "Souvenirs," I said. I tried to zip the suitcase but Jennifer insisted on rolling them up in socks.

Around four in the morning, Angel stumbled in, blind drunk. He laughed and climbed up on the motorcycle like it was a jungle gym. Jennifer tried to explain what had happened to us at the school. Angel tried to stand on the foot pegs. He fell off, but I steadied him before he could topple onto Jennifer. She tried again to get him to understand our situation as I lowered him to sit against the wall. He muttered something in Korean.

"He says don't worry," Jennifer said. "He is your real friend, and he will help you."

Angel fell over sideways, sliding smoothly down the wall like the second hand on a clock and passing out in an "L" shape on the floor.

We waited until well after 9:00 on Thursday morning, to be sure the base travel agent would be open.

"You walk ahead," I told her. "I'll follow, but farther back. We're harder to identify if we're not together. If you see the police, duck into a store. If you're bothered by anyone else, I'll run up and put a stop to it."

"The stores around here won't be open in the morning," she said. "We should run straight to the base."

"Okay, but let's still stay a distance apart. They're less likely to stop us."

We walked as quickly as Jennifer could manage, keeping our heads down, and made it to the gate. The MPs had seen the two of us before and paid little attention as I signed her on.

Our first stop was the post office, where I unlocked my mailbox and removed the brown envelope, its contents totaling $9,340. We left the box empty and hobbled over to the travel agency.

"Well, hi, you two!" the sprightly travel agent said. "Back already? How was Cheju Island?"

"We had a problem," I said. "We need to get out of Korea."

The woman's smile vanished as she looked from my face to Jennifer's, taking in our obvious exhaustion, the bruises, and the general disheveledness. "Let's see what we can do," she said quietly. "Do you have your passports?" We put them on the desk. She typed on the computer. "As an American, you have lots of choices. You can pretty much go anywhere, and stay for at least 30 days. That's not true for Koreans, though; I think fear of North Korea makes other countries stricter with South Korean immigration, too. Let's see …" She removed a binder from a drawer, scrutinizing a tattered sticky note inside the front cover. "Without getting visas in advance, Koreans can go to Singapore, Hong Kong, Macau, the Philippines, Guam, Thailand, and Saipan. They're all tourist and shopping destinations, so they let Koreans pop in like that, but only for a week or two."

"How about Singapore?" I asked. "I have friends there."

She clicked a few keys. "Hmm … not many flights, and all

booked solid with pretty long wait lists for the next few days."

"Okay," I said. "It doesn't matter so much where we go. We just need to leave as soon as possible. Is there anything today?"

She clicked keys. It felt strange, sitting on padded chairs in the quiet, carpeted office. There was a framed poster for Telluride, Colorado hanging behind the desk, and another for New York City on the wall next to Jennifer. A hidden stereo played barely audible bossa nova.

"I have two business class seats from Seoul to Guam this evening," the agent said, "but they're not together."

"We'll take them," I said.

"Flying to Seoul from Taegu, I assume?"

"No!" Jennifer said. Turning to me, she added, "They will look for us at the airport."

"Can you get to Seoul some other way?" the travel agent asked. "It's the only truly international airport in South Korea."

"Train?" I asked. "Bus?"

Jennifer shook her head. "They could check those stations, too. Can we fly from Pusan?"

"Yes," the travel agent said. You can fly from Pusan and make the connection in Seoul.

"How would we get there?" I asked. "The bike isn't legal on the highway. We'd be stopped for sure."

"Angel can take us," Jennifer said.

"Angel doesn't have a car."

"Angel has lots of friends. Someone can provide him a car."

"I guess, but it'll probably be stolen," I said. "Or full of stolen goods."

The travel agent's eyes widened.

"We don't have a choice."

"Okay," I said. "Let's book it out of Pusan."

The travel agent typed something and stared at the computer. When she spoke, her voice was even softer than before.

"I'll give you as much time to get there as I can … Looks like 3:40 this afternoon out of Pusan will still get you to Seoul in time to connect. Total cost in United States dollars is $2,620.62."

Jennifer counted the cash out from the brown envelope. The travel agent opened our passports and typed some information into her computer. "It's a good thing you're leaving today," she said. "You didn't get that visa straightened out and tomorrow would be too late."

"Do you have to put our names on the tickets?" Jennifer asked.

"It has to match your passport, especially the last name. I can just use your first initials, though, I think."

"Thank you," Jennifer said. "That might help."

We hustled back down the street toward my place. One of the little junk stands outside the base had opened early, selling bad knock-offs of popular designer goods. There was a pink baseball cap modeled after the trendy ones from the Gap store, reading "CAP." I bought it for her. "Here, put this on. It'll hide your face. Maybe they'll think you're an American."

She put it on.

It took physical shaking, loud music, and three cans of Bacchus F before Angel understood what we were asking of him. He muttered something.

"He says he's tired," Jennifer said.

"Listen, man," I said. "We need you. You're the only one who can help us." I gestured at the pile of things we were leaving behind. "I'm leaving all this for you. Just please help us get to Pusan." I took the key from the motorcycle and put it into his palm. "It's yours. Everything."

He nodded. We each downed another can of Bacchus F. Angel shrugged into his red and yellow satin jacket that read "CONVORSE" in big letters across the back. He unfastened the lock and went down the street to the payphone. I relocked the padlock and went to hide with Jennifer in my room.

Angel was gone for more than two hours.

He came back with a silver hatchback that was at least ten years old. The shattered rear passenger window had been patched with clear packing tape, and the same method had been used to secure the driver's side headlight. Angel drove cautiously, like a new driver, and it occurred to me that he might not have a license.

"We can make it on time, I think," Jennifer said. We piled in, with her in the passenger seat and me hunkered down in the back to hide my face.

"If it's supposed to be a two-hour drive, it's going to be close," I said.

The car drifted from side to side on the highway but Angel got into a groove. We began passing other cars, making up a little time.

Traffic slowed and then stopped. There were construction signs ahead, but still too far away for the characters on them to be readable. Angel shut off the engine and we waited. Nothing happened. Angel fell asleep.

We sat there like that, watching the clock as it first showed the time for check-in, and then the boarding time. Jennifer and I sat quietly, staring at nothing.

"It must be taking off right now," I said.

The cars started moving again. We woke Angel. There had apparently been a big accident where all the cars had tried to crowd into a single lane to pass the construction, and there were still a lot of road emergency vehicles and crew milling around as we passed.

Eventually we made it to Pusan's airport. I fought the suitcase out of the trunk and Angel shook my hand.

"Is like movie," Angel said. "You are star. I am extra." He took off the jacket and handed it to me, smiling. "It's yours," he said. He drove away.

The airline was able to put us on the next flight to Seoul, but there was no way we'd make the flight to Guam. Airport security confiscated the pepper spray from her purse, because it was an aerosol. They didn't seem to know that it was also a weapon. The sun set before we took off. Korea did indeed look weird from the air at night, with mountains forming big dark patches between bright lights.

It was after 10:00 p.m. when we reached Seoul. The ticket counters were all closed, but the Korean Air guy hadn't yet turned off his light. We ran up and told him we needed tickets, listing all the places we'd been told Koreans could go without getting a visa ahead of time. Jennifer was back in Korean-American mode, speaking primarily in English and periodically butchering the Korean language when she had to make something clear. He tried to tell us he was closed, but we kept talking to him as if we didn't understand. He found two seats on a flight to Hong Kong, leaving at 9:20 the next morning. He couldn't take dollars, but there was a currency exchange counter still open. Finally, the Korean Air guy issued the tickets, as we requested, with last names and first initials, and checked our bag. The brown envelope now contained $5,002.54

"But I must flag this one," he said, holding up my ticket. "Your visa will be expired by tomorrow morning."

We spent the night in stiff chairs at a closed gate. Jennifer wore the pink cap down over her eyes and wrapped herself in Angel's jacket to better disguise herself. I sat in a seat some distance away, watching her and monitoring the activity in every direction from which someone could approach.

The visa office opened at 8:00 the next morning. We found the gate for our scheduled flight but placed Jennifer strategically at a different gate nearby, so that she could observe anything unusual that might be going on where we were supposed to be. Her presence at the immigration office would not have helped my case.

I went in and stood at the counter. Next to me, a policeman was talking to one of the clerks in Korean.

I was dirty and unshaven. *Hairy, like animal.*

"Yes?" a dour, pudgy little Korean man said.

"Hi," I said. "I missed my flight yesterday, and the ticket guy said I had to come here. Some problem with the stamp on my passport, I guess."

He reached for my passport. I handed it to him, already opened to the SOFA ROK-USA visa stamp. Letting him see that I'd entered with an English teacher one would raise unwelcome questions. I avoided looking at the cop.

"Ticket," the man said. I produced it.

"Where is the rest of your documentation?" he asked.

"I ... what?" I said.

"Your documentation. The papers from your employer."

Oh, shit.

"What?" I said. "I don't have all that stuff with me. I have a valid passport and a ticket, and I'm on my way out of the country. Why would I carry a bunch of papers like that?"

"You are required to have documentation," he said.

A typical American with nothing to hide would challenge this guy. I spoke faster to keep his attention. This would be much harder if he started leafing through the passport. "Look, man," I said, in my best clueless-American voice. "I was here for a little while, working to keep Korea safe. I missed my flight. I'm on my way *out* of the country, and I don't know what you want from me."

The cop was staring at me.

I spoke more quietly but the cop kept watching. "How do we fix this, you and I?" I asked.

The cop did not move. The immigration guy hesitated, absentmindedly fingering the pages of my open passport.

He stamped something and gave me a paper. "This will let you board," he said. "Do not miss your flight. Be more careful next time you come to Korea."

"I'll do that," I said.

The cop watched me go.

I returned to the gate where I'd left Jennifer.

She was gone.

I turned around in a circle, looking for some sign of the satin jacket or the pink cap, but she was nowhere. I went to the gate for our flight, but she wasn't there, either. The gate where she had been sitting was filling up with passengers.

Our flight would board soon. Korean immigration would not forgive me for missing it. I paced slowly back and forth from our gate to the one where I'd last seen Jennifer.

A hand appeared on my shoulder.

I spun around, fist clenched and ready.

It was Jennifer. I let out the last few thousand breaths I'd taken.

"I thought I saw my sister," she said.

"Any idea where she is now?" I asked.

"No. I couldn't look at her because I was afraid she'd notice."

We stood close together, hiding our faces and pretending to look out the window, resisting the temptation to look over each other's shoulders. There was no reason to make ourselves more conspicuous by raising our eyes. What could we do if we saw one of them, anyway?

They were not above ambushing us as we boarded a plane, or even above using violence in an airport. If they spotted us, we'd never escape. There were cameras and cops everywhere.

The garish yellow and red satin baseball jacket made a decent disguise for Jennifer, or maybe I just hoped it did. It was a dramatically different look from her usual designer suits, in any case. Even with the clashing pink cap and my black plastic wrap-around sunglasses, too much of her face could still be seen. Bruises were still visible on her cheeks and neck, though she'd tried to conceal them with makeup.

As for me, a white American, I would stand out no matter what.

We chatted quietly, without looking at each other. Talking seemed less likely to draw attention than standing in silence. It also kept the two of us connected, akin to holding hands, in a place where actually holding hands in public came with the threat of being beaten to death.

Jennifer turned her passport over in her hands, twice. I had never before seen her fidget. "Lucky I tried to change my major in college," she said.

"Yeah."

I tugged at my sleeve to make it billow out around the bandage Jennifer had affixed at my elbow, in case it had soaked through.

She looked exhausted. We had now been running and hiding for five days. If they found us, there would be more violence. If we missed the flight, we would soon be discovered and separated, and we probably would never see each other again after that.

"They're boarding," Jennifer said.

We kept our faces down, but everyone stared anyway. This was where they'd cornered us before: at an airport gate, as we'd prepared to board a flight.

The trick we'd used, giving the ticket agent only a first initial instead of a full name, wouldn't be much help, at least not for me. My last name stood out as much as the rest of me did, and they would surely know my last name. Our former employer had only contempt for our privacy.

I slid my boarding pass out from my passport and examined it for the hundredth time, pinching it tightly between my fingers and white-knuckled thumb. It was smudged with ink from my new visa stamp. "If we have any chance of avoiding them, it's because we bought these after the counter was supposed to have closed," I said quietly.

"They could be checking right now," she said.

Ordinary Americans, lining up for ordinary flights, would probably look bored, so that was how we tried to appear as we shuffled toward the door. One passenger after another presented a ticket and made it onto the jet bridge. A gate agent motioned to Jennifer, took her ticket, and let her pass.

"Hello," a different one said to me, extending an open palm. "Boarding pass and passport, please."

I gave her the documents. The gate agent looked them over, and went to get someone else. Together they scrutinized the paperwork, especially the new stamp. Finally, they accepted the ticket and I proceeded into the tunnel.

I had almost caught up to Jennifer when someone pushed me against the wall.

I spun toward the offending hands. I would not go down easily.

It was an *ajuma* with a thinning perm, dyed coal black except for a quarter inch of gray roots, clad in thick black polyester. She shoved past me and continued down the walkway, using her elbows and shoulders to part the crowd. Two other *ajumas* followed in her wake, wearing the same hair and clothing. A Korean Air flight attendant stopped them at the front of the line, and passengers crowded behind them, waiting to board.

"She's asking for their tickets so she can show the *ajumas* where to go," Jennifer said. "They don't want to sit in their assigned seats."

The *ajumas* argued. The crowd at the end of the jet bridge swelled. It took four flight attendants to coax them from the door and into their correct seats.

We crossed the threshold. Jennifer was at the window and I was in the middle seat next to her. "It's a little cramped for a four-hour flight," I said. "And to think, just yesterday we were business class to Guam."

Together we watched as person after person stepped through the open door. What would we do if someone boarded the plane to get us? My mind ran through a possible scenario involving activating the emergency slide, running across the tarmac, and being gunned down.

Not easygoing people, Koreans.

It was the best plan I could come up with. If they got onto this plane, I would put an arm around Jennifer and dive for the emergency slide.

A man in a suit paused at our row. A fist in the gut would bend him over, and I could hit him in the jaw with the top of my head as I stood up to fight. I waited for a word or a grab, but none came. He placed his briefcase in an overhead bin and sat down next to me. A few minutes later, the plane door closed and a flight attendant stood up at the front to give her spiel about the exits and seat belts, first in Korean and then in English.

The plane taxied. I gestured out the window. "Want to take one last look?" I asked. "You may never see it again."

She gazed out at the concrete and glass, the tower, and the mountains in the distance. "I won't miss it," she said.

I didn't know it then, but more than two decades later, she still would not miss it.

The plane sped down the runway.

"The last time we thought we got away by airplane, it didn't work out so well," she said.

Our flight to Cheju-do had been just last week.

They would soon learn where we were.

"We may just be leaving one set of troubles for another," she said.

I took her hand as the plane accelerated, pushing us back into our seats, lifting off. Beneath us, the landing gear whirred and retracted, and I felt machinery clunking under the floor. Like taut rubber bands allowed to go slack, we collapsed against each other.

11

The plane landed in Hong Kong. We collected our bag and proceeded to the customs area. "Look how many white people there are in the crowd," I said. "And Indian and African, and Southeast Asian. I bet it's about 20 percent non-East-Asian here. Even as a couple, we hardly stand out at all."

We lined up with the rest of the crowd, passports in hand, and eventually got called up to different desks. Jennifer was allowed through immediately and she waited on the other side. My guy looked from my passport to my face, from my face to my bag, and from my bag to my passport. He leafed through the pages again, looked at my face again, and raised his hand, glancing over his shoulder. Two uniformed Chinese men with machine guns appeared—not with the weapons slung over their shoulders, but actually holding them in their hands. The man gave them my passport. "You go there," he said, gesturing to a narrow hallway. I picked up my suitcase and followed their directions, making sure not to look at Jennifer or show any connection with her whatsoever. They ushered me into a stark white room, where two other uniformed Chinese men opened my suitcase, carefully removing items and scrutinizing them.

The machine-gun men stood by the door. One of the two new ones stood with his face inches from mine, looking back and forth from me to the picture on the document. "Why you come to Hong Kong?" The accent was different than a Korean one; the sounds were shorter and they came faster.

"Big shopping trip before heading back to the United States," I said. "I finished my contract and I want to spend all my money on new suits and shoes."

"Where you fly from?"

"Korea."

"What your job in Korea?"

"English teacher."

"Why you come to Hong Kong?"

"To spend money."

"What your job in Korea?"

"English teacher."

They rummaged around in the suitcase, undoing much of Jennifer's meticulous folding and organizing. The butterfly knife and tap detector were in there someplace, and I fought to keep from cringing as the rubber gloves unfolded shirts and unrolled socks. They found aerosol cans of shaving cream and deodorant and sprayed them onto paper towels. Then they hastily shoved everything back in, gave me back my suitcase, pointed me at a door at the other end of the room, and disappeared.

Outside the door was a room twice the size of a basketball court, with every inch of its floor, walls, and columns covered in grimy ceramic tile that originally might have been beige or pale green. A dense crowd flowed through it. Many people were meeting loved ones who helped them with their bags and escorted them out of the airport into waiting cars. I spotted

Jennifer almost instantly. She smiled at me and shook her head, as if to say, "I knew you'd get out of it somehow."

"They only stamped my passport for two weeks," she said.

"That should be enough time to straighten out the visa stuff and buy tickets to the United States," I said.

"Now what?" she asked.

"Now we're free," I said, smiling. "Let's get a room and sleep for a week."

"No hotels, though," she said. "We have to save money. They must have something like a *yogwan* here. And right away, we need to set aside plane fare, which is, how much, do you think?"

"I don't know. $2000?"

"So let's first set that aside," she said. "In fact, to be safe, let's put $2200 away. We can keep that in the brown envelope, to be sure we don't overspend."

"I'm sure we can find a cheap place. Speaking of money, we should change some." I nodded toward a currency exchange booth.

"What do you think?" I asked Jennifer as we approached the booth. "Two hundred U.S. into Hong Kong dollars?"

"I don't know," she said. "I don't know how much dollars buy. We should change Korean won first, though, because we can use dollars when we reach the United States."

The guy behind the bullet-proof glass shook his head at our remaining Korean won, which didn't surprise me much, given Korea's strict currency controls. He pointed to a piece of cardboard with various bills taped to it, with the U.S. dollar at the top. Jennifer counted out two hundred dollars and got stacks of red, green, and blue Hong Kong bills back.

We exited the airport and found ourselves in a dimly lit area beneath the first floor of an adjoining structure. A few yards away, a diminutive Chinese guy stood leaning on a white minivan, smoking a cigarette. He was wearing black jeans, a purple satin jacket, and an unnecessary pair of dark sunglasses. "You need ride? Room?" he asked.

Jennifer backed up.

"What's wrong?" I asked.

"That's the kind of van they use in Korea, kidnapping girls," she said.

"Taxi'll be twice as much, and this guy says he can get us a room," I said quietly. "To me, he doesn't seem sophisticated enough to pull off a kidnapping."

Jennifer walked around the van, looking in every window. "Okay," she said.

He assumed we wanted to go to the *Kowloon side*. We didn't let on we had no idea what he was talking about. "Cheap shopping, right outside," he said.

"Sounds a little like Bong Duck Dong," I said.

"I guess," Jennifer said.

"What kind of room?" I asked the guy.

"Clean," he said. "Two beds, own shower, own toilet. Clean. 650 Hong Kong dollar."

Neither of us were familiar with Hong Kong dollars or their purchasing power, but we had just converted to them from United States dollars, with which I was familiar. Jennifer, however, was better at doing math in her head.

"What's that in U.S. dollars?" I asked.

"About eighty," Jennifer said.

"Eighty American?" I asked the guy. "We could get a nice hotel downtown for that. C'mon, man. I'll tell you what. I'll give you $25 U.S. per night for that room. That's ..." I raised my eyebrows at Jennifer.

"About 200 Hong Kong dollars," she said.

"200 Hong Kong," I said. "That seems about right for what you describe."

"Where you come here from?" he asked. "America?"

"South Korea," I said.

"Hong Kong more expensive than South Korea. Hong Kong more expensive than Manhattan. Nice hotel downtown, maybe 2,000 Hong Kong. You want room for 200 Hong Kong, I can get, but not nice. Nasty. Not by shopping. You want nasty 200 Hong Kong room, or you want nice, clean room for … 500 Hong Kong?"

"That's 60 American," Jennifer said.

"Well, obviously we're sophisticated people and it must be clean and not nasty," I said. "But yours sounds like thirty bucks to me."

"That's … 240 Hong Kong," Jennifer said.

"No," he said, elongating the word and shaking his head so it sounded like a mosquito buzz. "400 Hong Kong."

"300 Hong Kong," I said.

"350," he said.

"320," I said.

"That's 40 U.S., in case you didn't know," Jennifer said.

"I didn't," I said. "Thanks."

"Okay. 320. Plus 300 for ride."

"300?" I asked. "How far is it?"

"Taxi there be maybe 500 Hong Kong."

"What's 500 Hong Kong, again?" I asked.

"60 American," Jennifer said.

"But you're not a taxi," I said. "You have a van that makes her think of kidnappers. Let's add 100 Hong Kong for a ride."

"200," he said.

"That's 25," Jennifer said.

"Deal," I said.

I climbed into the passenger seat. Jennifer sat in the back, intently watching our driver. No chance of him and his van earning her trust. As we headed off for Kowloon, I looked out the window and took in my first glimpses of Hong Kong. The traffic, moving on the left-hand sides of the roads, was mostly buses, minivans that were usually white, like the one we were riding in, and red and white Toyota taxis. Crowded in among them were regular passenger cars of all descriptions, though the most common were Japanese, and every so often I spotted a high-end luxury sedan like a Benz or even a Rolls Royce.

Dominating the landscape were dozens of skyscrapers, clustered in groups of four or five, each of them tall enough to have served as a tourist attraction in most other cities in the world. Surrounding the towers were older buildings of maybe eight or ten stories that seemed not to have been built so much as stacked. Successive floors often had different windows, different exterior paint, and were occasionally even of different sizes, with some jutting out wider than the floors above or below. Laundry hung off balconies on arrays of long poles, and air conditioners dripped down onto the street far below. Narrow rectangular billboards of Chinese characters took up whole sides of buildings, sometimes with a logo or photo in one corner.

"It's so crowded," Jennifer said quietly.

"Glitzy," I said. "Shiny, gigantic, brand-new buildings."

"But more are really old," she said. "I've never seen a place this dirty. The whole city seems to be covered in hundred-year-old lime."

"Mm, maybe you mean grime?" I asked.

"Grime. Right."

"I guess that's why our driver made such a point about how clean the guest house is," I said.

He took us to a busy part of the city and parked in a narrow alley between several tall buildings. Three large Chinese men in filthy work clothes were standing in the permanent twilight, smoking cigarettes. Our guy swung open the van's side door and took our suitcase past them into the building. We followed him up four flights of stairs and down a long, grubby corridor, at the end of which were two other Chinese men, engaged in animated and not particularly friendly conversation. They stopped and stared as our guy opened a door into a little reception area that was, in fact, clean. He introduced us to a middle-aged Chinese woman—the Chinese equivalent of an *ajuma*, but with a white silk blouse and hair styled with curlers instead of a tight perm—who might have been the guy's mother or aunt. She led us to a room that was slightly larger than mine had been in Korea, with a tiny bathroom and two beds that looked like they might have been made for dolls. We paid the driver, he paid the woman, and she gave us a key. I pulled our suitcase into the room. We collapsed onto the two tiny beds and slept for about seven hours.

There was as much light coming through the window when we woke up as there had been when we'd arrived, but now it was electric, and pulsating in colors.

Jennifer moaned slightly as she sat up.

"How are you feeling?" I asked.

"Better, but still achy."

"You can keep sleeping," I said. "We got away. There's no urgency now, and we can rest as long as we like."

"That's not true," she said. "We are not safe. My brother-in-law does business in Hong Kong. We shouldn't let our guards down." Those words hung in the air for a moment before she continued. "I'm hungry."

"Oh. Actually, I'm hungry, too. Maybe we should go see what Hong Kong has to offer."

"Okay."

The guest house was small and cheap, but the guy's promise held true: Even our bathroom was clean. Jennifer sat on the bed for a while, gently applying makeup to the giant bruises on her face and neck. I changed the bandage on my forearm, replacing the blood-stained white tee shirt with a new black one. I washed the old one in the bathroom sink and hung it to dry on a wire hanger Jennifer found behind the radiator.

I dug into the black vinyl bag and removed the brown envelope, with its US$2200, and stuffed it into one of the front pockets of my jeans, where it would be hard to steal. I put the rest of the cash in my other front pocket. The butterfly knife went into my back-right pocket for easiest access.

"What are you doing?" Jennifer asked. "It's not safe to carry all our cash out on the street."

"Safer than here," I said. "How many people do you think have stayed here? How many keys might be floating around? Did you see the people behind the building and in the corridor when we came in here? Some of them looked pretty rough. I think our cash is safer with us than it would be just sitting here unguarded."

"I hadn't noticed rough people," Jennifer said. "It's all the same level of strange to me, but what you're saying makes sense. Okay."

The guest house was in a tall building facing Nathan Road, which, as our driver had promised, was a shopping area. There were plenty of tourist traps and souvenir shops, but it wasn't all cut-rate merchandise. There were a number of custom tailors and lots of jewelry stores. Those places were all closed because it was 9:00 at night, but they still had bright lights in their bullet-proof display windows, showcasing their glittering wares. Across Nathan Road from our building was a Hyatt hotel.

"We should find something cheap to eat," she said.

"I think we should celebrate," I said.

"We're going to need our money when we get to America."

"We fought like hell," I said. "We got away. We won! And here we are, in love, with thousands of dollars in cash, in one of the world's most exciting cities. We should acknowledge that." I took her hand. We stopped walking. I looked into her eyes. "We got away," I said.

Her tiny smile thrilled me. "We did get away, didn't we?" she said.

We continued on down the street until I caught sight of a backlighted green sign featuring an English Bulldog. Next to the dog was the name of a restaurant, spelled out in yellow English letters: *Mad Dogs Pub.*

"This place might have fish and chips," I said.

"I like fish," she said.

The restaurant was a basement done up in British pub style: hunter green paint, lots of wood paneling, and framed posters. It was packed, but two seats opened up just as we reached the bar. We sat down and ordered a couple pints of Guinness.

"That man knoos his beer," said the guy perched on the stool next to me. He was Caucasian, short, and going bald on top, though there was a full head's worth of brownish hair on each of his forearms. Over the next few pints, we learned that his name was Kyle, he was Scottish, and he worked as some kind of construction foreman. We told him how we came to be there that night, and an Irish waitress named Ailene overheard and took an interest. We related the whole story to her as well, in bits and pieces as she passed back and forth.

Kyle gave us his phone number so we could all get together again. "Thanks, man," I said. "We're just passing through, but it would be great to do this again before Jennifer and I leave Hong Kong. Could we just meet back here tomorrow night?" He agreed, and Ailene said she'd be working then.

"You wouldn't know where the American Embassy is here, would you?" I asked. "We have to get a visa for Jennifer to enter the United States."

He didn't, but Ailene said she had a big table of Americans. She asked one of the friendly ones when she brought them another round. "It's buey Hong Kong Poork," she told us.

"Where's Hong Kong Park?" I asked.

"Just take the tube," Kyle said. "Should be Admiralty."

"The what? How?"

"The train. You know, the subway. It's called MTR in Hong Kong—Mass Transit Railway. Take it to a stop called Admiralty."

Kyle had to get home. Jennifer and I stayed for one more drink and then waved goodbye to Ailene.

Climbing the stairs, Jennifer said, "You know, we talked with both of them all night, and I never understood anything they said."

We walked up and down Nathan Road a few times, bathed in light from the neon signs and jewelry store display windows, feeling victorious, invincible, and free.

12

ight, persistent knocking awakened us around 10:00 the next morning. The Chinese lady wanted to know if we'd be staying another night. We paid her for one more. I tried to go back to bed but Jennifer was already sitting up.

"We should find the embassy," she said.

"Yeah, okay," I said.

"My stomach is not right today," she said.

"Mine, either," I said. "I think we should avoid drinking the tap water in Hong Kong."

We each took a shower and got dressed, both wearing one of my tee shirts, and headed out. It was a bright, warm day. We found a pharmacy and bought some Pepto Bismol and bottled water.

Just down the street from the pharmacy, a young man was selling clothes out of cardboard boxes inside a storefront he seemed to have rented, or perhaps broken into, just for the day. Jennifer bought a pair of brown pants for about five American dollars.

We walked down Nathan Road in search of the MTR station. The thoroughfare was crowded in the middle of the day, but the current of pedestrians parted in several places, flowing around people begging. One middle-aged man sprawled on the sidewalk with his pant leg rolled up to reveal a deep, gaping wound in his calf the size of a grapefruit. He braced himself against the ground with one hand while raising a begging cup toward passersby with the other hand, which was missing three fingers. A few paces farther down the street, an old blind man pretended to play a plastic pan flute while a recording played from a box at his feet.

Someone pulled at my sleeve. I spun, shoving the offender up against a plate glass window. He was Indian, not Korean. His partner emerged from a store and explained they could make me custom shirts in any fabric.

The crowd became more diverse as we approached the waterfront, with a few Africans, Indians, white people, and other minorities mixed in with the Chinese majority. "Please! Please!" someone called from a doorway, in a decidedly British accent. It was guy about our age, in a fraying but still fashionable suit. His face was partially hidden behind a cardboard sign that read LOST MY MONEY, NEED TICKET HOME. His hair was growing out from what had probably been a stylish cut, and his head shook slightly as if he might be crying.

After approaching a few businessmen to ask for directions, we found the station in our area, Tsim Sha Tsui. We took the train to Admiralty, reaching Hong Kong Park by around 2:00 in the afternoon, and soon located the United States Consulate building.

There was a line at the front door. We should have expected that. It was 1994, and Hong Kong was still a British territory, but it would be reverting back to China in 1997. The Communist Chinese government had fired on civilians in Tiananmen Square, killing hundreds, in 1989, and Hong

Kong's most successful capitalists were justifiably nervous about what would happen after the transition. The crowd of wretched refuse trying to emigrate included a lot of meticulously groomed men and women with expensive clothes and jewelry. We recognized the desperation in their faces as we passed person after person, following the line out and back... and back, and back, joining it when we finally reached the end.

Some Indonesian guys in front of us gave us a couple of their clove cigarettes. After waiting in line for three hours, we made it inside just before the office closed. At the counter, we explained that I was an American citizen and we needed to get Jennifer a visa. They informed us that the line wasn't the one for American citizens, and that this window couldn't help us. There was a nearby window that could have, but it was already closed for the day. If we came back tomorrow, they said, we could go directly to that window. American citizens didn't have to wait in the line.

With nothing to do until we met Kyle and Ailene back at the pub, we explored Hong Kong Park. We were out together in public and no one we encountered paid any attention to us. We were anonymous. We were free.

Eventually we made our way back to Kowloon. Outside a tall building just down the block from our guest house, a mob of hustlers vied for foreigners looking to rent rooms. They shouted at anyone who looked foreign, offering low rates. As we approached, one woman pushed her way to the front and told us of some great deal she could offer us. A man she had shoved aside snubbed his cigarette into her cheek. She knocked his hand away and stared hatefully at him. There were still a few ashes sticking to the red burn under her left eye.

We hurried past and spent another night drinking

Guinness, eating fish and chips, and exchanging stories with Kyle. It was quite late when we returned to the guest house.

The next day, Jennifer made sure we were awake and out the door by 8:00. We paid the woman for another night there as we passed, and headed straight down Nathan Road to the Star Ferry, which we hoped would be a cheaper way to reach Hong Kong than the MTR.

At the Star Ferry docks it took a little while to figure out the system, but we found the ticket counter, paid, and boarded. The tickets were so cheap that paying nearly double for the upper deck didn't matter at all, even to us.

The upper deck of the Star Ferry was enclosed in glass and air-conditioned, with hard plastic seats. Because it was so high above the water, it rocked like an inverse pendulum. The ride was only a few minutes, but the combination of motion and stale air nauseated us both. At the Hong Kong docks, we asked for directions to Hong Kong Park, then found the correct window at the Consulate.

"We have to do this visa stuff fast," Jennifer said. "I worry about my family finding us here, and I worry about spending all our money."

"Tourist visas are issued quickly, I think," I said. "They require less paperwork, so let's just ask for one of those. They'll probably make us wait for a week or two like the travel agent back on the base said, so we might still be here for a while, but I think it'll be faster. We can wade through all the heavy bureaucracy once we reach the United States."

Having been one of a handful of white Americans in a city of nearly three million Koreans for so long, I found it strange to see all the Americans bustling around inside the Consulate. About two-thirds of them were white businessmen in suits.

Jennifer went into a room with rows of chairs facing a front counter area, much like a DMV waiting room back in Iowa. I was not allowed to go inside the room, but I could watch from a window in the hall.

"Waiting for someone in there?" asked a smiling, gray-haired American guy in an expensive looking gray suit.

"Girlfriend," I said. It had been a long time since I'd had a friendly conversation with another American. It felt weird.

"Oh, your girlfriend's from Hong Kong?" he asked.

I shook my head. "South Korea. Her family chased us out with the cops and we ended up here. We're heading to the States now."

"And then back to Korea?"

"What? Hell, no."

"But that room's for people getting tourist visas," he said. "She'll have to go back to Korea when it expires."

"We'll get married," I said. "They'll give her a different visa for that."

"So she's got a South Korean passport," he said.

"Yeah."

"Might be tough."

"It won't be *tough*," I said. "She's just going to ask for a tourist visa. We'll have to wait a couple weeks or whatever to get it, but that's okay. We'll sort it all out when we get to Iowa City."

"She can't get a tourist visa if you're going to get married. She'll need a fiancé visa. That means you'll be coming to my department."

"You work here?"

"I do," he said. He handed me a business card. It was embossed with a gold eagle, and read "James G. Baratona, Vice Consul of the United States." He was no longer smiling. "And I have news for you," he said. "South Korean citizens can't get U.S. immigrant visas from Hong Kong. You have to go back to Korea."

"Okay," the Vice Consul guy said as Jennifer and I entered his office. "Have a seat, folks. I'm Jim. Let's figure out what's going on."

We sat down in two chairs facing his desk. I gritted my teeth, silently chastising myself. At the first sight of an American, I had assumed I was back in familiar territory and let my guard down. Hong Kong was not home. Jim was not our friend. We should have practiced better OPSEC. Now that he knew most of the story, we had to fill in the details so at least he'd know we were telling the truth.

"Dang," he said when we finished. "You guys should write a book."

"Nobody'd believe it," I said. "All we need to do is get to Iowa City. Now that you know what's up, I'm sure you can help with that, right?"

"Jennifer is not a resident of Hong Kong," Jim said. "The visa you need is a fiancé visa, which is an immigrant visa, because you plan to get married. The United States can't check her background here, so we can't issue her a fiancé visa. To get one, you'll need to go back to Korea."

"Or we can forget I told you any of that stuff, and you can give her a tourist visa," I said.

"We won't be doing that," he said.

"We can't go back to Korea," I said.

"You can't go to the United States," he said. "Well, *you* can, Mark. You're a citizen. You can return at any time, obviously."

"But it's just a stupid stamp," I said. "It's a definition. Lots of couples plan to get married *someday*, but that doesn't mean they can't be tourists in each other's country first."

"You told me she's not going back to Korea, so that means she's not a tourist," he said.

"Just because she's not going back to Korea doesn't mean that she'll never travel again after hitting our shores," I said. "You're choosing to interpret it that way."

"I have to interpret it in the way that's most dangerous to the United States, and then take steps to ensure that whatever danger I find is addressed."

"Oh, give me a break," I said. "Just wave your magic wand and make her a tourist for a couple weeks. We'll file some extension or whatever from Iowa City."

"You're here because you bought last-minute plane tickets, with cash, at an airport from which you could practically walk to North Korea. The stamps in your passport show a strange pattern I don't yet understand. Maybe someone at the Consulate with experience in the military will be able to explain it." He pinched his chin with his thumb and forefinger, like the Thinker, leaning against the arm of his chair, staring at me with raised eyebrows. "Let's hope so."

"We can get married here," I said. "Then she's not a fiancé, she's my wife. I've got to be allowed to return to my own country with my wife, right?"

"Wrong. It's the same visa, for immigration, not for a visit.

It lets someone move to the United States permanently. You cannot get an immigrant visa of any kind unless and until you apply from your own country."

"What about second world countries like Thailand?" I asked. "Places like that will let Koreans enter without prior authorization."

"You can't immigrate from there, either," he said. "Or anywhere else. They'll know who you are."

"Because you'll tell them."

"They already know," he said.

"At least our money would last longer in a place like that," I said.

"But you'd have to fly there," he said. "That's going to eat up a lot of your cash."

"We'll have to stay here, then," I said.

"You have to go back to Korea," he said again.

"Do you know how marriage works in Korea, Jim?" Jennifer asked. "My mother goes to a government office where they keep family records. Every family has a book there. When daughters get married, our mothers go to the office, and tell the clerks to cross out our names from our family book, and write our names in our husband's family book. That makes us married. That might already have happened. They might already have married me to someone there, against my will. We can't go back to Korea."

"The cops were after us, Jim," I said. "Who knows what kind of fake charges I might be facing back there? Who knows what kind of arbitrary bullshit they'll subject me to? We can't go back to Korea."

"If you stay here, you'll run out of money," he said. "Then Hong Kong authorities will deport each of you to your own country."

"Won't happen," I said.

"Mom and Dad can send you money?" he asked.

"I don't come from that kind of family," I said. "But I'm resourceful."

"I can see that," he said, flicking a few fingers toward where my recently scrutinized passport sat on his desk. "You'll do well to remember that Asians take law and order very seriously."

"You don't say."

It was Jim's job to deal with problems involving Americans in Hong Kong. My best move was to show him that if he couldn't find a way to let Jennifer come to the United States with me, I would be here, causing problems.

He watched me with his lips pursed and his eyes narrowed, like a chess player.

"Look," I said quietly. "I'm no prince. But I am an American. That has to count for something with you people."

"Tell you what," he said. "My wife works here in the Consulate, too. She's from Thailand, and her parents didn't like me much, either. We'll both be off work in a few hours. What say we meet for a few beers at the outdoor café in Hong Kong Park after work? My treat. Maybe we can come up with a solution."

I shrugged at Jennifer.

"Sounds great," she said. "Thank you."

"Yeah, thanks," I said.

Jennifer and I left the Consulate offices and wandered around Hong Kong Park. We found the café where we'd be meeting Jim later, and then we discovered the aviary. It was free to enter, and inside we found shade and fresh air. There were real trees, beautiful songbirds, and even some little deer, though it was difficult to determine just how little they were, from our position suspended on the walkway some distance above their heads. We stayed there, breathing the air and watching the birds, until it was time to meet Jim and his wife. She was a Thai lady who looked about the same age as Jim, but without his gray hair. Her name was Kamon.

We chatted and got to know a little about each other. Jim explained why the building they worked in was called a Consulate and not an Embassy (embassies are permanent diplomatic missions that are usually in a capital city, and Hong Kong was just a colony). They told us a little about Kamon's background in Thailand and about Jim's experience with the Peace Corps there many years before. Finally, we got around to discussing how we might address our situation.

"Mark can go to the U.S. and get a job, and Jennifer can stay here," Jim said. "That's allowed, of course."

"I'm not leaving her here," I said. "I didn't do all this so I could abandon her in Hong Kong. Besides, I'd have two rents to pay."

"You're going to have to figure this out pretty fast," Jim said. "Your visa's for 30 days, but hers is only for two weeks."

"We just have to get jobs here," I said.

"Might be tough," Jim said. It was apparently his go-to phrase. He'd reverted to the same *I-know-better-than-you* tone he'd used at the Consulate.

"You could hire me," I said. "If I'm working at the Consulate, I'm on American soil, right? Gotta be something I can do for the good ol' U.S. of A."

"Everybody gets hired in D.C. and shipped over here," Kamon said.

"Yeah, and here I am, ready to save shipping costs," I said. "Don't you guys have some mandate to cut expenses when you can?"

"Everyone gets shipped over?" Jennifer asked. "Even for jobs like taking out the garbage?"

"Those services are all contracted with local companies,"

Jim said. "To you it'd be the same as any other job in Hong Kong, requiring Hong Kong authorization to work. You could call the U.S. Chamber of Commerce here, though. They might have a few leads. They'll be in the phone book. Start there and see what you come up with."

"I have a notebook with contact information for some international friends," I said. "Nobody from Hong Kong, but maybe one of them knows somebody here."

"It's worth a try," Jennifer said. "But for right now, we're going to have to find a cheaper place to stay. We might be stuck here a while."

"Check around," Jim said. "Stop by my office in a few days to let me know how it's going. Maybe I'll have some more ideas by then."

In the morning, an Australian couple at the guest house told us they'd looked at a place down the street that was much cheaper per day, though they themselves had refused to stay there. We followed their directions to a tall building called Chungking Mansions, which we recognized as the site of the earlier cigarette-face-snubbing incident. We negotiated with a few of the hawkers, and came up with a room on the 15th floor for around US$10 a night. The sprawling ground floor of Chungking Mansions had the feel of a bus station or perhaps the area under stadium bleachers, crowded with garishly lit shops selling Indian saris, clocks, Chinese cloisonné, Arabic food, bolts of fabric, sacks of grain, radios, and anything else one could want, from every corner of the world.

The shops expanded from their tiny concrete boxes with display cases, tables, cabinets, coolers, and even seating areas. People, mostly men, milled everywhere, shoulder-to-shoulder between the swelling stores. In contrast to the crowds on the street, only a small fraction of this one was Chinese. Most were Indians and Africans. I was the only white guy I saw, but I felt less conspicuous here. Plastic signs, most of them white with red letters, announced goods, services, quantities, and prices, in English, Chinese, Hindi, Arabic, and a dozen other languages.

The winning hawker escorted us through the crowd and into the line for the elevator. We waited with men who seemed to have come from every country on Earth, all of them there to work menial, survival-level jobs. Just outside the elevator, an Indian guy had a little stand where he sold clocks and Indian CDs. His music played loudly from a boom box, filling the area with sitars and words that sounded like *eeeayaeeeaya*. A bit farther away from the line was a Middle Eastern restaurant with a seven-foot-tall bearded man guarding the door.

"We need to be careful, here," I said quietly into Jennifer's ear. "Look around. All male, mostly from desperately poor places. Grim expressions, hollow eyes. They left their women behind so they could come work like slaves here. They're hungry and don't have much to lose. The richest man in Chungking Mansions has to watch his back, and with you by my side, I'm the richest man in Chungking Mansions."

Though to an observer it may have seemed that this was intended as a sweet or romantic comment, I knew Jennifer was practical enough to take it as the warning I meant it to be.

After more than half an hour in line, we were able to enter the elevator. It was built to hold maybe three people, packed in tightly, but the crafty residents of Chungking Mansions had discovered that by having people push against the sides, they could climb partway up the walls and double the capacity. They were dirty and sweaty and exhausted, which made the agonizingly slow ascent as unpleasant as it was terrifying. Nobody bothered us about the suitcase taking up extra space or adding extra weight, though.

The hallways upstairs were all beige tile, with stenciled numbers spray-painted in red over doors and on corners. Our hawker introduced us to the proprietor of the place, another Chinese version of an *ajuma*, who informed us that our room would actually cost US$11 rather than the US$10 our hawker had promised, "because aia-con."

"We don't want air-con," I said. "We'd rather have a window."

"Tomorrow," she said. "You move tomorrow, have window no aia-con. Now, only this one." The windowless room she had available was poured concrete with a bare bulb hanging from a wire on the ceiling. It did indeed have an air-conditioner installed along the top of one wall that blew cold air around in a circle, incubating some of the world's most pungent strains of mildew.

"Are there windows in all the rooms across the hall?" Jennifer asked. "We get one, no matter who moves out?"

"Yeah, yeah. Window tomorrow," the woman said. Faced with the choice of accepting the only available room, which was basically a refrigerated gym shoe, or going back downstairs to negotiate and stand in line with the suitcase again, we took the room.

We put the suitcase under the bottom bunk and went back out, taking the stairs. Around the 8th floor, a broken pipe had turned the painted concrete stairs into running rapids, but Jennifer and I were able to lower ourselves one slippery stair at a time by clinging to the railing. Back on the streets, we explored the area behind Nathan Road and discovered a

7-Eleven store whose offerings included instant ramen (not ramyun) and quarts (not liters) of Pabst Blue Ribbon. It was easier to convince Jennifer to buy beer than I'd thought it would be, since we'd determined we'd have to buy bottled water anyway. We also bought some prepaid telephone cards, which would be necessary for international and even local calls. We shared a quart of PBR and each had a cup of ramen, and then bought more beer to take up to the room. We climbed rung by rung up the handrail, making it past the 8th floor cascade without any broken bottles.

Because the smell of mildew was so overpowering in our room, we kept the door open to get as much "fresh" air inside as possible. As a result, we met a few of our neighbors. There was an old Israeli woman named Ruth who told us she would die soon and had come on a trip to see the world with her college-aged son, Alon. Upon hearing our story, they gave us a special piece of cloth Ruth said would bring us luck. An hour later, we met a black guy with a British accent who introduced himself as Micha, and told us he was from Germany. He was working illegally as a bouncer at a night club and said he might have a lead on a job for me, which would've been great if we'd ever seen him again after that. A young Italian woman named Stefania claimed that she was merely passing through, but she seemed to have some kind of underground employment. She didn't say what it was and we didn't pry. She did, however, know a great trick for extending Jennifer's visa.

"You take the, the boat, the jet boat, to Macau," Stefania said, in a thick Italian accent that tended to add extra syllables to the ends of words like a bad cartoon. "It does not cost much." *Cost-a much-a.* "You stay one night, come back, and they give you a new stamp. You can do it maybe four or five times."

The guest house had three shared toilet stalls, with rubber

hoses hanging down over the bowls that had plastic shower heads on the end. To get clean, you leaned over the bowl, turned the lever, and rinsed off, letting the water run into the toilet. Alternatively, one could sit on the toilet and hose off that way, letting it run into the floor drain. The system ensured that the toilets were usually relatively clean, but they were never dry, and there was no free paper.

Eventually we got tired, and, regrettably, we closed our door. The air conditioner blew directly onto the top bunk so we both shared the bottom one. By 2:00 in the morning we were both coughing, so we pulled clean tee shirts over our heads and then back up over our faces without putting our arms through the sleeves, in hopes of filtering the air.

The next morning, we packed our suitcase and waited for the old lady. Either we'd move to a room with a window as she had promised, or we'd fight our way back down the stairs with the suitcase and try again.

Some guy moved out of the room next to Stefania's, so we were able to move in. The room was the size of a twin bed, with a plywood shelf from wall to wall covered with an inch-thick foam mattress. We were able to put the suitcase underneath it with the door open, but retrieving it would require opening the door again. The walls were covered in shiny brown tiles. It had a window, though, so the air was breathable, thanks in part to the ceiling fan that clocked me in the head as we climbed up onto the bed. The noise and fumes of Hong Kong were tolerable that high up, but this was mostly because our window overlooked a sort of courtyard instead of Nathan Road. Looking down, we noticed that the exterior of each floor level was darker than the one above it. Air conditioners were covered with Styrofoam takeout trays, paper cups, eggshells, and broken bottles. The walls of the lowest levels we could see were entirely black.

"People have probably been throwing garbage down there for 50 years," Jennifer said.

We made our way out to Nathan Road and looked up the American Chamber of Commerce in a pay phone directory. We called to make an appointment and got directions on how to find the place, which referenced a few different MTR stops.

Across the street from Chungking Mansions was a chain restaurant selling coffee and pastries that played French music for patrons dining at its four tiny white tables. "Should we get something?" I asked.

"We need to be careful with money," she said.

"We need to eat," I said. "It's 10:30 in the morning and we haven't had anything since cups of ramen for dinner."

"We need to get things we can make for ourselves," she said. Maybe we can find a grocery store to get things we can have in the room."

"What if we don't find a grocery store today?"

We decided to get two coffees and split a single chocolate croissant. It took no time at all to finish our breakfast, and then we were off again, searching for the subway. Jennifer found the signs and got us where we needed to be, so we were early for our meeting.

At the Chamber, we met with Carson, a pleasant young Chinese man. "Oh, dear," he said, in an accent with Chinese and British influences. "My, my, that's quite a story you have. Well, we'll surely try to help you."

"We need jobs, Carson," I said. "We need a source of

income, right away, and a source of legitimacy."

"Yes, well, that is a problem, though—the legitimacy part, you know. Such things rarely happen on a schedule like you would need. It is a difficult problem, surely. We have an extensive list of companies, but I expect they will move quite slowly with international hires."

"Slowly would be bad," Jennifer said.

The three of us sat in silence for a while. "There is one man I might recommend," he said. He leafed through a three-ring binder from a shelf behind his desk. Inside were plastic sleeves with pockets for business cards. Finding the one he was after, he jotted down a name and number. "Burt Pomroy is an American who has been in Hong Kong for a long time. I'm not familiar with his business, but he may be a good source of information about settling into Hong Kong without the help of a major corporation. Oh, and let me get you a flier about our upcoming networking events. There's one for young professionals coming up in a couple of weeks."

We thanked him and left the office. Our next stop was a nearby payphone. Burt Pomroy was brusque and irritated when I called, but he brightened at the mention of Carson's name. "I'm extremely busy," he said, "but I can give you a little time next week." The way he said it, in a tone that was more demanding than gracious, made it seem like my meeting with him might actually be more like an interview.

There were English conversation schools in Hong Kong, but in a British colony they had no need to sponsor foreigners for visas. My calls to them were all dead ends.

Using the prepaid phone card from 7-Eleven, I called every friend I could think of who might have a connection in Hong Kong. Nobody I knew in Japan had any leads. None of my international friends back in Iowa City knew anyone. Then I got in touch with my friend Nina in Singapore. Her dad ran a bar there, where Texas and Oklahoma oilmen listened to live country music performed by an all-Chinese band and caroused with local prostitutes. "I thought maybe you or your dad would have a Hong Kong contact."

"I do have a Hong Kong contact," Nina said. "Cashel is there right now."

"Your boyfriend? Really?"

"Yeah, I'll give you the number."

"Great! Thanks. Tell him I'll call him at his office tomorrow."

Jennifer and I had the rest of the day free. "We need to find a grocery store and get some supplies," she said. "We can't keep wasting money like we did this morning with the croissant."

"You're right, of course," I said. "But we have some time right now. Let's go back to the aviary."

"Yes, I like that idea," she said.

Jennifer and I met Cashel, boyfriend of Nina, at the Star Ferry dock on the Hong Kong side. It had been a few days since I'd called him and told him the story, and now, on the weekend, he was taking us to meet some people he knew in Hong Kong. "Preston is from Britain, and his wife Helen is from Korea," Cashel said. "He might have some ideas."

He took us to a different dock, to ride a different ferry, smaller and newer than the Star, out to some island. It felt wealthy there, with new residential construction, fresh paint and professional landscaping everywhere we looked. We found the right building and took the big, new, wood-paneled elevator up to their floor. There was no line, and nobody had to push against the sides to avoid tripping a weight alarm.

We met the couple in the entryway of a small but nice apartment, and we all sat down in the living room. They had a new baby they'd just gotten to sleep in the crib in the bedroom. Helen turned out not only to be Korean, but also from Taegu. Like Jennifer, she was from the upper class, and it was immediately clear that they probably knew a lot of the same people. Helen had even graduated from the same university, a few years before Jennifer had. Jennifer happened to have a gift certificate in her purse that was from some shoe store where they both had liked to shop, given to her by one of her private tutoring clients. Having no use for it, Jennifer told Helen to keep the certificate.

The women sat together, conversing in Korean. "Since the baby I've had to have fags in the toilet, but with three of us I think we can justify the kitchen," Preston said. Cashel and I followed him into the kitchen to smoke. Preston was from an aristocratic British family, and could only make small talk about sports cars, equestrian events, private planes, and other things that reminded me of my father.

I told him our story, with Preston interrupting after every couple of sentences to joke or share an unrelated anecdote. I finished telling it and asked him what he thought, which was a less direct way of asking for help.

"Let her parents have her," Preston said. "Take her back to Korea, and go to the United States alone. Helen's parents didn't like me, either. Trust me, it's not worth the fight."

"That's not going to happen," I said. "We just need to find some kind of employment so we can stay here."

"Well, what can you do?" Preston asked.

It was a valid question. Corporations wanted people with specialized skills, like Cashel and Preston had in investment banking, which they'd acquired by attending upper-crust schools. People like this, or perhaps like my half-brothers, were the ones who got international jobs. People like me...

Well, people like me had to hustle.

Preston couldn't have helped us if he'd wanted to.

We ferried with Cashel to Hong Kong Island. He had a flight back to Singapore early the next morning, and was unlikely to return to Hong Kong for several weeks. We said thanks and goodbye, and then headed back to Kowloon via the Star Ferry. To save money, we rode on the lower decks, and discovered that it was a much nicer way to ride. The lower level was open and breezy instead of air conditioned, and it didn't rock so much. We stood at the front railing, watching the waves as they crashed against the bow.

"Preston told me to just give it up," I said. "It was an awkward and painful conversation."

"Helen told me to return to Korea, forget about you, and beg my parents for forgiveness," Jennifer said. "I said, 'but you married Preston. How is it different?' 'Preston is British, and he has a pedigree,' she said."

When Jennifer imitated Helen, she looked down her nose at me, but was otherwise deadpan. "'The English have a long history," Jennifer-as-Helen said. "In English culture, they appreciate breeding and keeping the bloodline within the class, just like Koreans do. Once I explained what kind of family Preston is from, my parents decided that it was okay for me to marry him. America is a new country, and they don't understand the importance of family and tradition. They're simple and crude; obviously Korean parents will always reject them.'"

"The two of them definitely seemed to be on the same page as far as how worthy and important Preston is," I said.

"Apparently that's the most important part of their marriage," Jennifer-as-Jennifer said.

"That's how he caught her," I said. "He dangled his pedigree at her, and she snapped it up."

We hadn't yet found a grocery store, so we went to a 7-Eleven by the Kowloon docks to get more ramen. "We shouldn't drink so much beer," Jennifer said. "Our cash is disappearing fast, and beer is just extra."

"I disagree," I said. "Ramen is nothing but salty noodles mixed with bad stuff like fats and waxes. Beer is made from the same grains as noodles, and instead of bad stuff, we get good, wholesome alcohol. We also get an activity for the evening. I say we shouldn't eat so much ramen."

She agreed. We got a couple quarts and drank them there, looking at the Hong Kong city lights across Victoria Harbor.

We sat in Jim's office. He sat behind his desk wearing another gray suit, this one slightly darker than his other one and with a bit of texture to the fabric. It reminded me of one of the suits I'd abandoned in Korea. Behind him was a window looking out at Hong Kong Park.

"So, how's it going?" he asked.

"We've been busy," Jennifer said.

"We're looking for work every day," I said. "Got this." I held up a new pager we'd bought from some Pakistani guy in one of the Chungking Mansions stalls. It was the cheapest one we could find, long and narrow, and made of bright blue plastic, with a number display but no message function. "Nothing yet, but I do have a meeting the day after tomorrow."

"That's great," he said. "Good lead?"

"American guy. Carson at the Chamber of Commerce thinks he runs his own business. The guy made it sound like it might be more of an interview than a meeting, so I'm going to see him alone and meet up with Jennifer later."

"Sounds like a good plan," he said. "Well, I'm sorry I don't have any real news for you. I don't have any new ideas or leads to follow, but I do have these papers you can fill out. I can submit them for Jennifer's visa application, though I truly don't think they'll get you much."

Jennifer leafed through the stack. "I need to have an X-ray?"

"And a blood test," he said. "There's a list in there of approved, English-speaking doctors who will do the chest X-ray for you. I don't know how much it costs. You also need a set of photos taken a special way, but there are places everywhere for that."

"This one asks for our current employment," she said. "Should we say we're unemployed?"

"Well, you didn't officially quit your jobs back in Korea, did you?"

"Oh, hey, that's right," I said. "Thanks for that. It would be quite a commute from here, of course."

"So fill those out and leave them at the window," he said. "It's something you can do. Don't get your hopes up, though. I sincerely doubt you'll be approved."

"I guess we can go back to the park," Jennifer said.

"Before we go," I said, "I have a favor to ask. If we're going to get jobs, we're going to need resumes. Can I borrow a type-writer and some paper?"

"Uh, sure, I think so. Let's go downstairs. I bet we can find something."

He took us down to where some clerical workers sat at computers behind a low wall. Between them were a few abandoned desks with electric typewriters. Jim arranged for me to go in and use a typewriter. He opened the gate to let me in.

"Only you!" said a matronly American woman who might have been managing the area. "Special accommodations like this are only for American citizens." Jennifer had to wait on a bench on the other side of the little wall.

This rigid distinction between Jennifer and me demonstrated something important: The Consulate wasn't doing these things out of altruism. As an American citizen, I had the right to ask for help.

Early the next day, we found a doctor from the list and made our way to her office. We paid cash and waited. They took the X-ray of Jennifer and drew some blood, and we waited again. They handed us a chest-sized envelope with the X-ray inside, and a paper saying she was free of HIV. Places that took passport and immigration photos were indeed all over Hong Kong, so it was easy to stop into one and give them the printed sheet of directions for her photos, with her face turned ¾ to the side and with her full ear exposed. These activities took a substantial bite out of our cash.

We dropped off the documents at the appropriate Consulate window and, with nothing to do until my meeting the next day with Burt Pomroy, we returned to the Kowloon Star Ferry docks and hung out in the shade below an elevated walkway. A white couple strolled slowly past us, and the woman dropped a small fanny pack right in front of us. They continued moving away.

I picked up the bag. "Hey!" I yelled. "You dropped this! Hey!"

Jennifer and I caught up to the couple and returned the bag. "Oh, my!" the woman exclaimed. The guy was an American named David, and his wife, Elena, was from Spain.

"Let us buy you lunch," David said. "To say thanks."

Neither of us had eaten yet that day, so this sounded great. We followed them to a Chinese open market, and then into a restaurant which was much bigger than the storefront in the market had made it appear. They ordered some kind of Chinese thing with lots of greasy noodles. It tasted like old French fries, but Jennifer and I gobbled up as much as we could hold. David and Elena ate sparingly and told us about how they'd met in Spain. We told them our story.

"You should think of marriage as just a tool, to get what you want," Elena said. "It will get you what you need, right? So you should just do it."

"No, it's not like that," I said. "We do actually want to get married."

"The Consulate guy says it won't make a difference to get married, though," Jennifer said. "Are you okay?" she asked Elena.

Elena was a bit pale and her eyes were wide. "I'm okay," she said. "I was just thinking about what would have happened if we'd lost this bag. All our money is in it. It's so scary to imagine."

"We're the same way," Jennifer said. "Everything we have is with us all the time."

"Do you know the American Express office?" David asked. "It's right around here. I have to go there now to get some more cash. People can wire you money there."

"We don't have an American Express card, and we don't have anyone to wire us money," I said.

"I don't think you need the card," he said. "It's not far from here. I'll show you."

"Yeah, we can hang out a while," I said. "Not much on the agenda this afternoon. Don't forget the fanny pack," I teased Elena. "I won't," she said, holding it up, clutched together in the same hand with her purse. Together we set off. It was a somewhat longer walk than David had led us to believe. We went inside and David spoke to the guy behind the counter, asking him to explain to us the various American Express services. I listened politely to the entire sales pitch and then excused myself to go back out to the sidewalk as David did his business there. Those services were for people with access to money.

On the curb outside the place was an old, mostly toothless Chinese man with a plastic garbage bag full of women's panties. "You see this occasionally in Hong Kong," Elena said. "Someone steals inventory from some sweatshop factory, and then a relative peddles it on the street. It could be anything, like clothes, radios, or dishes. Whatever they make at that factory."

"This happens to be just what I need," Jennifer said. Through a series of gestures, she negotiated with the guy, who spoke neither of her languages, and got two weeks' worth of underwear for about US$4.

David and Elena told us they had to get going. We asked if they wanted to hang out again, but they said they were leaving, heading next to mainland China. We said goodbye and headed back to the docks.

Later that day, we waited in line to exchange more American dollars for Hong Kong dollars at one of the currency exchanges in Chungking Mansions. Across the crowded hallway, two African men leaned against a storefront, watching us. Their focus was too intense, and they stared much too long, for their interest in us to be casual. They looked away as I met their gaze, but in my peripheral vision, I could see that their eyes were fixed on us again as we stepped up to the counter. I turned away from them and pulled the butterfly knife out of my back pocket. I held it, still folded, in my open palm, angling my hand to be sure the two men could see it. Though a steady stream of people passed between us, I figured only someone casing us like they were would be likely to notice what I was doing.

They moved away, presumably to find somebody easier.

"And they're crispy, like potato chips?" Jennifer asked. We had found an American-style grocery store in the basement of some tall building. It had taco shells.

"They're thicker than that, and the edges are sharper when they break," I said. I pointed to other products and explained taco assembly.

"Should we get those?" she asked. "You seem to really want them."

"No, thank you, hon. I miss being able to do the whole thing, but it'd take a kitchen. I'm sure we can find something with more nutritional value per dollar, and that won't spoil without a refrigerator."

"Well, you'll have to do that," she said. "I don't recognize much of this stuff."

"Ah, look at this," I said. "Peanut butter. There are probably better nutrition-per-dollar items that locals know how to use, but this is something I'm familiar with. It has protein and fat, and I think it's pretty satisfying to eat, even when we won't be having much. Are you familiar with peanut butter?"

Jennifer nodded. "My mother bought peanut butter because it was imported and it made my sister feel sophisticated," she said. "She ate it with hot rice."

"Yeah, see? Sophisticated. That's us."

We found a grainy bread that we thought would keep us feeling full for a longer time, and we took it up to the room to dine on the comfort of our own sponge mattress. Later, we went out and sat on a bench by the Star Ferry docks, drinking beer and looking at the lights.

Jennifer kept track of our schedule and logged every call in the little notebook. She recorded details of each meeting we had, and every outlay of cash. She always knew exactly how much money we had, to the cent, in Hong Kong and United States dollars, and kept a running calculation of how many days we'd be able to survive based on our rate of expenditure.

I showed up right on time to meet Burt Pomroy.

"When I got to Hong Kong 20 years ago, I thought it was Cincinnati with chopsticks," he said. "What the hell is this place? But since then it has grown on me."

I noticed that in all that time, he had managed to hold onto his gold neck chains, Elvis glasses, and I.D. bracelet. His office was a single fourth-floor walkup room, only about three times the size of our Chungking Mansions room, with a big opaque window in the door like an old detective movie. Neither the door nor the man gave any indication of what his business might be. Piled everywhere were cardboard produce boxes, stuffed with paper and assorted junk. He made it clear that this was not an interview and that he was only giving me some free advice, and then proceeded to insult my clothes, my haircut, my notebook and pen, and my informal mannerisms. He said that he'd be willing to give me some job leads, but he didn't have time to dig them up at the moment.

"Come with me," he said. "I'll find them when we get there."

He had me follow him to his manicurist. I stood next to the table with my notebook as he dictated names, flipping pages in his vinyl binder with a nail file.

Most of the names and numbers he gave me turned out to be for people and offices that hadn't been there for years. The first few of his contacts I was able to reach all rushed to get off the phone at the mention of his name. With the last two calls, I tried to claim that I'd been referred by one of the other names on the list, but neither took the bait.

13

Jennifer mapped out how to get us to the Hong Kong-Macau Ferry Terminal via the MTR. Once there, she scrutinized a few boards and determined the kinds of tickets we needed. I spoke to the man behind the glass and counted out the cash for them.

The boat to Macau was built by Boeing, and was about the size of three double-decker buses driving side by side. It was red, and shaped like a ship from Star Wars, not a cool kind of fighter but some big, boxy one for hauling spare parts or space onions.

"It looks like those little cars at an amusement park, where you slam into other people," Jennifer said.

"A bumper car!" I said. "That's exactly what it looks like: a giant bumper car."

The jet boat didn't sail to Macau so much as it flew, hydro-planing above the water. It had threadbare red carpeting and a grainy TV on a cart at the front of the seating area, showing Chinese movies on Betamax. At the terminal in Macau, we presented our passports and got new stamps. We exited the immigration area and were immediately besieged by hawkers, but of a classier variety than the ones in Hong Kong. This crowd wore suits and ties and booked actual hotel rooms in real hotels, which I thought maybe we should have for once. We found a guy who represented Holiday Inn, and, tag-teaming him as we'd learned to do in Hong Kong, Jennifer and I negotiated a price that wasn't much more than the US$40 we'd paid for our first Hong Kong guest house. We exchanged Hong Kong dollars for Macau patacas at a currency exchange counter and paid him. They had a van that took us to the hotel.

It was mid-afternoon, and though there was construction underway everywhere, the streets were deserted. According to Kyle, our friend from Mad Dogs Pub, Macau was mostly about prostitution and gambling, so it wasn't too surprising that few people were out and about in the daylight. We settled into our room and went out, looking for something to eat.

We found a little café not far from the hotel that seemed like a good bet. The linoleum and Formica reminded us of Korea, but also suggested the place was affordable. We sat down and a waitress appeared, dropping menus written in two different languages; Jennifer's was in Chinese and mine in Portuguese. I had taken some Spanish in college, and Jennifer's library program had required a course in Chinese characters, so between the two of us we were able to make enough sense of the offerings to at least place an order. We ended up with two similar plates of spaghetti and a plastic basket of bread.

After dinner, we stopped at a little store, and I talked Jennifer into buying a bottle of champagne. We returned to the hotel and were joined in the elevator by a Chinese man with his arm around a white woman in high heels and a mini dress, and two men who might have been German, standing with another woman of similar appearance. The two women exchanged a few words in Russian. The elevator button for the top floor read "CASINO."

Everyone got out on our floor. The two German men escorted their Russian lady into the room next to ours. We filled our sink with ice and buried the champagne, then decided to check out the casino.

The elevator doors opened at the top floor, revealing a room with bare white walls, brown industrial carpeting, and bullet-proof glass windows and doors. Positioned outside the doors to the casino were a metal detector and an attendant holding a machine gun. Jennifer suggested we go back downstairs, but I thought it would be a good idea for us to give the neighbors a little time to finish their business. Machine-gun guy didn't speak as he gestured at Jennifer's purse and dug through it. We passed through the metal detector and into the casino.

The place was brightly lit, but there were no decorations of any kind, not even colored lights. There was none of the festive atmosphere one might expect in Las Vegas casinos. There were no black jack tables or slot machines. Men holding machine guns milled around, parting the crowd like sharks in a school of fish. I recognized mahjong, played with small, chunky white tiles, and fan-tan, where people guessed how many bead-like things were hidden under a metal bowl, but all the other games were completely foreign, with dice in little popcorn-popper things, cards the length and width of a finger, and weird lines and circles on the tables that made no sense to me. We made one lap around the room, drawing angry glares from the serious gamblers at the various tables and contraptions, and went back downstairs.

The bed was real. The room had no smell. It was quiet. We both lay down, intending only to rest for a few minutes, and fell deeply asleep.

I awoke a few hours later. This was going to be a big deal; I needed to think, I needed to plan. But I was comfortable and warm, and instead of thinking and planning the very best way to do it, I just lay there and watched Jennifer as she slept. Eventually she opened her eyes and saw me looking at her. She stared back at me for a long time without speaking.

There was supposed to be a right way to do this, but I couldn't remember it. I was aware only of what I wanted, and expressing what I wanted, and any thinking beyond that was suspended. There was no elaborate speech, no big production. I heard my own voice breaking the silence.

"Will you marry me?"

"Yes," she said.

On the jet boat back to Hong Kong the next day, we sat close together, sharing the bread and peanut butter we'd brought with us to Macau. Although we'd been talking about marriage for a while, it felt different having made it official. It was heavier, but not in a bad way. More like being anchored.

Going through Hong Kong immigration again, we each got new entry visas, since officially we were returning to Great Britain from Portugal. My stamp was good for a full month and hers was for a half, again.

We returned to Chungking Mansions and made a slightly better deal this time around, securing a room on a lower floor. That was important, since we always took the stairs.

We went to see Vice Consul Jim the next day, filling him in about our new official engagement to be married and the fact we'd been able to extend our visas somewhat. "We know getting married won't help her get to the U.S.," I said, "but at least we'll have that, no matter what else happens to us."

Having nothing else to do that day, we returned to the aviary, where the birds could fly around and imagine themselves free.

The American Chamber's networking meeting for young professionals was exactly what we should have expected. We each had to pay about US$5 to get in the door, which by this time was somewhat painful to do. The crowd was 90% male and 100% smug corporate tools. We introduced ourselves as people who were already working, as if we were truly there to network rather than find a way to survive.

Nobody wanted to talk to me. They were very eager, however, to buy drinks for Jennifer. I managed to steal a few drinks for myself from tables. After about 90 minutes, we were both pretty drunk and hadn't identified any job prospects, so it was no longer worth putting up with the scene.

We bought another couple quarts of beer and sat down by the docks for a few hours before stumbling up the stairs to our room.

The marriage registry was a typical government processing area, with no interior decoration of any kind. The woman gave us a form to fill out: "Notice of Intended Marriage." It was in English and Chinese, and the spaces to answer were square, to accommodate Chinese characters, rather than just the underlined blanks of a purely English form. We stood at a counter in the middle of the waiting area to fill it out. Across from us at the corner of the counter was an old woman with no teeth, who was eating something out of a cone of newspaper that smelled like boiled cat shit. She saw us looking and turned a shoulder to us as if we might try to steal it. I wondered how long it would be until we were desperate enough to consider that.

"What date you want your wedding?" the woman behind the window asked when we brought up the completed form.

"Oh," I said. "We were thinking right now."

"No. You give me this form, then you have to wait. Two weeks minimum. Then you can come back get married."

"Two weeks from today, please," Jennifer said. The woman filled in the date.

"Why do we have to wait two weeks?" I asked.

"To see if anyone objects to your marriage."

Jennifer and I exchanged a look.

"How do you determine that?" Jennifer asked.

"We post it on the board there," she said, gesturing. "Anybody wants to know about a marriage gonna happen, they come to the board and see who getting married and when."

"My brother-in-law comes into downtown Hong Kong for business all the time," Jennifer said quietly to me.

"I know," I said. I turned back to the woman at the counter. "Her visa will be expired in two weeks," I said. "Is there a way we can extend it for our wedding?"

"Yes. Take the receipt from filing your Notice of Intended

Marriage to this office." She handed me a sticky note with an address.

By the time we found the address on the sticky note that afternoon, the office was closed.

We headed back to the MTR station and studied the map to determine which train would return us to Tsim Sha Tsui, the stop near Chungking Mansions. Jennifer found a newspaper on a bench. "We should start picking these up," she said. "There could be jobs advertised in here."

Using prepaid phone cards, we stood at a payphone outside the 7-Eleven and answered job ads from the newspaper, with no success. Afterwards, we called Kyle and Ailene to invite them to our wedding.

"I don't know what to do about my mother," I said. "She tends to feel trapped and manipulated when I ask her for anything, and then she'll accuse me of trying to take advantage of her. I do think I should tell her I'm getting married, though."

"Will you tell her how we got here?" Jennifer asked. "Or how we're living here?"

"I think I can do that without seeming to demand anything," I said. "If she decides to try and help us on her own, it might actually lead to something good."

I called my mother. Floyd was out. I told her I was getting married. She was shocked by our story but offered no solutions or money. "You should know that we are very worried about you," she said.

The card ran out, and the line went dead.

The next day, we returned to the visa office and got both our visas extended for another month, explaining that we wished to stay in Hong Kong for a few weeks of honeymoon. Since we'd already paid for the MTR, we decided to stay on the island a while, wandering aimlessly around the crowded streets.

It was a slip dress, like the party girls wore. It was all white, but the shimmery material had a lacy, floral effect. The gruff old woman selling it from a single rack at the back of a tiny warehouse stall refused to take less than US$35 for it.

"We can't do it," Jennifer said. "It's too much."

"We should get it," I said. "Our wedding is in exactly one week, and as yet you have no dress."

"Are you sure?" she asked. We backed away from the woman to discuss it.

"Nobody's buying us a house," I said. "You won't have four changes of clothes, or a reception, or any of that. But you should have a dress."

"I won't have to bow to anybody, either."

"Nor will I. But, look. In Korea, I was a novelty. That made it suck to live there, but relatively easy for us to get cash. Here, I'm just another hoodlum, one with no connections and no friends. I have some ideas and I can keep us safe, but Hong

Kong is going to be hard. Our lives are going to get hard. Shouldn't we have one beautiful day first?"

We bought the dress.

The ring was a harder sell. We found a thin gold band at a real jeweler for around U.S.$85. Jennifer argued that it was foolish to spend money on a ring, which it was. The jeweler offered to throw in my wedding band for free because it was cheap electroplate. "I want you to have it," I said. "For the wedding, and for always."

"We might not live long after the wedding," she said.

"But we can have one beautiful day."

We bought the ring.

Vice Consul Jim had told us that he and his family had guests coming in and out all month, but we could come stay at his place over the week of our wedding.

We showed up at his door that Saturday. What we paid for the taxi to take us there would've paid for almost four nights in Chungking Mansions, but Jim's place would have warm showers, dry toilet seats, and real beds. It was a high-rise building with its own parking garage, out away from the main part of the city. They gave us their seven-year-old son Matthew's room, done in royal blue with rocket ships. Their nine-year-old daughter Danielle had pet turtles she kept in a plastic tub.

The building had its own grocery store, and Jim asked me to come with him on a beer run. Jennifer said I should buy taco stuff and make it for everyone, to say thanks. I asked Jim whether I might use their kitchen, and he said sure.

Jim suggested we have a party at his house Friday night, the day after our wedding, to celebrate. He said he'd invite some friends, and we used his phone to call Kyle and Ailene.

While Jim and Kamon went to work every day, Jennifer and I mostly stayed around the apartment with the kids and the elderly maid, Yanisa, who spoke no English. She had apparently been Kamon's maid since childhood but seemed too feeble to contribute much labor to the household anymore.

The family had a subscription to the local newspaper, the South China Morning Post, so we were able to scan the classified ads. One from the local Korean school was seeking a librarian, and Jennifer was perfectly qualified.

"They might ask who your father is," I said.

"They probably won't ask right when I call," she said. "But I'll have to put it on some form. It's a standard question in Korea."

"Will you have to put your actual father's name and address?"

"No. I'll just make it up. I don't think they'll check it as long as I tell them I'm married. They'll care about my husband, then, but not who my father is."

"So, what are you going to tell them about being married? Are you going to tell them about me?"

"I've been thinking about it. If I don't, they'll want to know all about my Korean husband, his company, maybe his father. If I tell them I married an American, they might not ask so much."

"But if you tell them you're married to me, they'll treat you like they did when we were there."

"My parents were impressed by my sister's awful husband because he was rich. Maybe it will work with these people the same way. I can't tell them you have some great pedigree like Helen told her parents, but I might be able to make them think you're rich."

"That would explain why we'd be here in Hong Kong without jobs," I said. "I feel like it's a good idea to tell them as close to the truth as we can. It's simpler."

"Okay."

She called. She spoke in Korean, presumably to a receptionist or secretary. Her words got shorter and faster, with abrupt pauses. She hung up.

"The secretary asked me whether I was already legal to work in Hong Kong," she said. "There won't be an interview."

We sat together quietly for a while. Jennifer flipped the pages of the newspaper back and forth a few times, then got up to throw it into the trash.

"This apartment is great," I said. "But I don't want to stay here on our wedding night."

"You want to go back to Chungking Mansions on our wedding night?" Jennifer asked.

"No. To a real hotel. A cheap one, just for one night."

"We can't afford it. We're really in trouble with money, Mark."

"I know, hon. I know. But we're only going to get one wedding day, and one wedding night. It's special. It's *ours*. I don't want to let your family take that from us."

"Okay. Let's do it."

We called all the low-budget places I recognized from the phone book, like the Holiday Inn and the Ramada. Everything was booked solid. I started calling more expensive ones, and eventually found a room.

"The Island Shangri-La has a room available," I told Jennifer. "They'll let us pay in cash when we arrive. It's on the 50th floor, and it's 4,000 Hong Kong.

"That's 500 United States dollars," Jennifer said.

"I know."

We looked at each other for a moment, without speaking. Booking this room would be financial suicide.

"Get it," Jennifer said. There were tears in her eyes. "For one beautiful day."

Jim and Kamon had prepared Thai food. "So, tomorrow's your wedding," Jim said. "Did you find a hotel like you wanted?"

"Yeah," I said. "We appreciate the offer to stay, but, you know, wedding night and all that. It should be a special day."

"Uh-huh," he said. "Where will you be staying?"

"The Ramada," I said. There was no reason to tell him just exactly how foolish we were being.

He nodded slowly. His expression remained blank, but his lips tightened in what might have been anger or suspicion. It was only for an instant, but I caught it, because I'd been watching for it.

In our aimless wandering around Hong Kong, we had come across an outdoor market table selling cheap plastic beads. I had found a few strands that looked like freshwater pearls, and I spent the evening before our wedding restringing them with a few black ones mixed in, so Jennifer had something to match her clunky black shoes from Korea.

In the morning, I asked the daughter, Danielle, whether she had anything blue Jennifer could borrow for the day, and she came back with a pastel blue plastic barrette shaped like a fish, which Jennifer tucked up under her hair at the back. "This wedding's got to be by the book," I said. "Cross every 'T' and dot every 'I.'" Jennifer had heard that saying before, but the wedding tradition involving "something old, something new, something borrowed, something blue" was an unfamiliar part of my culture. She was happy to play along with it, though.

The wedding was scheduled for 10:00, in the same building where we'd filled out the paperwork. We got there an hour early and sat outside the building, watching the front door.

"Could my family have gotten here earlier than we did?" Jennifer asked.

"Depends on how involved a plan they have," I said. "How likely do you think it is that they'll come here?"

"I'm sure they checked the airlines and found that we left Korea," she said. "It worked when we went to Cheju, so they must have thought to do it again. That means they know we're in Hong Kong. Our marriage has been posted here for two weeks."

"All this, just for the family name," I said.

"It's really important there. It's not just prestige. It's about how my younger brother will marry. People in my family have sacrificed like I was made to do, for their whole lives, for hundreds of years, to establish this great family and marry my brother into another great family. He's the future, for all of them, and my leaving lowers his chance of getting a wife from a high-status family, which means power, wealth, and security, not just for him, but for my parents, too. If they bring me back, as long as I'm unmarried, they'll show they're still in control, which will reassure matchmakers and other parents that my brother is a desirable match for their daughter."

What could I say to that? We sat silently, me in the one suit I'd brought from Korea and Jennifer in her new white party-girl wedding dress, watching until it was time to go inside. Nobody from Jennifer's family had entered the building during our watch, at least not through the door we could see from our stakeout location, but the threat loomed as we went inside and rode up in the elevator. Nobody was waiting when the doors opened and we checked in at the window.

Kyle and Ailene arrived to serve as witnesses. Jim showed up and took pictures of us with his own camera as we waited in a little hallway. Finally, we were called into a room with a long table and handed sheets of red Plexiglas with vows printed on them in white silkscreen, one side in English and the other in Chinese. The disinterested magistrate read from the cards, and we answered in turn. He pronounced us husband and wife, and we kissed. We stood around for a few pictures in the elevator lobby, and then Jim left to return to the Consulate.

Kyle had brought a bottle of champagne and some paper cups. We stood by a little fountain in the park outside the building, toasting and drinking. I discovered that Kyle had accidentally purchased non-alcoholic champagne, and we all laughed. Then he had to go back to work, and Diane had worked the night before until three in the morning, so they both went off to their lives. Jennifer and I sat in the park, finishing the last of the champagne with our paper cups, alone together as a married couple for the first time.

"We're married," she said. "I'm out of my family book."

"We're married," I said. "You are my family book."

Jennifer had packed a few things in the plastic grocery bag I'd gotten when I'd bought the taco stuff. The Shangri-La was accessible from Hong Kong park. We waited and watched the birds and animals at the aviary, with Jennifer in her white silk slip dress and me in my dark wool suit, holding our grocery bag, until check-in time.

The staff was not friendly as we checked in. We had to pay up front for the room because we were paying in cash. The desk clerk begrudgingly pointed us toward the elevators at the far side of the expansive, glittering lobby, and one carried us up, up to the 50th floor. I carried Jennifer across the threshold, which felt much the same as lifting our single plastic bag of clothes. The room was richly decorated in shades of gold, peach, and champagne, with thick curtains and dense carpet. It was quiet. The furniture was classic and elegant, upholstered in deeper shades of the same colors. The bathroom was five times the size of our room at Chungking Mansions, done all in gold marble, with a gigantic whirlpool tub. The view through our window, which was one full wall of the room, included most of the Hong Kong skyline. For this one night, we were living on top of the city.

"It's a clock," Jennifer said around 3:00 in the morning, looking out of our dark Shangri-La room. She was watching the color-changing lights on the spire of a nearby building we later learned was called Central Plaza. We'd seen it every night from the Star Ferry docks, but now it was directly out our window, level with us. "Each section changes color every 15 minutes."

"I think you're right," I said. "If you know the order of the colors and you can see all four segments, you know the time.

Like, right now, I see it's a quarter past... purple, because the top one has turned yellow."

"Exactly," she said. "When the next one down turns yellow, it will be half past purple."

"I have a very smart wife," I said.

We remained in the room until checkout time. It was raining outside, and the previous night's spectacular city view was now washed out and distorted. At 11:00, we took a picture out the window and then descended in the elevator. We had one more night to stay with Jim and Kamon, our party night, a handhold before we crashed down onto the streets. Jim had said he'd give us a ride if we could make it to his office.

We wandered around Hong Kong until 5:00, purposely avoiding food stands and their aromas, and then rode to Jim's place in his right-hand-drive Honda. On the way, we were forced to slow down as three lanes of traffic became two. A clean, new Rolls Royce sat with its hood open, blocking one lane, and I rolled down my window as we passed. "C'mon! Move that piece of shit!" I shouted.

"Why did you do that?" Jim asked me.

"I was helping him," I said. "I turned a minor inconvenience into a life lesson. Guys like me get yelled at that way all the time. Just for five seconds, some rich guy got to experience what it's really like to be broken down."

It was true, but it was only part of the story. Tomorrow we'd be lower than ever, and I could feel myself growing colder and meaner, steeling myself for the struggles ahead.

At the apartment, Jim and Kamon insisted that we rest, rather than helping with the party. "You're the guests of honor!" Jim said. We went into Matthew's room and slept. Jim woke us at 7:00 and the guests arrived at 8:00. Jim's coworkers, four other members of the diplomatic corps, arrived first, precisely on time, as a group. Ailene hadn't been able to get off work. Kyle showed up about an hour late, with two other Scottish guys.

The consular officers weren't unfriendly, just excessively cordial and not fun to be around. They each had a drink or two and left, all within a few minutes of each other. Jennifer and I drank with Kyle and his friends in the living room until Jim announced there was no more beer and the Scots vanished as if someone had pulled a fire alarm. It was only around 10:30, but the five of us had consumed a lot of alcohol. Kamon and the kids were already in bed.

"I can give you a ride tomorrow," Jim said after the last guests had staggered off toward the elevator. "I know you guys are low on money, and at least I can save you the taxi fare."

"Yeah, we are," Jennifer said. "Thank you, Jim. This has been nice, staying here with you."

"Where are you going tomorrow?" he asked.

"Back to Chungking Mansions," I said. "We have enough to hold out for a little while there."

"Then what?" he asked.

"Then we have to decide," Jennifer said. "We have enough money put away to buy plane tickets. Will we use it to stay in Chungking Mansions?"

"Too bad you can't stay here longer," he said. "Just a really busy month for us."

"You know what's funny about that, though, Jim?" I asked. "Your son Matthew didn't know that anyone was coming to stay with you tomorrow."

"Well, Mark, Matthew is seven. We don't tell him our day-to-day plans."

"Uh-huh," I said. "He also didn't remember anyone staying with him last week."

"Mark," Jennifer said. "Jim has been very generous. You are being rude."

"Oh, fuck this," I said. "Generous, or curious? You want to see rude?" I went to our bag and dug out the tap detector, plugging it in. I picked up the receiver and the red light came on. I held it up for them to see.

"I got this for twenty-five bucks from a magazine ad," I said. "How likely is it that another country is bugging a United States diplomat's house with tech this can catch?" I shook my head. "This is you. I bet you've got cameras, too, somewhere. That's why you can leave complete strangers in your house with your kids; we were watched every minute." I raised the receiver to my ear. "Hello? With whom am I speaking now? My guess is it's David and Elena."

Jim's eyes and mouth were wide open. Jennifer was smiling her Mona Lisa smile. I realized I was going to spend the rest of my life trying to see that smile again and again.

"Mayday, mayday," I said into the phone. "We are an American citizen and his lawfully wedded wife, in severe distress, requesting assistance. Our need is dire but simple: Please stop spying on us and let her have the goddamned visa, already."

I hung up. "You said there was only one week available to stay with you, because you wanted to see us on our wedding night."

He said nothing. Just stood there.

"Look, man," I said. "I understand that you have a tough job to do here. I know that you spied on us because you wanted to help us and needed to be sure doing so was safe.

You're doing your duty to our country, and I'm not mad about that. But it's getting dangerous for us. It kind of looks like you might just let us die here."

"You have options," he said quietly.

"We will not go back to Korea and we will not separate. If you've got anything else to offer us, I'm all ears."

"Think about it, Jim. What have you learned about us that suggests we'll go down easy? Before Hong Kong takes us under, we are going to make a lot of waves."

"What're you talking about?" he asked.

"Well," I said. "For example, have you ever seen us do anything reckless?" I lowered my voice. "If we stay here, I'd say it's quite likely that I will get into serious trouble, maybe the kind that'll get me on the news. Remember that kid in Singapore a few months ago, who got permanent scars for vandalism? I saw him on the news even in South Korea. Hopefully the good people of Hong Kong will understand I was driven to any misdeeds because of my country's refusal to let me bring my wife home. In any case, I will be an embarrassment."

I unhooked the tap detector and extended a hand to Jennifer. "Come to bed, darling, where we shall sleep ... *apart*."

Jim did give us the promised ride back to Chungking Mansions, but he made the entire trip without saying a word. As I got out of the car, he said, "Check in with me in a week or so."

At the same store we'd visited before, we bought the same grainy bread and the same peanut butter. Standing in the warm sun outside the building, we made the hawkers haggle with each other and were offered a room for US$9 per day, but the window let in too much noise and vapor from the road below, so we turned it down and went with the next lowest bidder. We knew how to live this way, now. We dumped our suitcase, bread, and peanut butter in the room without opening any of them, and headed back outside.

Sitting at the docks was free, but there would be no more beer.

"We could go up into mainland China," I said. "I could probably teach English there. Teaching peasants wouldn't pay much, but we could stay alive."

"It wouldn't cost much to get there," Jennifer said. "We might even be able to walk."

The pager went off.

We called back to the number it displayed. A receptionist at the American Chamber of Commerce answered. I asked for Carson.

"I have what I think is good news," he said. "I met a man recently who said he was looking to hire a few people, and he was interested to meet you." Carson gave me the name and number.

It turned out that the guy ran an operation that brought in Christmas trees from China and sold them over the phone to expatriate Americans and Brits. I set up to meet him the next week.

"We should go out," Jennifer said.

"To celebrate an interview for a short-term telemarketing job?"

"To celebrate your birthday today," she said.

"Oh, yeah, I forgot. I'm twenty-five."

We got a single scoop of ice cream with two spoons at the Haagen-Dazs by the Kowloon Hyatt, and I got to choose the flavor. It had chocolate and orange.

Jennifer had calculated how long we could live, paying US$10 a night and sharing a single piece of grainy bread with peanut butter per day, before we needed to dip into our airplane money.

"Nine days," she said.

We stayed out late on the street, watching the hawkers and the hustlers.

"I'm wondering whether we should start staying only every other night in Chungking Mansions," Jennifer said. "We don't need to shower every day."

"I've been watching the fake Rolex guy," I said. "Do you remember when we first arrived in Hong Kong, and there was that British guy with the cardboard sign?"

"Yeah," Jennifer said. "That was when I first realized Hong Kong could be dangerous for us."

"Think about this, though. Here's this shifty-looking Chinese guy with a pony tail and a stringy mustache, and he comes up to people saying, "Copy watch?" with four of them on one wrist. People know what they're getting from him, and they're not willing to pay much. But if that British guy with the cardboard sign happened to be wearing one, just one watch at a time, it would appear to be his own, from his prior life. If I get to know that Rolex guy, I might be able to get those watches in bulk, then sell them on the street one at a time, as the poor American down on his luck and parting with something precious. There'd be a good margin in that, maybe enough to pay for a room."

"He doesn't seem very friendly," Jennifer said.

"No, I don't suppose he would be. It may be worth considering, is all. And I do still have a suit."

Around 11:00 that night, we trudged up thirteen floors to our room and went to bed. We'd decided to forego the bread and peanut butter, having eaten already that day, not just once, but twice: breakfast at Jim's and our celebration ice cream.

Just after 3:00 in the morning, we were awakened by noise and loud voices in the hallway. Someone was pounding on every door in the guest house and shouting, "Immigration!"

We opened our door to see four uniformed men with holstered handguns, who instructed us to line up against the wall with our passports, which they snatched from our hands to examine. One of our neighbors was roughly escorted out. Our documents were in order, so they let us go back to bed.

A chain restaurant had been promoting a cheap deal on bread bowl soup, for half price. Every day, we'd walked past two or three free-standing signs on the sidewalks, featuring pictures of the thick bread bowl and its steaming, creamy soup. After days of telling each other how it really did look good, we decided we could allow ourselves to split one, even after the birthday ice cream indulgence the day before. The restaurant was basically a fast-food place, but with table service by teenage waiters. Ours slapped down the brown plastic tray in front of us with one hand, and a third of the soup spilled out. "Here is your one bread bowl of soup," the scrawny, acne-riddled kid said, in a thick Chinese accent. "Eat it and go back outside."

We'd have lost even more of our dignity if we'd argued. We sat there, taking turns with the single plastic spoon. "There's another mixed-race couple in here," Jennifer said. "Why was he like that to us?"

She looked around the dining area, at the other mixed-race couple and the other people in the place. Then she looked down at herself, wearing one of my rugby shirts that was maybe 10 sizes too big for her. It ballooned out below her shoulders. Her brown pants were starting to tatter and fray from being worn, washed, and wrung out every other day. Her nail polish was gone. Her hair was frizzy with split ends from being outside eighteen hours a day. She had used most of her makeup back when she'd been covering bruises, and the last of it on our wedding day.

"Oh," she said.

We quietly finished the soup and tore off little pieces of the bread bowl. It would have been lovely to savor its softness and warmth, but hunger, and the need to escape the place, drove us to devour it quickly. I was proud that neither of us tried to mop up the spilled soup.

"I need to find a bathroom," I said. We went into a nearby shopping mall and followed the signs. The bathrooms were locked and only accessible when a merchant gave you a key. We didn't try.

There was a hotel attached to the mall. There would be a public bathroom in the lobby, certainly. People passed in and out through glass doors. A tall, muscular man standing just inside the door stepped in front of us. He was wearing a black suit and sunglasses that obscured his ethnicity. A small translucent earpiece he wore had a tightly coiled cord running down under his jacket, to where a radio probably hung at his belt. "Hotel guests only," he said. "May I see your room keys, please?"

The only accessible public toilets were in little concrete shacks provided by the city. There was often a line to get in. The men's rooms usually had a couple of urinals, and perhaps three "squat-type" toilets, but most often these were broken, and the bowls filled up with fifteen-pound mounds of shit after days of deposits. We found one of these buildings and made the best of the accommodations.

Having nothing else to do, we stayed a long time at the docks, coming back in well after midnight. The ground floor marketplace at Chungking Mansions was quiet. The stores and restaurants had all been packed away in their concrete boxes and sealed behind steel overhead doors.

Working our way through our usual shortcut to the staircase was easy with the crowds, tables, and merchandise out of the way. As we turned a corner, I saw two Indian men holding a severely injured African man against a store's closed steel shutters, which were smeared with blood. Both Indians had knives. Jennifer didn't realize what was happening, and she took a few steps down the hallway before I grabbed her by the shoulders and turned her around, gripping her tightly as she stumbled. "Hey!" she said. "What are—?"

"Back outside, as fast as you can," I said, pushing her ahead of me. "They won't want witnesses."

Our own feet made too much noise to hear whether anyone was following. Thick cigarette smoke rolled out of a tiny storefront with a single fluorescent tube hanging from a cord. The six or seven Indian men sitting inside watched us pass. I held the butterfly knife in my hand but didn't flick it open. We made our way through the warren of closed shops and burst out onto Nathan Road.

"Here," I said. "Stop right here. The jewelry store window. It's brightly lit, and there are security cameras."

We stood there a long time. They didn't come out.

"Should we have done something to help that guy?" she asked.

I shook my head. "I promise you that we will survive here," I said. "But that's all we can worry about."

We stayed there for a while, huddled against the bullet-proof glass, looking back the way we had come and turning to see what was coming up the street in the other direction, but nobody came. She turned to look into the window.

"Wow, look at that one," she said.

"The one with the round central stone and narrow triangle diamonds on either side of it?" I asked.

"Yes. How did you know which one I meant when I didn't point to it?" There were probably two dozen diamond rings glittering there, of all shapes and sizes.

"I don't know."

"I never cared about jewelry, but looking at that one, I can see why people say a ring can be breathtaking."

"It's pretty," I said. "But I think the knives, the blood, and the run may have had more to do with taking your breath away."

"Yeah, probably."

A man slowly approached, walking up Nathan Road slowly from the direction opposite of Chungking Mansions. He stayed out of the brightest lights by the window but we could see him clearly, tall and skeletal, with sunken eyes, thick dark hair and dark skin that seemed more gray than brown. He could have been from any of a hundred countries.

"Want coke?" he asked quietly. "Hash?"

"How much for hash?" I asked. I had no intention of buying, but this was an opportunity to understand the market here.

"2,000."

"For how much?"

"One."

"One what?"

"Bullet."

"What the fuck is a bullet? How many grams?"

"Seven. Seven grams."

"So that's a quarter ounce for 2,000 Hong Kong. Hon, help me out, here. What's 2,000 Hong Kong in American dollars?"

"250," Jennifer said.

"What?" I said. Street hash was like decent quality weed. Primo stuff went for about $125 a quarter back in Iowa City, and that was certainly better than street hash. Hong Kong was not Iowa City so the markets weren't going to line up perfectly, but it did seem there was probably a lot of room to negotiate. "I think a bullet should be, like, 500 Hong Kong," I said. He went up from there and I dragged him back down, and after a few volleys it turned out he was indeed willing to take five hundred Hong Kong for a bullet. In fact, it had been a little too easy to get him to five hundred. A good street price for what he had was probably lower than that.

"And where's a price break?" I asked. "How much more do I buy to get a discount? Four bullets?" Price breaks for quantity were the nature of the business.

"Four bullets 400 each," he said.

"That's $200 US but I don't think you should buy it," Jennifer said.

$200 an ounce. It was probably still too high for the quality I'd estimated.

"Yeah, you're probably right," I said. "We're on a tight budget."

"Four bullet 350 each," he said. "350."

"Nah," I said. "She's right. We can't today." To show I meant it, I gestured to guide Jennifer back toward Chungking Mansions.

"Did you learn what you needed to know?" she asked quietly.

We began spending much more of our time in the room. Interacting with the hectic and hostile world outside only seemed to intensify our feelings of hopelessness and desperation. Plus, we weren't taking in many calories, and too many trips up and down the stairs in a day made us lightheaded.

A butterfly knife has two thin handles attached to the blade with pins. When opened, the handles rotate around the blade, exposing it with a bit of flash and style that demonstrates the wielder's level of skill, functioning to warn attackers in much the same way as a rattlesnake's tail. However, a butterfly knife is not made to handle torque, and is not suitable for the repeated scooping of peanut butter over a period of weeks.

The brittle die-cast metal of one of the handles cracked and fell off. For two days we scooped up peanut butter with our plastic spoons from Haagen Dazs and tore little pieces of bread to top each spoonful, but one spoon broke and we decided to save the other. On the next day we got our daily portion out with our fingers and pinched bits of bread, but then the bread was gone.

"Maybe we should wait a day before buying more," Jennifer said.

We sat across from Jim, who sat at his desk, in his concrete office, in front of the window and the expanse of green outside it. It had been exactly a week since we'd seen him.

He handed Jennifer an envelope of photographs from our wedding. We thanked him for the pictures. "You know,

I think your wedding kiss was the first time I ever saw you two touch each other," Jim said. "It probably wouldn't kill you to show a little affection from time to time."

"That has not been our experience," Jennifer said.

Jim exhaled, looking from Jennifer to me and back a few times. Then he pushed a thick folder across the desk.

"What's this?" Jennifer asked.

"It's your visa," he said. "Congratulations. You're cleared to enter the United States."

Jim gave us the name of a travel agent he said he'd used to arrange a trip home for Christmas last year. "They're good at working with whatever parameters you give them," he said. We took the MTR straight there from his office.

We sat together on the train, stunned but cautiously hopeful, chatting quietly about what had just happened. Leaving Hong Kong was a monumental turn of events, but it was hard to let ourselves believe in it just yet. There were many remaining hurdles to clear between us and safety, including two sets of customs and immigration officials, the cost of transportation, and even mundane challenges like surviving the night. "You think it'll really happen?" Jennifer asked.

"I think Jim really wants us to leave Hong Kong," I said. "That doesn't necessarily mean we'll be admitted into the U.S. when we arrive."

We asked the travel agents to get us to Iowa City as cheaply as possible, and they came through for us. Our itinerary would take us from Hong Kong to Taiwan, then to

Tokyo, then to Seattle, then to Chicago, and then to Cedar Rapids, Iowa, the airport closest to Iowa City. With all the plane changes and layovers, we'd be traveling for more than 35 hours. "They might have a meal on every flight," Jennifer said. "That would be five free meals for each of us!"

The next day, we boarded the plane. We did not hide, we did not run, and we had no issues with our passports or visas. We ate, slept, and changed planes, over and over.

They let us through customs in Seattle with no problem, and Jennifer entered the United States as a legal resident. Waiting in Seattle for the next flight, I called friends from a payphone, using some spare United States coins I'd had since getting them as change on the military bases in Korea. Danny said we could sleep on his floor.

We filled up on airplane food and wandered around Chicago's O'Hare Airport for hours. Finally, the last plane began its descent into Cedar Rapids. "This is the American Midwest, where I'm from," I said, pointing out the airplane window.

"Look how flat it is!" Jennifer said. "I can't believe those gigantic farms."

"They produce more grain here than just about anywhere else on Earth," I said. "I never felt connected to this place before. That's why I could just pick up and go wherever: It didn't feel much like a home to me. Now, with you, it does."

"I feel like that, too," Jennifer said. "Like I'm coming home, for the first time."

Epilogue

We never learned who sent us the jumbled page that brought me to Jennifer's workplace that day in Taegu.

A few months after we reached the United States, Jennifer's parents appeared in Iowa City, armed with my personnel file from SNM Academy showing my mother's house as my "permanent" address. My mother sent them to our apartment, a single room behind a gas station, where they showed up unannounced at our door. Officially we all made up. They gave us $5,000 as a wedding gift, which Jennifer wanted me to have. I used it to have a jeweler recreate the ring that had taken Jennifer's breath away in Hong Kong.

Now Jennifer talks to her family on the phone once or twice a year, which is more contact than we have with anyone in my family. We have never returned to Korea, and we have no plans to do so.

Jennifer's sister's toad-faced husband went bankrupt, which in Korea meant that creditors came to their house in "Korea's Beverly Hills" and threw them out, keeping the home and all its contents in partial payment of the debt. They fled the country and ended up in Indonesia.

Jennifer earned two master's degrees and now works in healthcare information technology. She's back to wearing designer suits, which she still prefers to wear with pants. I went to law school and practiced for a while, and then I began writing novels. From time to time, friends who have heard our story have told me I should write a book about how we came to be married, so now finally I have.

We recently celebrated our 24th wedding anniversary, and we now live in Maine. We have built our life from the ground up, and we own every part of it together. We have a strong and intelligent daughter, who we have raised to believe in justice, independence, and herself. As far as we're concerned, she can marry anyone she chooses.

I took this on the roof of some building, which might have been where I was living at the time.

My camera had a remote for self portraits, but we never figured out how long the delay was before it snapped. This was the best we could manage. Note the maps I'd taped on the wall behind us.

The War Machine

Chungking Mansions Inside. This is the entire room, taken from outside the door.

Chungking Mansions from outside

Jennifer in Kowloon with the Hong Kong skyline behind her. Note Central Plaza, the building towering in the center of the shot.

Hong Kong night skyline. This was our view most nights.

Deep into the struggle in Hong Kong, Jennifer looks tired, but determined. This is one of my favorite pictures of her.

This was the scene from the stairway window on maybe the 8th floor of Chungking Mansions. Someone had purposely grown this plant on the roof, where it only got maybe an hour of sun between all the buildings.

We stood a distance apart on the same street and handed the camera back and forth, to capture the feeling of the entire street.

Discussion Questions

1. Mark and Jennifer come from very different worlds.

   What do you think attracted Mark and Jennifer to each other? Are they a good match, in your opinion? Why?

2. Early in the story, we learn the following about Mark:
   He used to procure drugs for his friends back home.
   He drinks a fair amount of alcohol.
   He reads books like The Anarchist Cookbook.
   He manufactures and consumes a hallucinogenic drug made from banana peels.

   Might parents be justified in attempting to keep a daughter away from guys like this? Do you feel the actions of Jennifer's parents were justified? Why or why not?

   To what degree does Mark have a corrupting influence on Jennifer's thoughts or behavior? A liberating one? What kind of influence does Jennifer have on Mark?

3.   In describing her childhood, Jennifer explains the many disadvantages of being a second daughter in South Korea. Mark shares his experience as the first-born son of a divorced American family.

Which differences in their upbringing stood out to you? Which similarities?

In what ways did the disparate approaches to parenting in their respective families shape the personalities of Mark and Jennifer as they grew up?

4.   As a couple, Mark and Jennifer are judged and treated harshly by Mark's landlady, their employers, and strangers. Those holding their relationship against them are often far from model citizens themselves.

Are their experiences the result of racism, or merely of cultural differences? Are you surprised by the overt hostility and discrimination they encountered?

Do Mark and Jennifer change their behavior in response to these encounters? Would you?

5.   We see that alcohol plays a different role in Korean society than it does in the West, with respect to business relationships, gender roles, and friendships. Mark occasionally drinks in accordance with these societal rules, but also drinks on his own, as well as consuming and manufacturing other drugs.

Do you feel the norms relating to alcohol consumption in Korea are consistent with the rules of Korean society in general?

Consider Mark's friendships with Jae Won and Major Byun, as well as the depictions of businesspeople going out to drink with their superiors. If you had to follow Korean formalities in your own socializing (such as refilling the glasses of superiors), would it change the nature of your relationship with those friends or coworkers? How might it influence your feelings about those relationships?

Would you hang out with Major Byun, if you were in Mark's situation? Why or why not?

6. Mark and Jennifer discuss the strictness of Korean society, and Mark concludes that "all over the world, resources keep dwindling as it gets more crowded. Other places are becoming more like Korea. We're not stuck in the past, here. This is the future."

Do you agree that factors such as Korea's population, land area, and available resources contributed to the social hierarchy described in this story? Is Mark correct when he says this is the future for all of us? Why or why not?

7. A number of characters tell Mark and Jennifer that it is wrong for them to be together, that it's selfish behavior, showing disrespect for Korean values. Mark and Jennifer defy these admonitions to do what they feel is right for them.

How does one strike a balance between personal morality and respect for social norms? Did Mark and Jennifer do it in this story? Do you judge this differently with regard to Mark, who comes from outside Korea, than with respect to Jennifer, who is struggling from within her own culture?

8. It is explained in the story that Korea has been invaded more than 900 times in its history, and Mark observes that Korea's restrictions on women's freedom might have developed because there were "always invaders outside the door." It is also revealed that Jennifer had narrowly escaped being kidnapped off the street and sold into prostitution, and Katherine, another of the female English teachers, was raped in her apartment.

Does the desire to keep women safe explain all of the rules for Korean women we observe in the story?

9. Mark says he's underqualified to teach English, and his teaching style varies greatly from that of the other instructors at the school.

Based on the classroom scenes in the book, is Mark an effective English teacher? In what ways do his unconventional methods benefit his students? Would you prefer the traditional style of English instruction to Mark's way?

10. Mark and Jennifer talk about the Korean education system, with its high pressure, long hours, and little sleep. For example,

Jennifer was at school six days a week, from 6:00 a.m. until 10:00 p.m. as a teenager, and for boys it was even more intense.

Are there aspects of this system that you feel other nations should emulate? How well do these practices prepare kids to succeed in our increasingly competitive world?

What roles should parents and educators play in raising children to be productive members of society? Is there a limit to how hard they should push?

11. Mark and Jennifer break laws and risk punishment, especially relating to Korean immigration and visa restrictions, and Mark extends this behavior to the American military bases.

Are these transgressions justified, given their circumstances?

Would you have taken these risks, in their situation? Why or why not?

12. Jennifer's family allowed her to work at the academy so that she could build her "wedding resume" and show that she has valuable knowledge to teach children. Mark and Jennifer discuss the possibility that early exposure to Western literature may have helped make her different from other Koreans.

Do education and exposure to other cultures make one a better spouse and/or parent, in your opinion?

Do education and exposure to other cultures necessarily challenge traditional values? Is this good or bad?

ABOUT THE AUTHOR

It's strange that "About the Author" pages are always written in the third person. Why pretend that someone else wrote this? I'm Mark D. Diehl. I write books.

I grew up in Iowa City, Iowa. I lived alone with my mom, who I will generously describe as unpredictable. Eventually everyone learns that life is unfair, but some of us figure out early on that usually it is made so by someone in a position of power. By the time I was twelve, I had a seething contempt for authority, and my heroes were criminals. After failing classes in junior high and high school, I somehow managed to attend and graduate from the University of Iowa.

Without money or family support, there was no way I could start my own business, but the idea of working my way up through the ranks of some company sickened me. South Korea was developing rapidly at that time, and I imagined that finding inroads to the economy there might allow me to become my own boss sooner than I would any other way. I took a job teaching English in Taegu, South Korea, which is where I met my wife, Jennifer. (The first year of our relationship, which culminated in our escape from her powerful family and Korean authorities, inspired my memoir, *Stealing Cinderella: How I Became an International Fugitive for Love.*)

Korea's hierarchical and authoritarian society both fascinated and terrified me. Its control over everyone there was so total and so brutal that Jennifer and I consider ourselves lucky to have escaped it. Ours is not so much a story of fighting against people as it is one of resistance to a system, one which I came to warily respect. In the Korean people, I saw strength and resolve that could only have developed over thousands of years of invasions and shortages, and I recognized that the parts I treasured most about my own culture had evolved in an environment of relative abundance. It became clear to me that the rigidity I struggled against was the very thing that made Korean society so efficient, productive, and strong.

In the years following our return from Korea, I went to law school at the University of Iowa and ended up practicing with a multinational law firm. There I recognized the same kinds of structure that I'd seen in Korea, with level upon level of hierarchy, stifled individuality, and institutionalized suspicion of anything different. Knowing I wouldn't survive there for long, I attended a two-year graduate workshop in creative writing at the University of Chicago, where I began working on a dystopian science-fiction trilogy set in an oppressive, hierarchical future world whose supply of natural resources has nearly been exhausted.

Jennifer and I have lived for the last decade or so in Cape Elizabeth, Maine, along with our daughter Myra, a slew of rescued reptiles, and a one-eyed dog. I founded a local-centric business networking group here, hoping to help preserve the American respect for independence and individual will, and even ran for the Maine State Senate. I've now accepted that there's no way to halt our society's (and really, the world's) momentum, so these days, I mostly sit by myself and write.

Please visit www.MarkDDiehl.com for a complete list of titles available from the author, including his *Seventeen Trilogy*, the dystopian science fiction series inspired by Mark's experiences in East Asia. Interviews, photographs, reviews and press coverage are also highlighted on the website, as is Mark's blog, through which he shares information about ongoing projects, book tours and more.